the house of
Krupp

the house of
Krupp

THE STEEL DYNASTY THAT ARMED THE NAZIS

PETER BATTY

Cooper Square Press

First Cooper Square Press edition 2001

This Cooper Square Press paperback edition of *The House of Krupp* (originally published in the U.K. in 1966) is an unabridged republication of the edition first published in 1967 in New York, here updated with a new afterword by the author. It is reprinted by arrangement with Random House U.K., Ltd., and the author.

Published by Cooper Square Press
An Imprint of the Rowman & Littlefield Publishing Group
150 Fifth Avenue, Suite 817
New York, New York 10011

Distributed by National Book Network

Library of Congress Cataloging-in-Publication Data

Batty, Peter, 1931–
    The house of Krupp : the steel dynasty that armed the Nazis / Peter Batty.
        p. cm.
    Originally published: New York : Stein & Day, 1967.
    Includes bibliographical references and index.
    ISBN: 0-8154-1155-3 (pbk. : alk. paper)
    1. Fried. Krupp AG—History. 2. Krupp family—History. 3. Steel industry and trade—German—History. 4. Weapons industry—Germany—History. I. Title.

HD9523.9.K7 B3 2001
338.7'67'0943—dc21   2001053814

TO MY MOTHER AND FATHER

Contents

List of Plates

Introduction

To AT least one group of people in Germany, the night of 5 March 1943 has a particular significance, such that they will never forget it. That group is the citizens of Essen, the great iron and steel town of Germany's industrial heartland, the Ruhr—and the reason for their remembering that night in March twenty-three years ago is that it was the occasion for their first major air-raid of the Second World War.

After the flares of the Royal Air Force's Pathfinder Mosquito bombers had pierced the smoky haze above the sleeping city, within minutes the heavier loads of the hundreds of Halifaxes, Wellingtons, and Lancasters following had laid waste some 160 acres in the centre of Essen and badly damaged another 450.

And that was not all, for this first raid was merely a taste of what was to come, a grim sample of what lay in store for the people of Essen. Essen was to be the target for many, many more bombing raids—for Essen was the home of Krupp's, of the Krupp armament factories that had forged Bismarck his cannons in his wars against Austria and France nearly a century before, that had made Kaiser "Bill" his notorious Big Bertha to smash the Belgian forts standing in the way of his army's advance on Paris in 1914. And now thirty years later this selfsame Krupp's was turning out tanks and guns and U-boats for Hitler.

Before the war was won, RAF bombers alone were to make some 11,000 or so individual sorties over Essen, and in nearly 200 full-scale air-raids were to drop more than 36,000 tons of incendiary and high-explosive bombs, most of them on the three square miles of Krupp factories. Goebbels was to record in his diary that he thought Essen was the city hardest hit by Allied raids, while General Heinz Guderian reported to his Führer the final Christmas before Germany's defeat that the home of Krupp's was already prostrate.

When British and American troops finally captured the city in April 1945, they found almost total destruction. Nothing worked any more—there was no gas, no electricity, no water. "It was a place of the dead", wrote home one American corporal. "It is impossible to imagine this city ever living again", a British intelligence officer reported to his superior. What little Krupp machinery that still remained undamaged was earmarked to be broken up and shipped piece by piece by way of recompense to some of the countries formerly overrun by the Nazis. The rest was expected to be sent as scrap to either British or French blast-furnaces.

In November 1945 a British chartered accountant from North Harrow was put in charge of Krupp's. He announced to all and sundry that it was intended to prevent the Essen firm from ever rising again. "No Krupp chimney will ever smoke again", he told the few workmen who were left— and amidst the rubble and the ruin that was the Ruhr in those chaotic months immediately after the war, who could have doubted him? Except of course that the selfsame thing had been said by the victorious Allies in 1918 and yet within a relatively short time Krupp's had been back in business.

History was indeed to repeat itself. Today, Krupp's are bigger, busier, and boomier than ever before. In twelve months between 1965 and 1966 they sold nearly £600 million worth of goods, a record for the firm, and they were giving employment to 112,000 people—roughly the number of inhabitants in a town the size of Oxford or Preston.

Yet just one man owns this monolithic factory-kingdom— Alfried Felix Alwyn Krupp von Bohlen und Halbach. Like Gustav Krupp, his father, who was arrested and imprisoned after the First World War, Alfried was arrested and imprisoned after the Second. American judges at Nuremberg in 1948 found him guilty of war crimes and sentenced him to be stripped of his wealth and to be jailed for twelve years. But again, just like his father, Alfried was soon released. His properties were returned to him, though on the clear understanding that he would sell off his coal-mines and his steelworks. Today, his private industrial empire remains intact.

What is more, he is one of the richest men alive, worth, it is said, every penny of £1,500 million. No wonder his family have been called the "Incredible Krupps".

But the Krupp saga is full of paradoxes. Perhaps the most pertinent one of all is that even the very name symbolises different things to different people. Outside Germany, Krupp has become identified with that country's aggression and that country's beastliness in two world wars. As a word it fits easily into a newspaper headline; and it is one of the four or five German family names that are known the world over. Even when you pronounce *Krupp*, it sounds like a shell exploding!

To Frenchmen, it was Krupp guns that ravaged France three times in a century. To Americans, it was Krupp tanks that spearheaded the German Army's counter-offensive through the Ardennes in November 1944 with its terrible toll of doughboy dead. To Russians, it was the Krupp giant railway-guns that decided the siege of Sevastopol and devastated many of her ancient cities. To British people, Krupp is remembered for having built the first U-boat and most of the hundreds that followed—while the coastal batteries that shelled Dover and Folkestone in the Second World War were Krupp-made too.

But to Germans, Krupp means something entirely different. It is the symbol of their country's industrial prowess. Furthermore, Krupp's have always had the reputation in Germany of being an excellent employer of labour. Once taken on, workers tend to stay with the firm: son following father, father following grandfather. Even the title "*House of Krupp*", the title preferred as the name of their firm by Krupps themselves, suggests a kingly dynasty.

In Germany there is a saying, "As the Fatherland goes, Krupp goes"—a sort of Teutonic version of "what's good for America is good for General Motors". Indeed there are striking parallels between the triumphs and disasters of Germany under Bismarck, the Kaiser, or Hitler, and the rise and fall in the fortunes of the House of Krupp. What is more, this habit of matching the mood of the moment has been continued by Alfried in the Germany of Konrad Adenauer and Chancellor Erhard. If slavish devotion to whoever happens to be controlling the political power-strings is considered a virtue, then the Krupps must be numbered among the most virtuous of men. But, equally, if such blinkered compliance is thought of as something less than praiseworthy, then the family of which Alfried is the present head must suffer the appropriate obloquy.

The Krupps are always proud of their loyalty to the State —and whether this loyalty leads them into supporting a Kaiser's vanities or a Führer's megalomania is immaterial to them. It happens usually to be good for Krupp business— and the Krupps are first and foremost businessmen; being human is only incidental to their way of doing things. Accordingly, the story of the House of Krupp is the story, purely and simply, of an exercise in industrial power. That the cast-steel cannons old Alfred made and perfected were to be used to maim and to murder thousands of luckless men never entered his thinking. That the subterfuges Gustav got up to in duping the Allied disarmament commissioners after 1919 could only end in another bloody holocaust never occurred to him or worried him. That the thousands of Jewish workers forced to make weapons for Alfried during the Second World War could be living in abominable conditions, could be being brutally treated by their Gestapo guards, could be being needlessly exposed to Allied air-raids, and could be dying off in their hundreds, evidently never caused him then or even now to lose a single night's sleep.

The Krupps are insensitive men—unscrupulous, grasping, materialistic, but thoroughly able. There is a continuum in their behaviour and in their attitudes. To understand them fully you must go back to their origins and to their past.

The Krupps of course created Essen—at least they created Essen in the sense that without them Essen would probably still be just another insignificant market-town, unsung and unknown to the rest of the world. The family, like none other, were totally responsible for Essen's tremendous growth during the second half of the nineteenth century. Equally, it was the presence of the firm there that made the Allies determined to destroy Essen during the Second World War.

Today, Essen is no longer dependent upon Krupp's for its

livelihood, but the Krupp presence and the Krupp influence
is nevertheless still strong there. Alfried, for instance, owns
the city's best hotel and hence its smartest rendezvous for
visitors. There again, some one hundred or more streets in
Essen are still to this day named after members of the family
or firm, not to mention of course the many parks, hospitals,
and other public institutions that were originally founded by
the Krupps.

But the story of the House of Krupp is not just the story of
the growth of an industrial family, of an industrial city, and
of an industrial area—albeit the most famous, or perhaps the
most infamous, industrial area in the world, the Ruhr. It is
also the story of an exercise in public relations, particularly
in their selling themselves successfully to their employees and
their receiving in return their employees' loyalty and respect.
It can of course be argued that the Krupps, along with other
German industrial families in the nineteenth century, stepped
into the shoes of the landed aristocracy whom Napoleon
had diminished both in quantity and in influence. The
factory barons of the industrial revolution came in for that
compliance and devotion that had previously been the
prerogative of the feudal lords. This submissiveness and
veneration they repaid in their turn by their well-nigh
fatherly concern towards their employees—concern which
found its best expression in acts of welfare, especially the
provision of housing, and also in the benignant gestures of
charity on the part of wives and daughters to the workers
and their families. Such attitudes were clearly at odds with
the political and social trends of the age. Indeed, the Krupps
in keeping with the other German industrial dynasties were
strongly antipathetic to any groupings of workers or in fact
to any activity by their men that savoured of socialism, self-
help, or syndicalism. Alfred Krupp's writings on this subject rank among the most virulent manifestations of the
reactionary point of view in the whole of the nineteenth
century. Krupp workers, along with German workers in
general, were probably disposed to accepting meekly this
state of affairs, yet Krupp's success in this sphere of internal
public relations must be regarded as perhaps their most
astonishing accomplishment of all.

As a French diplomat once described them, Krupp's are
indeed "a state within a state". In Bonn, the new West
German capital, they maintain an office which in its outward
appearance and interior splendour can only be likened to an
embassy—in fact its occupant is sometimes referred to as
"the ambassador from Essen". For its part too the Federal
Government tends to look upon Alfried as its industrial
prince, for when heads of state come visiting the country a
trip to Essen and a meeting with Alfried is usually on their
schedules. Even some of the titles of the top Krupp executives
have a stately ring about them: for instance, the Krupp man
in London is occasionally known as their Commonwealth
Delegate, while Berthold Beitz, the number two in the Krupp
hierarchy, is often called in Krupp literature the General
Plenipotentiary.

The saga of Krupp's, stretching backwards in time to the
sixteenth century, is one of the most fascinating and fantastic
stories of all time. It is a story of intrigue and greed, of the
lust for power and of the possession of power. It is a story of
men apparently strong and ruthless, but in fact weak and
fallible. Above all it is a story of dangerous men.

It is a story of the growth of big business and of gigantic
industrial organisation. Unfortunately it is the story of our
times and of our fathers' times, of our grandfathers' times
and of our great-grandfathers' times. It is in many ways
almost unbelievable.

The Krupps are already a legend, already a lore unto
themselves. But they are also a lesson—and theirs is a tale
worth the telling.

One has not embarked on such a project without a certain
trepidation. Many books have already been written on the
Krupps and many more will follow mine. I by no means
claim for mine the epithet *definitive*. Indeed, but for the encouragement of my family and my friends, and above all my
colleagues at Associated TeleVision, I doubt whether I would
have ever started to write it at all.

Let it be said straightaway that the idea for attempting a
book on Krupp's sprang out of a television documentary I
made for Associated TeleVision in the winter of 1964-5,
which was subsequently shown twice on the independent

television network here in Britain at a peak hour in February and September 1965. On each occasion the audience estimated to be watching was between nine and ten million people. The programme was also transmitted overseas in nearly twenty different countries, including both East and West Germany, Italy, Holland, Belgium, Sweden, Switzerland, and the United States. It brought, too, to the writer a *grand prix* for television documentaries at both the 1965 Venice and the Leipzig film festivals.

My interest in Krupp's, however, dates from long before joining Associated TeleVision. It is to my father that I owe the first mention of the name of Krupp in my consciousness. Like many of his generation who had to fight in the First World War, and for whom that terrible experience was a lasting and deeply felt one, he has what might be called the conventional British ex-serviceman's view of the Krupps: he loathes and despises them. Accordingly, the name Big Bertha, inevitably as it was included in his stories and tales of that war, came to have a very real menace and at the same time a certain mythical charm in my early childhood. Although I was fortunately too young to be called upon to fight in the Second World War, I was nevertheless old enough to know and to fear the Krupp U-boats and the Krupp Tiger tanks. Therefore, to my parents, and to those of their generation for whom war has unfortunately loomed large in their lives this century, I respectfully dedicate this book.

Many people have helped me in this project. My colleagues at Associated TeleVision, in particular Robert P. Heller, Norman Collins, Lew Grade, and Robin Gill, who both encouraged me to get started and then made possible the opportunity for me to finish it: to them I am permanently grateful, as I am also to Ingrid Floering who assisted with the research for the television documentary, and to Ann Scorer, who over the months aided me in a multitude of ways. I am indebted too to George Clark, Guy Ambler, Roger James, and Cyril Hayden, for their forbearance at a certain key-moment in my saga of the Krupp saga! To the press clippings library at Chatham House I owe an enormous debt, especially for their thoroughness and their patience in dealing with my persistent queries—as I do also to Margaret

Duerden who helped me obtain books, and indeed to every library I have plundered unmercifully and to every mind I have picked uncharitably over the years.

Without the substantial aid of officials of Essen Public Library, I could not have compiled the earlier history of the family, since my primary sources for that particular period include the various official Krupp histories, monographs, anniversary brochures, company reports and picture-albums which were kindly put at my disposal there. I have also had access to the files of British newspapers and magazines of the last century. In particular, Wilhelm Berdrow's edited collection of *Alfred Krupp's Letters* (Gollancz, 1930) was of immense value.

For the period between the wars, I have again largely relied on the newspapers and magazines of the time, together with the talks I have had with key principals such as Gottfried Treviranus, a Cabinet Minister in the Weimar Republic, a close acquaintance of both Bertha and Gustav Krupp, and a frequent visitor to the Villa Hügel. It goes without saying of course that I have needed to refer closely to the proceedings of the Krupp Trial (*Trials of War Criminals before the Nuremberg Tribunals, Vol. IX, Alfried Krupp, et al.*).

Most of the recent material, especially that from 1945 onwards, has in fact come from conversations I have had with people privy to certain crucial episodes of the Krupp story, as well as from a sedulous perusal of the newspapers and periodicals, German, American, French, and British, of the day. In particular, I would like to record the invaluable information and comments I received from Lord Shawcross, Lord Robertson, Sir Christopher Steel, Airey Neave, Goronwy Rees, Harris Burland, Rex Malik, Harold Edge, Professor Francis Carsten, Terence Prittie of the *Guardian*, Reginald Peck of the *Daily Telegraph*, Karl Robson of *The Economist*, Frederick Fischer of the *Financial Times*, and Lee Brawand and Dr. H. Alexander of *Der Spiegel*. The latter was kind enough to put his own collection of back numbers of *Der Spiegel* at my disposal. Many, many others—some former and some present employees of the Krupp concern —talked to me in strict confidence: a confidence which I intend to respect, come what may. The book's merits, if it has any, can be laid at many doorsteps, its faults, alas, are purely mine alone.

A final word of gratitude must go to my wife and to my small children for being so tolerant in what has been a difficult time for me. I trust and hope that my two young sons and my young daughter will perhaps wonder in the years to come what was all their father's fuss about guns and U-boats and tanks and slave-labour. For myself, if another Krupp cannon is never again fired in anger then it will have been worth while.

Richmond, Surrey, 1966

THE KRUPP FAMILY TREE

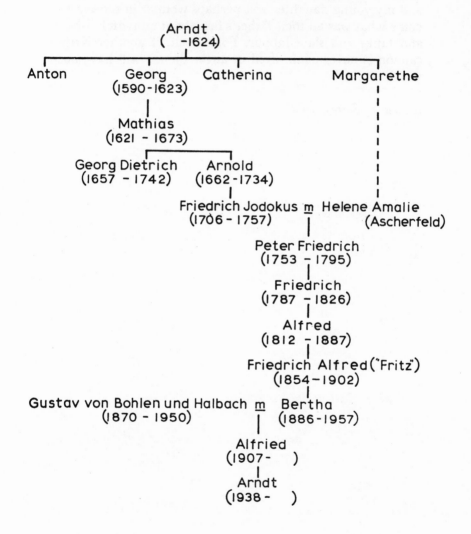

Arndt
(-1624)

Anton   Georg   Catherina   Margarethe
         (1590-1623)

Mathias
(1621 - 1673)

Georg Dietrich   Arnold
(1657 - 1742)   (1662-1734)

Friedrich Jodokus m Helene Amalie
(1706 - 1757)   (Ascherfeld)

Peter Friedrich
(1753 - 1795)

Friedrich
(1787 - 1826)

Alfred
(1812 - 1887)

Friedrich Alfred ("Fritz")
(1854 - 1902)

Gustav von Bohlen und Halbach m Bertha
(1870 - 1950)   (1886-1957)

Alfried
(1907 -)

Arndt
(1938 -)

CHAPTER ONE

"The Place of Ash Trees"

IF HISTORY as taught in English schools is anything to go by, then 1587 is mainly memorable as the year when Mary, Queen of Scots, was beheaded for plotting against her Tudor cousin, Elizabeth, Queen of England. Or else as the year when Drake's little ships set fire to the bulk of the Spanish Armada as it lay at anchor in Cadiz harbour—the daring raid which has gone down in English folklore-history as "the singeing of the King of Spain's beard".

London theatre audiences were then about to hear the first play of a new author called William Shakespeare. The play was *Love's Labour's Lost*, and in 1587 the Immortal Bard was barely twenty-three years old. In Italy, the Renaissance had just lost its high bloom, though Michelangelo and Titian had not been long dead, while Tintoretto and Veronese were still painting; elsewhere, El Greco was thirty-two, Rubens ten, and Rembrandt was not yet born. Spanish and Portuguese empire-builders were transporting Negro slaves by the thousands to their colonies in the New World, but it was to be at least another thirty years before English settlers in Virginia and the Carolinas started following their example.

For us, the year 1587 is important in that it represents the beginning of the recorded history of the House of Krupp. Among the new members listed in Essen's *Register of Merchants* for that year appears one Arndt Krupe. Where he came from, or exactly when he arrived in Essen, no one knows for certain. Researchers by the score have been commissioned over the years by the Krupp family to pinpoint their forebear's origins, but with little success.

Some have argued that Arndt might have once lived in the

little town of Ahrweiler, lying near the west bank of the
Rhine about seventy miles south of Essen. Their evidence
is simply that the names *Krupe*, *Kruyp*, and *Krup* were
recorded there during the sixteenth century and that, what
is more, the Abbess of Essen once owned vineyards in the
area. On top of this, not far away from Ahrweiler, where the
river Ahr meets the Rhine, there was once a village called
Kripp in which a family named either *Kripe* or *Kruppe* were
ferrymen at this time.

Other Krupp historians in their turn have claimed that
Arndt was a descendant of the *Krops* and *Kroppens* who lived
along the banks of the lower Rhine between its junction
with the Ruhr at Duisburg and the present Dutch border.
But whether Arndt's forefathers really called themselves
Krup, *Krupe*, *Kripe*, *Kruyp*, *Kruppe*, *Kripp*, *Krops*, or *Kroppens*,
his descendants soon began writing their names as plain
Krupp.

Essen was of course a vastly different place in 1587 from
what it is today. Three centuries in fact were to pass by
before she came to be totally identified with the particular
industry that was to make her famous the world over—steel.
The only manufacturing sixteenth-century Essen could boast
of was flax-spinning and linen-weaving: "a very strong kind
of linen", according to the archives. When an iron industry
eventually began to appear there, it was very small and
confined simply to supplying the needs of local farmers.

The city of the Krupps takes her name from *Eschen*,
meaning "the place of ash trees". She was known to the
Romans as *Assindia*—indeed her citizens are still sometimes
termed *Essenders*. In 874 a Christian nobleman called
Altfridus built a cloister there, of which his sister became the
first Princess-Abbess. Later, the abbey, together with a
few square miles of land surrounding it, was made into a
citadel and became a devout retreat "for the daughters of
the aristocracy". That it also grew rich can be judged from
the relics remaining today—relics such as a *Golden Madonna*
and several processional crosses encrusted with precious
stones or ornamented in enamel.

Essen lay on the Hellweg, that ancient mule-track linking
the two rivers Rhine and Weser, which travellers had used

since earliest times. When the Franks had invaded Germany after the collapse of the old Roman Empire, they had transformed it into a recognised trade-route by establishing fortified villages along the way to provide shelter and protection for the many merchants and pilgrims using it. During the Middle Ages some of these villages grew into towns—among them Essen, Dortmund, and Duisburg. In the fourteenth and fifteenth centuries Essen belonged to the Hanseatic League of Trading Cities. Engravings of the city dating from the middle of the seventeenth century show the old walls still intact then—and Essen had changed little in outward appearance or in function even by the beginning of the nineteenth century. Never a beautiful or a particularly wealthy place, Essen only began expanding beyond her mediaeval defences after 1823. Until then her citizens had never numbered more than 4,000.

Ruled by a Princess-Abbess, Essen was one of the many so-called Free Cities in the mosaic of tiny territories and petty principalities that went to make up the Germany of the Holy Roman Empire. Even the very name of this empire, established by Charlemagne at the beginning of the ninth century, was a confidence trick, since the only connection Germans had had with the previous Roman Empire was that their ancestors, the Barbarians, had helped to destroy it! Never a very cohesive empire, it started really falling apart during the century Arndt Krupe arrived in Essen.

That century had in fact begun well for Germany. Her merchants were enjoying great wealth and her burgesses' self-confidence was knowing no bounds under the civilising balm of the High Renaissance. Yet the sixteenth century closed amid social turbulence and economic despair in nearly every German city.

In the first place, the opening of the sea-route to India around the Cape of Good Hope prompted an enormous shift in the pattern of world commerce. Locked up as they were in the middle of the European land-mass, mercantile communities such as Venice and the German cities along the Rhine declined within a generation or two from great centres of international trade to mere economic backwaters. While for Britain, France and even Holland, the centuries that were to follow were among the most prosperous and expansionist their peoples had ever known, for Germans they were merely years of stagnation and depression—a condition from which they were not really to recover until the end of the nineteenth century and the age of Bismarck and Kaiser William.

The other big cataclysmic event for Germany was the Protestant Reformation. When Martin Luther in 1517 proclaimed his ninety-five objections to the sale of papal indulgences, many of the German princes, especially those living in the north, joined in his protest simply in the hope of securing yet more independence from their political overlord in Vienna, the Holy Roman Emperor, who was preferring to remain faithful to the Pope. Although in theory the Emperor was elected only for life, by the beginning of the sixteenth century the post had become the heirloom of one particular south-German family, the Hapsburgs—a fact of constant annoyance to the smaller princes of the north. Thus was created that division in Germany between Protestant North and Catholic South: the division which held up the development of a unified German state for three hundred years and which persists in some form or other even to this day.

A series of local wars among the princes gave way in 1555 to what was only the first of many attempts at peaceful coexistence between loyalists and protestants. But the particular Treaty of that year, while permitting each and every petty German despot to pursue the religion of his choice, was in effect a victory for what has come to be known as the Balkanisation of Germany—that is the breaking-up of the Holy Roman Empire into myriads of separate, sovereign territories.

Although the Emperor tried to reassert his authority over the whole of his German domains through that series of bloody conflicts from 1618 to 1648 known in school textbooks as the Thirty Years War, he was prevented from succeeding by the intervention of the French and Swedish kings who saw nothing but advantage in having a weak, divided Germany on their doorsteps. Thus began the fragmentation of the country—a process which was to go on until

Napoleon's conquest of Central Europe a century and a half later destroyed the Holy Roman Empire altogether and compelled Germans to think afresh how they wanted to be governed.

Until then Germany was indeed merely a geographical expression: simply the shorthand name for a collection of virtually self-governing states many of which were no bigger than a London postal district. It was calculated that the area we now term Germany contained at one time no fewer than 77 major principalities, 51 Imperial Cities, 45 Imperial Villages, and 1,475 Imperial Territories under the sway of so-called Independent Knights of the Empire, owing only a slender allegiance to their emperor in Vienna.

And being disunited, Germany was a tempting prey to foreign invaders—the armies of Louis XIV and Louis XV of France moved freely and without much harassment over a large part of the country. People today, particularly those in the Anglo-Saxon world, tend to forget that the Germans, although the largest, were also the last of the major European nations to unite: the centralised, homogeneous German State was not achieved until 1871.

Free Cities such as Essen were, for the most part, corrupt oligarchies—their councils in the hands of greedy merchants who had seized the chance of the chaos into which the religious squabbles had plunged the Empire to throw off the rule of their former ecclesiastical or lay overlords. Indeed, after the Reformation the suzerainty of the Princess-Abbess over the citizens of Essen came to an end and the city's government passed into the gift of a hereditary clique of tradesmen who interpreted the holding of public office as simply yet another opportunity to feather their nests and to extract an extra profit from the poverty-stricken peasant. Goethe, perhaps the most distinguished man of letters Germany has ever produced, likened the lot of the German peasant at this time to the plant-lice he had been observing so lovingly in his biological studies: for he noticed that almost as soon as these lowly creatures had fed themselves on the rose bushes they were sucked dry by big, fat ants. As in most other German cities, Essen's Guild of Merchants, which Arndt Krupe was now joining in this year of 1587, fixed the

import tariffs and the transport tolls within their jurisdiction
entirely to suit themselves and so as to exploit to the full their
customers, the luckless tillers of the local soil, the plant-lice
of Goethe's allegory.

An early convert to Luther's Protestantism, Arndt Krupe
survived not only the rancour of the Reformation but also
the ravages of the Great Plague of 1599 when, according to
the local archives, entire streets of Essen were like a cemetery
"in their sad desertion". What is more he prospered, though
exactly how he did so is still uncertain. For hostile historians
of the Krupp legend the answer is simple and clear: Arndt
profited from the plague. The Black Pest, as the deadly
disease was known, caused many citizens to panic into thinking that the end of the world was nigh: they sold everything
they possessed so as to enjoy to the full their final days on
earth. These Essenders scrambled to dispose of their
businesses and their lands to the first bidder, who in many
cases happened to be Arndt Krupe. He purchased every
property that came his way at what would today be described
as "bargain-basement prices"—and when the scare was all
over he sold them back again, more often than not to their
original owners, for something nearer their true value.

What is certain is that within a short time of the end of the
plague Arndt Krupe began to be numbered among Essen's
wealthiest burghers, for thereafter the city's records mention
his name with growing frequency. We are told, for instance,
that he was a merchant dealing in wines, spirits, and
sometimes cattle; that he later added Dutch spices to his
list; that he acquired yet more land and yet more property,
including a substantial house near the City Hall; that he was
elected to the City Council; that from time to time he loaned
money. A typical Arndt loan was that of £40 at 6 per cent to
a Johann Osterfeld and his wife Anna. The security was the
Osterfelds' house, two brewing-vats, "and all their heirlooms,
present and future, to cover any possible loss"—which makes
Arndt Krupe sound a very prudent businessman indeed. That
he was also thorough can perhaps be judged from the fact
that just before his death in 1624 he bought from a local
quarry a tombstone for ten shillings.

Arndt left four children: Anton, Catherina, Georg, and

Margarethe. Catherina married a rich, elderly Essen merchant, Alexander Huyssen, and so set the pattern for a great many of the Krupp womenfolk who were to come after her in outliving her husband by several years—in her case by fifty-five years—and in increasing the family's fortune during her widowhood. Indeed if the official Krupp historians are to be believed she died "probably the richest woman in Essen".

Although Essen did not become a notable centre for making or using iron until the early nineteenth century, gunsmiths and armourers had been listed among her craftsmen since the Middle Ages. Their customers were neighbouring German princes or else agents for foreign armies such as the British and the French. By all accounts it would seem to have been a lucrative line of business—so that when Germany became the battlefield for the Thirty Years War, Essen was especially well-placed to supply all comers. She sold alike to both Protestant Holland and Catholic Cologne. The city's records for 1608 mention some two dozen gunsmiths and dealers in weapons doing business within the bounds of the mediaeval walls—but already by 1620, after barely two years of war, the number had grown to fifty-four.

It so happened that Arndt Krupe's eldest son, Anton, had married into one of Essen's most prosperous and well-established gunsmith families, the Kroesens. And although Anton kept to the same line of business as his father—he is listed as dealing in spirits, Spanish wines, and spices, and as paying taxes on imports and exports—during the Thirty Years War he took the opportunity of his father-in-law's connections to extend his wares to embrace weapons. At one time he was selling 1,000 gun-barrels a year, which was evidently quite a hefty slice of Essen's total turnover in that particular product. Other members of his family are said to have peddled bayonets and cannon-balls to the God-fearing armies who warred around Essen's walls. So within just one generation of arriving in Essen the House of Krupp was already associated with the industry from which all its later notoriety springs—armaments.

Anton also followed his father's example in seeking out

public office in Essen. Apparently he was a shrewd nego-
tiator, for there are frequent references in the records to his
being included in the many delegations from the city that
dealt with the inevitable disputes arising over the billeting
of foreign troops there. After 1641 his stock in the city must
have been especially high, for in that year single-handedly
he successfully persuaded Frederick William of Brandenburg
(the "Great Elector" of Prussian history) to include Essen
in the neutral zone separating the contestants in the Thirty
Years War.

But for Anton this evident facility to argue was to bring
him nothing but trouble in later life. According to the city
archives he appears to have been particularly litigious in his
old age. He was constantly in the courts over matters to do
with his wife's legacies—and this liking for the due processes
of law seems on occasion to have given way to truculence and
even to violence, for it is recorded that he was once fined fifty
shillings for beating up one of his legal opponents in thestreet.

However, there was at least one Krupp who could be
relied upon to keep his head at all times—and that was
Anton's nephew Matthias. In 1648 the twenty-five-year-old
son of Anton's younger brother Georg, who had died from
the plague when Matthias had been just two years old, was
elected Town Clerk of Essen. It was a job for life. Although the
official salary was low, there were numerous fees and other
honorariums—and Essen Town Clerks usually prospered.
Matthias was to be no exception. He bought land outside
the city walls, including some that nearly two centuries
later would be the site for the great Krupp steel foundries.
That he must have also been a success in his public duties
can be judged from the fact that when he died in 1673 his
son was allowed to succeed him as Town Clerk and that the
post now became an heirloom of the Krupp family.

Matthias' son, Georg Dietrich, was Town Clerk of Essen
for sixty-four years. He too prospered, adding yet more land
and yet more houses to the already long list of Krupp
properties. He speculated with great success and became a
money-lender, though by all accounts he was harsh and at
times unscrupulous in his dealings: it is said that once when
the chairman of Essen's Guild of Merchants tried to oppose

one of his schemes, Georg Dietrich simply had him removed from office and a Krupp put in his place.

Georg Dietrich's younger brothers had also become wealthy men holding public office in Essen: one was elected Mayor at the age of thirty while another was appointed superintendent of the local orphanage and a collector of taxes to boot. In fact by the end of the seventeenth century the Krupps were already becoming known as "Essen's uncrowned kings". This rise to riches and respectability within just four generations of Arndt's unheralded arrival in the city coincided with the succession to power of another German family, and one with whom the Krupps' later destinies were to be indissolubly linked—the House of Hohenzollern.

Until 1415 the Hohenzollerns had held imperial posts in Nuremberg, but in that year the Emperor Sigismund had made Frederick of Hohenzollern the *Elector* of Brandenburg. The title of *Elector* meant that he cast one of the seven votes for the emperorship, but Brandenburg, with its capital at Berlin, was a State so poor in natural resources that it had been derisively dubbed "the German Empire's sand-box"— hence the electorship of Brandenburg was considered by some to be a form of banishment from the civilised delights of imperial Nuremberg. If the original Frederick's appointment had been a joke on the part of the Hapsburgs then it was the Hohenzollerns who certainly had the last laugh!

As the eighteenth century began, the Hohenzollerns, principally through the efforts of Frederick William, the Great Elector, had outgrown their adopted Brandenburg, had absorbed Prussia together with a few small though populous principalities along the Rhine and Ruhr on each side of Essen itself, and were about to seize Silesia and a hefty slice of Poland. What is more the Hohenzollerns' army and the Hohenzollerns' administration had become the envy of every German ruler—indeed, the army was considered a force to be reckoned with even by the major military powers of Europe, such as Britain and France.

Georg Dietrich Krupp outlived his only son, and when in 1742 he died at the incredible age for that time of eighty-five, the town clerkship of Essen passed to one of his nephews, Heinrich Wilhelm. Unfortunately, this particular Krupp did not turn out to be as competent or as ruthless as his forefathers had been. His business ventures, almost without exception, were disastrous—so much so that before he died in 1760 he had been forced to sell even his own house to help pay off his debts. He too had only one son who died soon after him. When the widow left Essen on the day of the funeral her creditors claimed that she had in fact fled from them. No Krupp was ever again Town Clerk of Essen—and it seemed that with the fifth generation the golden days of the family were over for ever.

But one of Georg Dietrich's nephews *had* flourished—Friedrich Jodokus Krupp. And it is he who is the link between the family's mediaeval eminence and its later industrial prominence. Born in 1706, Friedrich Jodokus was both a grocer and a cattle-dealer. When barely twenty he married a wealthy heiress twelve years older than himself and in 1737 they had purchased a magnificent house in the centre of Essen, on the corner of the Flax Market and the Limbeckerstrasse. Although their marriage produced no children, their house was to see the birth of many Krupps, including perhaps the most famous Krupp of all time—Alfred, the "Cannon King" of nineteenth-century Europe.

Jodokus' wife died when he was still only in his forties. She left him a rich, eligible widower. He was elected to the city council where he filled many minor public posts. One of his colleagues on the council was a distant cousin of his called Ascherfeld: they were both great-great-grandsons of Arndt Krupe! Ascherfeld in time introduced Friedrich to his nineteen-year-old daughter, Helene Amalie—and Jodokus was smitten enough to ask the gay, good-looking girl to marry him. Thus a Krupp married a Krupp—and in this way a new dynasty was being launched upon the world.

Helene Amalie was an extremely intelligent and remarkably industrious young woman. Straightaway she set about bringing a new look and a new drive to Jodokus' old business. Nor did it take her very long to master the running of his affairs—which was just as well, for he died when she was only twenty-five, leaving her in sole possession of the firm. Undaunted, Helene Amalie proceeded to bring up her two small children while at the same time improving and expanding the family business. In doing this she showed that tenacity and stubborn resolve which is the hall-mark of the Krupps, and which never ceases to astonish the chronicler of the family's story.

One of her first actions was to change the name of the firm to the rather imaginative *Widow Krupp*. Then she went on to find new things to sell in her store: cotton goods, linens, paints, lottery tickets. Amsterdam and Cologne public markets came to regard her as one of their regular traders. She even opened a factory for making snuff, at that time a relatively new craze in Germany. Woman friends in Essen were badgered into making towels and handkerchiefs for her to peddle in her shop. She even acquired half a dozen sizeable farms and shares in at least four big coal-mines. But it was when she had already passed her sixtieth birthday that she took the historic step of buying her way into heavy industry: first with her purchase of an iron-fulling mill, and then, much more significantly, with her taking-over in 1800 of the Good Hope iron-foundry at Sterkrade near Essen. It is with this particular acquisition that the House of Krupp became finally associated with the industry to which it owes its present immense wealth and prominence.

The Good Hope had been founded nineteen years earlier by one Eberhard Pfandhoefer, who although apparently sound in his mastery of the technicalities of iron-making was certainly a duffer when it came to business. He had been forced from time to time to borrow money from Widow Krupp, but finally, finding himself unable to repay her, he absconded. "As he fled privily, his estate went into bankruptcy due to my heavy claims on it, and I was forced to buy into it at the public auction paying 15,000 thalers Berlin currency (£4,000) for all the buildings, plant, rights, and goodwill." Helene Amalie was sixty-eight when she opted to try to make the foundry a going concern. After first endeavouring to run it through a manager, in 1807 she put her grandson Friedrich in charge, although he was then not yet twenty-one years old; his father had died twelve years before.

Helene Amalie must have been an immensely forceful and

intolerable woman, certainly in her middle and later years. She had completely dominated her only son, Peter Friedrich, who appears to have been a somewhat insignificant Krupp as Krupps go. He had much preferred to copy his father, interesting himself in public affairs and intellectual matters rather than in business, becoming a lieutenant in the Rifle Association and a member of the city council. He had married a Petronella Forsthof, the daughter of a yeoman farmer from near Düsseldorf, and they had had three children. In fact his main contribution to the Krupp saga would seem to be that he fathered the particular Krupp from which the firm *Fried. Krupp of Essen* still takes its name even to this day.

But he had also looked after his mother's accounts—and it is from Peter Friedrich's careful inventory of her wealth that we learn not simply that she was at one time worth nearly £40,000 (a considerable sum for those days and equal to about £400,000 at today's prices), but more interestingly that her fortune like many another trading fortune of the period had been built up largely through lending money to local peasants at high rates of interest.

So far the Krupps have been traders, usurers, and office-seekers—none of them ever farmers or simple artisans. They had preferred peddling the products of other people's labours to producing things for themselves. Moreover, in contrast to most other German mercantile families at this time there was not even a cleric or a scholar, a doctor or a soldier among them. With single-mindedness of purpose, the Krupps for six generations had interested themselves solely in the amassing of wealth. They had been capitalists pure and simple. The next stage in the Krupp saga is how the capitalists became entrepreneurs. It also happens to be the story of the beginnings of the industrial revolution in Germany.

CHAPTER TWO

"... for the manufacture of English Cast Steel and all products made thereof"

HELENE AMALIE's grandson, Friedrich Krupp, had been born on 17 July 1787, exactly 200 years after the first casual mention of Arndt Krupe's name in Essen's archives: 200 years that had seen not only changing fortunes for the House of Krupp, but also momentous happenings within Europe itself. The protracted wars of the Reformation, the terrible years of plague and economic depression, had given way to the growing military power of Brandenburg–Prussia in the east, while in the west across the Rhine the glamorous reign of Louis XIV of France, *le Roi Soleil*, had come and gone. By the year of Friedrich's birth, France was already a bankrupt nation—a factor of immense consequence for every European no matter how humble. And since Essen lay in the centre of Europe, midway between rising Prussia and stumbling France, it was clear that no one in that city was going to escape the tumult of those turbulent times.

Never a great seat of learning, Essen's college was evidently in a sorry state by the closing decade of the eighteenth century—and so Friedrich's formal education, despite all the years he devoted to it, left much to be desired. Throughout his whole life he could scarcely ever compose a letter properly. It would seem too that these early faults in his training helped to make him a peevish, petulant young puppy, reluctant to persevere at anything—the exact opposite of what today we have come to picture a Krupp.

In the years that followed the French Revolution—that event which so alarmed central Europe's despotic rulers that they hurried in vain to suppress it before some of its liberalising yeast might leaven their internal stodginess—Essen became a see-saw of capture and evacuation. First she was occupied by the armies of Prussia and Austria on their way to attack France in 1792. Then the French troops forced them out and took Essen for themselves. But in 1802 Prussia saw fit to seize the city again, this time for her own self-aggrandisement, and thereby to proclaim the end once and for all of Essen's thousand years of independence—until of course Napoleon retaliated and defeated Prussia, when the city once more reverted to French rule. Bonaparte's men were finally driven out by Marshal Blücher's forces in 1813, and at the Peace Settlement twelve months later Essen was given to Prussia—an arrangement which at least has proved lasting!

During the final French occupation, Friedrich became a municipal councillor. But to do so he had had to take an oath of loyalty to Napoleon. The month he had chosen to make this quislingite gesture was a particularly inopportune one—December 1812, when Bonaparte had already been checked at the gates of Moscow and his retreat was setting off a wave of nationalistic sentiment throughout Germany. But apparently all this patriotism left Friedrich singularly unmoved, as wearing the red and white cockade of Revolutionary France he went about his public duties of seeing to the safe billeting of Napoleon's soldiers within the city.

Almost a year later, during the autumn of 1813 when the Prussian Army was fast advancing on the Ruhr, Friedrich helped the French dig trenches in front of Essen. But as soon as Bonaparte's men had withdrawn, Friedrich offered his services to the new occupiers and in fact became an adjutant in the Prussian Home Guard. Some Krupp historians have tried to dismiss all this as simply youthful enthusiasm on the part of Friedrich (he was only twenty-six at the time), while others regard it as the first instance of what was to become a lasting trait in the Krupp character, namely that of shrugging aside the politics of any particular issue and preferring instead to go along with who ever happens to be in power at that moment. To these critics, the Krupps are not the patriots their eulogisers would have us believe, but are merely opportunists with a keen eye for whatever is expedient.

When Essen had first become Prussian in 1802, Helene Amalie had sought to enlarge her Good Hope iron-foundry by trying to persuade the new authorities in Berlin to give her a subsidy. Instead they had given her orders for cannon-balls. This was the first of a long series of attempts by the Krupps to get Government assistance for their firm. Although they were out-and-out capitalists and staunch believers in unfettered private enterprise, they were never averse to State aid if they could possibly get it on their own terms.

Helene Amalie had evidently acquired the Good Hope with the clear intention of presenting it to her grandson whenever the opportunity arose. In 1807, after he had spent only a short time managing the store in the Flax Market, she let him take over the running of the iron-works although he knew next to nothing about either engineering or metallurgy. His commercial experience to date had been confined merely to the buying and selling of paints, linens, and spices for his grandmother. What is more, it would appear from his letters that he was a churlish and impulsive youth—indeed one of his earliest actions at the foundry was to sack the old foreman who had been looking after the place quite successfully before him. Another was to switch from making kitchen stoves and cooking utensils, all of which had hitherto been profitable lines, to manufacturing parts for steam engines, products they had had no experience of selling and which in addition were much more expensive to produce. Friedrich also set about enlarging the Good Hope —in fact entirely rebuilding it. But his grandmother had become rather anxious at the sharp drop in the foundry's profits, and so while Friedrich was recovering from a sudden illness she seized the chance in November 1808 to sell the concern after only a year of his management. Nevertheless, despite her grandson's follies, she got more than three times what she had originally paid for it! and there the brief flirtation of the Krupp family with the making and selling of iron might well have ended, and they would perhaps have returned for all time to the profitable peddling of other men's labours. Incidentally, the Good Hope later became one of the greatest industrial undertakings along the Ruhr and is today the twelfth largest business concern in West Germany, only marginally smaller than Krupp's themselves!

But Friedrich would not seem to have been disheartened by his grandmother's obvious lack of faith in him. Perhaps his mind was taken off it all by his marriage to Therese Wilhelmi, the sixteen-year-old daughter of another Essen merchant. The young couple went to live with Helene Amalie in the house near the Flax Market, while Friedrich returned to looking after his grandmother's store.

Meantime of course Napoleon had conquered most of central Europe. The Holy Roman Empire was at long last dissolved, and all Germany outside Prussia and Austria organised into a French Confederation of the Rhine. German cities such as Essen began experiencing for the first time some of the liberalising leaven of the French Revolution; religious persecution was prohibited, Church lands confiscated, serfdom abolished, the privileges of the landed aristocracy ended, and the restrictive practices of the mediaeval guilds removed for all time.

Yet in giving the German people a taste for liberty and equality, Napoleon also gave the German princes a reason for fraternity. It was hatred of the French that in the end united Germany's rulers and gave German nationalism a voice. And after their traditional leader Austria had dithered in taking up their standard, German nationalists looked to the second most powerful State in Germany, Prussia, as the instrument for ridding them of the French. This was a decision of paramount significance to the rest of Europe, and one of incredibly good fortune to the businessmen of Essen, located as they were within Prussia's orbit. It was particularly fortunate for the House of Krupp since they had already established business relations with the Prussian Government.

The year Helene Amalie sold the Good Hope iron-foundry, Napoleon still occupied most of Germany. By blockading Continental ports to English shipping and trade he was also trying to starve Britain and her allies into submission, or at least to cripple them financially. But despite a tight chain of Customs posts, intensive evasion of the embargo now began. It was of course at this time too that the Rothschilds, the famous banking family, were laying the foundations for their great fortune by smuggling gold and other contraband between Britain and Napoleon's Europe—and evidently such dangerous undertakings appealed to young Friedrich Krupp as well.

In November 1809 he formed a partnership with some Dutch merchants of Borken to smuggle coffee, indigo, soap, and sugar between Holland and Germany. Krupp put up £1,500 as his share of the partnership—a sum which he could have only got from his grandmother, so presumably the project must have had her blessing. But it soon became clear that the risks were immense, for as Napoleon tightened his blockade many of the smugglers were caught and shot. Nothing daunted, Friedrich even began to ply for business as far south as Frankfurt, which was of course Rothschild country, though there is no evidence of the two families having any contact with each other at this time. In the end, however, Friedrich's Dutch partners took fright and dropped out, which forced him to give up too.

Meanwhile Helene Amalie had died: on 9 March 1810. Having outlived her husband by fifty-five years, Friedrich's grandmother had become one of the wealthiest women in the Ruhr. Her fortune was made up mostly of land and property, together with a few well-secured loans. In addition to the store in the Flax Market, Friedrich inherited an initial £6,000. Twelve months later he became wealthier still when a great-aunt died leaving him another considerable legacy. Friedrich at first threw all his energies into enlarging the store and into improving the wholesale side of the business, but his brief experience at the foundry had evidently whetted his interest in iron, for it was to this that he now turned his main attention.

For reasons we have already discussed Germany had been much slower in starting her industrial revolution than either Britain or France. Even in the year of Helene Amalie's death, she was still predominantly an agricultural country. The great stimulus which nations like Britain had received from the opening up of new continents had passed Germany by. Moreover, she had missed out too on the expansion in world trade. On top of everything the protracted wars of the Reformation had ruined her handicrafts and diminished her population. She had no prosperous manufacturing-class as in Britain, and her mercantile community was perhaps the most aggressively conservative of any on the Continent. In contrast to Britain, Germany's earliest industrialists were mainly financiers, hardly ever inventors.

But far and away the most debilitating factor of all for German businessmen was the lack of political unity. This meant not only that there was no large ready-made domestic market for the products of their burgeoning industries, but also that with the fragmentation of the country numerous petty restrictions held up the free movement of goods even between neighbouring towns: for instance, in 1800 thirty-two separate tolls had to be paid, many of them involving lengthy delays, on a journey along the Rhine between Strasbourg and the Dutch frontier, while the valley of the Ruhr was divided among eight different territories, each with its own individual systems of revenue-taxes and Customs-dues.

Yet Germany was not lacking in natural resources. She had ample supplies of coal and iron-ore, as well as plenty of fast-flowing rivers to power the primitive forges and the other early machinery. Coal in fact had been mined in the Ruhr valley since at least the thirteenth century—and iron too had long been dug out of the hills south of the river. But it was only the English discoveries of steam-power and *puddling*—a process for converting cast-iron into wrought-iron by smelting with coal—that enabled the iron industry to come down from the hills and to move away from the charcoal forests to the valleys and plains of the north where the collieries lay. Essen was doubly fortunate in having abundant coal and iron-ore close by.

When Prussia grabbed Essen in 1802 there were no fewer than 127 coal-mines within a few miles radius of the city. Most of them lay in the valley of the Ruhr, and traces of these early mines remain even to this day. But the Prussians closed the older pits, concentrated production on the larger collieries, and halted the indiscriminate sinking of new shafts.

Many local mine-owners, already fearing competition for their coal, took still more fright when the authorities at Berlin set about improving river navigation so that goods could be shipped more quickly and more cheaply—and the alarm spread to other Essen tradesmen when the French having reoccupied the area proceeded to sweep away all the petty tolls and import tariffs that had grown up there over the centuries. These narrow mercantile communities were beginning to feel the chill wind of outside competition for the first time.

But the new machinery of the industrial revolution demanded a material tougher and more reliable than iron. In 1740 an English watchmaker called Benjamin Huntsman had created such a material with his invention of cast or crucible steel. Since it was carbon that gave iron its inherent drawbacks and weaknesses, Huntsman's process was designed to get rid of the offending ingredient by fusing in sealed earthenware crucibles. The finished product he called steel and his method of making it remained a British monopoly for one hundred years. It led for instance to Sheffield's phenomenal rise.

Germany hitherto had got all her supplies of cast steel from Britain, but now Napoleon's blockade was putting an end to all that and was threatening to kill many German industries into the bargain, particularly those located in the Ruhr valley. Bonaparte realised the crucial importance of this steel, for he had offered prizes of £1,000 to anyone on the Continent who could match the British product. Similar monetary inducements to get round the shortage of other essential goods shut out by the blockade had produced a spate of inventions in Essen, including one from Friedrich's brother-in-law for brewing "approved patent coffee". South of Essen, in the town of Solingen, there was even an Inventions Company formed at this time to take part in all these competitions. Two Belgian brothers and a Swiss competed in fact for Napoleon's steel prize in 1807. It was their failure that spurred young Friedrich to enter the race.

In their naïve wish to whitewash the family, many Krupp biographers have endeavoured to claim that either Friedrich or his son Alfred invented the German variety of cast steel.

The truth would seem to be that neither did, but that Alfred eventually developed a way of making cast steel based on the British process. So far as Friedrich is concerned, he had not attempted to compete for Napoleon's £1,000 until he met up with two retired army officers by the name of von Kechel. These brothers claimed they possessed a secret formula for making a steel every bit as good as the British product. However, they did not tell Friedrich—and he would appear not to have asked—the source of this formula. It was in fact taken from a school textbook on chemistry! Nor did the von Kechels tell Krupp that a previous venture of theirs for making steel in another part of Germany had recently gone bust.

Unknowing, yet undaunted, Friedrich entered into a partnership with the von Kechels. He was to contribute the capital for establishing the plant and keeping it running, in return for their providing their "secret formula"; the profits were to be split two ways. And so on 20 November 1811, when he was just twenty-four years old, having announced to his friends that he "had no further interest in spices", Friedrich founded the firm of Fried. Krupp of Essen to build and to operate a factory "for the manufacture of English Cast Steel and all products made thereof"—the firm which, surviving many changes of fortune, is still the basis of today's multi-million-pound Krupp industrial empire.

Spellbound by the vision of immense profits which he felt sure would soon be his, Friedrich straightaway took on fifty workers to help build his smelting shop and forge, and immediately began buying immense quantities of coal and iron. He proclaimed that he was prepared "to supply all Europe with his steel" and he commissioned scores of price-lists from the well-known Essen printing-house of Baedecker —the selfsame family who later published the famous guide-books.

But Friedrich and the von Kechels never produced any steel—and after three years of fruitless experimenting, during which he lost more than £5,000, Friedrich finally took his family's advice in the autumn of 1814 and closed down the works. His partners tried to milk him even further, before the courts came to his rescue and decided the factory's ownership in his favour. Following a stormy scene with the workmen, the von Kechels hurriedly left town.

Yet within a year Friedrich had reopened the works, this time with a new partner: a former captain of the Prussian Hussars by the name of Nicolai. Nicolai had advertised his abilities in the local Ruhr newspaper as "a useful member of society who has journeyed widely throughout most of Germany, Holland, England, and France to form his artistic talents, and has garnered on these journeys a wealth of the most practical knowledge, notably about every kind of machine". Evidently this kind of blurb was enough to persuade Krupp, particularly when Nicolai claimed to have had experience in making cast steel for the Prussian Government and said he held a royal charter granting him the sole right to produce such steel in the area between the Elbe and the Rhine.

On this occasion Friedrich was slightly shrewder in drawing up the partnership agreement with Nicolai; perhaps he had learned something from his venture with the von Kechels. Although he once again put up the money for the machinery and the materials, he insisted on Nicolai providing the funds to operate the factory day by day. But when Nicolai soon fell behind in paying the workmen their wages, and a visiting Prussian official pronounced his letter of credentials to be a fake, Friedrich realised he had been swindled a second time. His foundrymen had to be forcibly prevented from harming Nicolai, and in July 1816 the doors of the works were once more closed.

But although he had been conned twice—and at great cost—Friedrich had at least learned a little about foundrywork, enough to give him the confidence to branch out on his own. Within a few months he had re-opened the factory and begun producing a steel of sorts. The times, however, were far from favourable to small manufacturers like him. Although Napoleon had been defeated and the wars which had devastated central Europe, and Germany in particular, for twenty-three years were now over, the hopes of those who had looked forward to an immediate economic recovery were quickly dashed. Almost straightaway after her victory at

Waterloo, Britain began flooding the Continent with her goods, selling many of them at prices below those prevailing at home. This hit Germany's budding businessmen, whose position was then made worse by the petty German princes insisting on their country being divided up yet again into numerous different despotisms. Thus the German trader was deprived of that large home market which ironically he had known only under the occupation of the hated French. Friedrich even tried competing with his powerful British rivals by pinching their trade-marks to use on his own products—but all to no avail.

As Essen had been granted to Prussia at the Congress of Vienna that had decided the peace after Bonaparte's defeat, Krupp looked to Berlin to provide work for his foundry. In 1817 he was successful in obtaining orders from the Prussian Royal Mint for several steel dies for making coins—and it was this, together with a few local sales of mechanics' and artisans' tools, that put Friedrich on his feet. But once again he wanted to run before he could walk. Not content with his modest success, he immediately began planning massive extensions to his existing works, even for a new factory on a different site. Although he already owed them about £5,000, his mother and brother-in-law advanced him still more money. He even put up his prices, which immediately brought protests from his regular customers and a sharp falling off in their business with him.

The site he had chosen for his new factory lay just beyond Essen's Limbecker Gate, on land that had been in Krupp ownership ever since Matthias the Town Clerk had bought it a century and a half before. But inevitably Friedrich's plans were over-ambitious. They provided space for sixty smelting furnaces, though only eight were ever put up in his lifetime. The building was complete by August 1819 and a further £3,500 was spent on fitting it out with fresh equipment. To Friedrich, the new factory was "lovely and expensive". More orders came his way from the Prussian Government, this time for steel blocks for gun-barrels and bayonets. One of his clerks even managed to place an editorial plug for the firm's products in an influential Frankfurt newspaper, which brought in yet more business.

By 1823 Friedrich's output was considerable, though nearly two-thirds of it was work for the Prussian Mint. But his luck did not hold. The extensions to his works had swallowed up all his available capital and he had run into debt—even his family was refusing to lend him any more money. This shortage of funds hindered his buying the proper raw materials and on occasion he had to make do with inferior scrap iron, which lowered the quality of his goods and brought constant complaints from his customers. On top of all this, he was often late with his deliveries, for he had run into a crop of technical troubles, the chief of which was the frequent cracking of the cupolas in which he fused his steel, so that the molten metal sometimes ran away. He had also erred in siting his new factory near a stream which usually ran dry in summer. It meant that his forging hammers lay idle for weeks on end so that he had to sub-contract out the forging work, all of which resulted in yet more expense and yet more delays.

His sales dropped and dropped. He began to lose interest in the firm. His book-keeper had to drag him out of taverns to sign essential papers. He tried and failed to get a subsidy from the Prussian Government. He sought the post of super-visor at the new State-owned steel foundry, but was not even considered. He approached the Czar with a view to establishing a steel mill in Russia, but again got no response. Soon his relatives started worrying him to repay their loans, and family accord was only restored on many an occasion by his mother giving them some of her own land. Then in April 1824 his wife's father secured a legal injunction for the immediate settling of £2,000, and when as expected Friedrich could not pay, the courts insisted that he hand over the deeds to the house in the Flax Market which Friedrich Jodokus had first bought in 1737—the house in which Helene Amalie had lived for most of her life and in which her great-grandson Alfred, the future "Cannon King", had been born in 1812. Reluctantly, Friedrich did so, and a short time later the house was sold, passing out of the family for ever. Today its site is occupied by a shop selling washing machines and refrigerators.

Friedrich moved his wife and their four children into the

little cottage he had originally built near the factory for the foreman. His wife told her friends that the air outside the city walls would suit their health better and that Friedrich could also "keep a closer eye on affairs at the works"—not that much was happening at the works, for almost all their customers had left them. But Friedrich's health was really broken now. In fact he spent most of his time in bed. The rest of the family did not bear these tribulations temperately —and their noisy arguments became the talk of the town. Friedrich had long since resigned his seat on the city council and his name had already been struck off the list of taxpayers. In 1825, the year after giving up the Flax Market house, he had to suffer the final indignity of being removed from the Register of Privileged Merchants: a sort of local *Who's Who*. To date, his various enterprises had swallowed up more than £30,000. His only daughter was working as a governess while his eldest son was billeted on relatives because Friedrich could no longer afford to feed him. On 8 October 1826, although just thirty-nine years old, Friedrich Krupp succumbed to pectoral dropsy.

The year he died, coal from the Ruhr was borne for the first time by rail and the Rhine saw its first passenger steamship. His had been an era of great change. Essen was discarding the final traces of mediaevalism, while all Germany was at last beginning to throw off the lethargy into which she had fallen during the long decline of the Holy Roman Empire. The stage was being set for what would have seemed to him incredible material progress and prosperity, for the final forging of German political unity through Bismarck's "blood and iron". If Friedrich had been born perhaps only a few decades later, it is conceivable that he might have been more fortunate. His failure mirrors the immense difficulties under which the early German industrialists had to labour. The year before Friedrich's death, Goethe wrote, "Wealth and rapidity are what the world now admires and what everyone now strives to attain . . . this is the century for men with heads on their shoulders, for practical men of quick perceptions, who, because they possess a certain adroitness, feel their superiority to the multitude."

Friedrich's body was laid to rest in a little churchyard near the centre of Essen. Not many years afterwards, when the city began to outgrow its ancient walls, the cemetery was built upon. Today no gravestone indicates the spot where he lies. What is more no painted likeness of him has survived the passage of time. Yet he has perhaps the most concrete memorial of all the Krupps, for it is his name after all that the firm bears today—Fried. Krupp of Essen.

CHAPTER THREE

"We have no time for reading, politics, and that sort of thing"

ON 26 APRIL 1812, just five months after Friedrich had founded the firm, Alfred the future "Cannon King" was born—ironically those two rogues the von Kechels were his godfathers. When Friedrich died, his eldest son was barely fourteen years old. He had already been taken away from school the year before because of the expense—nor had his family been able to afford to apprentice him to some master-craftsman. Instead, he had been sent to help out in the foundry. In later life, when visitors used to ask him about his formal education, Alfred would invariably growl back, "I got my schooling at an anvil".

The son was a vastly different kettle of fish from the father. In fact they were opposites—and this was to be true of Alfred and *his* son. Whereas Friedrich had been by and large a Romantic, weak but sentimental, Alfred on the other hand was to be a Stoic, resolute but unimpassioned. In the same week as his father's funeral, he was writing to tell their most important customer, the Director-General of the Berlin Mint, that the business would not suffer as a result of the family's misfortune, "as my mother, who has instructed me to present to you her most obedient regards, will continue it with my help"—and he went on, "The satisfaction of merchants, mints, etc., with the crucible steel which I have turned out during the past year has gone on increasing, so that we often cannot produce as much as we receive orders for." This last statement was of course a blatant lie, but then Alfred throughout his life was never to be a stickler for truth—he was never to see anything amiss in bending it a little to suit his own advantage. In point of fact, work had almost ceased at the foundry when Friedrich died. Only seven men remained, and most of them had not had any wages for several weeks. The firm's debts amounted to nearly £4,000, £1,500 more than the total value of all the machinery and buildings.

To shield her four children from the shame of a possible bankruptcy, Therese Krupp put the property in her own name. She was then just thirty-four years old herself—and no matter how disgusting or repellent one may find the Krupp saga, yet at the same time one cannot fail but be touched by the determined way in which the widowed Therese and her schoolboy son set about restoring the family's fortune. "I learned a great deal more from my mother than from my father", Alfred was to say in middle age. "I inherited from her the industriousness by which she rescued the family." Life became very hard for Therese. For one thing there was not always the money to buy food —and so like many another impoverished widow in Essen at that time she grew a few potatoes and reared a few live-stock of her own, either on the communal pasture or else around her tiny cottage near the works. In this way she could make sure that her children never actually starved.

While other boys of his age were playing with their chums in the fields or else hunting alongside their fathers in the woods around Essen, Alfred devoted every hour of his waking day to the firm: helping the men in the foundry one moment and during the next writing letters to customers for his mother. His youth was without those softnesses and those light-hearted moments with which other parents seek to surround their maturing offspring. Small wonder then that with every passing year he should become a little colder and have a little less warmth of feeling in his relations with his fellow beings. Small wonder too that in place of his heart should burgeon a terrible obsession—an obsession solely to do with the making and selling of steel.

Before success and fortune finally came his way, Alfred had to endure twenty years or so of perpetual grind and near-gloom, though the first ten were by far the worst. There were weeks for instance when he did not have enough money to pay his men—and there were other weeks when there was no work for them to do. But Alfred himself never slackened for one moment. He used to visit all the smithies and forges for miles around Essen, seeking custom, but he was having to compete with steel from England which still dominated the Prussian market. Even when the orders came in they were small and far from regular in flow: a few tools here, a few fleshing knives there, and only very occasionally the more lucrative coin-dies for mints.

As prosperity began to pick up in Prussia, so Alfred's business gradually improved. He started venturing farther afield in search of work for his foundrymen, visiting the valleys of the Main and the Neckar in south Germany— trips which proved quite profitable. However, like his father before him, as soon as any money began to come in Alfred immediately plunged into schemes for rebuilding and extending the works. The smelting-shop was fitted out with a new forging-press—and he even installed a wooden power-hammer. But the hammer was something of a white elephant, because there was seldom enough water in the stream to drive it. In the end it was to be another sort of drive and power that would save Krupp, that would put him on the path to eventual fortune—the drive and power of Prussia.

At the Peace Conference following Napoleon's defeat, Prussia had been given most of the former Rhineland states in the west as compensation for the loss of her Polish terri-tories in the east. In making this territorial transfer, the statesmen of the day did not of course consult the wishes of the luckless people who happened to live in these lands— it was merely a question of counting heads, or *souls* as the diplomats called them then. Prussia in point of fact would have much preferred to have kept her part of Poland, or at least to have got a bigger slice of Saxony, and not to have had anything to do with the Rhineland—indeed when she was given it she suspected the whole manœuvre as a piece of skulduggery on the part of her former allies. What she certainly did not realise at the time was that she was giving up some relatively worthless agricultural land in the east and obtaining in return what was to become the richest industrial area in the world. Nor did her allies realise that by granting Prussia the Rhineland they were really forcing her to become a German State, a prospect she had hitherto been reluctant to face up to. What is more, because the new Prussian lands in the west were cut off from Prussia proper in the east, they were in effect creating problems of defence and pure administration for the Prussians which could only be satisfactorily solved by annexing all the territories in between—and once Prussia had done that she would be not only the most powerful state in Germany but also well on the way to becoming the most powerful state in Europe.

Three years after the 1815 peace, in an attempt to help unite their scattered provinces, the Prussian Government lifted all internal Customs barriers and at the same time abolished most of the remaining petty restrictions on the movement of trade. At first many of the other German states retaliated by coming together in groups themselves to form their own Customs unions. However, these never proved very popular, and on 1 January 1834 they all joined up with Prussia in a single Customs union which within two years had been extended to cover most of Germany except 'for Austria, Hanover, and a few of the tinier territories. This *Zollverein*, as it was called, created what many German businessmen had been longing for—a single economic unit of twenty-five million people. In many ways it was the forerunner of today's European Common Market—and of course Ruhr businessmen such as Alfred Krupp were well placed to serve this new community.

Indeed, three months after the *Zollverein*'s creation, Alfred was setting out on a business trip that took him to all the principal centres of Germany—a trip that was so successful that by the end of 1834 he had trebled his output and had increased his labour-force from eleven to thirty. A year later he had doubled his production yet again and was then employing nearly seventy people. At long last he was able to purchase a steam-engine to power his forging-hammers and in this way could turn his back once and for all on the seasonal variations of drought, flood, and ice in his mill-streams. As fate would have it he obtained his steam-engine—a £750 twenty-horsepower one—from that self-same Good Hope iron-foundry which his great-grandmother had once possessed and which his father had nearly inherited a quarter of a century before. Alfred was then just twenty-three years old!

But even the expanded market of the German Customs union was not big enough for him. He took on a couple of travelling salesmen and began looking for business in other parts of Europe. Soon the orders were coming in from as far afield as Russia, Italy and Turkey, as well as from France, Holland, Austria and Switzerland. He made coin-dies for the Royal Dutch Mint and for the Royal Sardinian Mint.

His younger brother, Hermann, now joined the firm and together they spent much of their time flitting from city to city, from capital to capital, both often being away from Essen for months at a time. But all this gadding about was swallowing up the profits: Alfred's correspondence is littered with pleas to suppliers to extend their credit, appeals to bankers for loans, excuses to customers for late deliveries. His mother made at least eight different applica-tions to Berlin for Government assistance—to be rebuffed every time. And all the while, of course, Alfred continued to face competition from Britain, for as in his father's day English steel still led the world, and he in effect was merely picking up the few titbits the Sheffield manufacturers cared to let fall from their rich tables.

Alfred as a matter of fact was for ever trying to ape his English rivals, even to the extent of seeking out the same sources of iron for his steel as they used in theirs, hoping that this might lead him to the secret of the superior British product. But in the end he decided that perhaps the best solution of all was to go and see for himself how the English made their steel: in other words to play the spy.

And so in the summer of 1838 he set out for London and checked in at the Hotel Sablonniere in Leicester Square under the name of A. Crup. He had chosen this way of spelling his name because he thought it sounded more English and therefore might come in useful if he needed to take a job in a Sheffield foundry. But all this amateurish cloak-and-dagger stuff was not to be necessary, for Alfred got what he wanted by simply marching up to the factory gate and asking to be shown around. "Only yesterday", he wrote home to his brother, "I saw without any introduction, a new rolling-mill for copper-plates which has only been working for a short time and where no one is admitted"—and he went on, "I was properly booted and spurred, and the proprietor was flattered that such a good fellow should deign to inspect his works." On another occasion he boasted to his brother how the English had been so hospitable that "I have not had my meals at home one-third of the time and so I have learnt English at less than one-third of the cost!" That Mr. Crup had little difficulty in fact in getting the English to accept him socially is confirmed by a German diplomat who met Alfred in England at this time and who later wrote of him: "We called him the 'Baron' and he was quite young, very tall and slim, looked delicate, but was good-looking and attractive. He always wore little swan-neck spurs and was quite a gentleman. I did not hesitate to introduce him to many families of my acquaintance."

Ironically, Alfred was most particular about protecting his own manufacturing secrets, such as they were—perhaps because he had seen how easy it was to pinch other people's. Only his most trusted workmen were allowed into those parts of the factory where the special processes were being carried out, and he even applied to the Prussian Government on one occasion for authority to make his workmen take an oath of loyalty to him. Although Berlin rejected his request he nevertheless required his men to promise solemnly on their honour not to give away any information—and he even exacted this ritual of a workman who had been sent by him to spy out a secret from a competitor.

In fact Alfred was obsessed with security. When he was not lecturing his brother from afar on the fire hazards in the factory—even to the extent of insisting that he compile a list of all the workmen who smoked—he was probably warning him that "the role of the night-watchman even is not above suspicion, for he certainly walks around too much in the factory by day".

Like everything else he did, travelling was a very earnest affair with Alfred. While in Paris, he wrote to his brother, "I make notes all day, stop in the street ten times an hour to jot down what occurs to me." But what was occurring to him was nothing whatsoever to do with the delights of that most civilised of capitals. Invariably it was something to do with steel, steel, steel—and if not that, then perhaps a grumble or two about his health. Alfred was a hypochondriac. Even on his twenty-seventh birthday he was writing home to say that he was celebrating it with enemas and pointing out that he had toasted himself on his last birthday with cough medicine.

Alfred suffered also from insomnia and had taught himself to write in the dark so that there might be no let-up in the opportunities for note-taking. And this habit of scribbling on pieces of paper stayed with him all his life. He much preferred sending written commands to people rather than instructing them face to face. One of the results of all this was that when he died he left behind him something like 30,000 letters or memoranda.

Unlike his father, Alfred never filled any public office. He was a youth in a hurry—in too much of a hurry to think of his fellow citizens, unless they would buy his steel. A youth, you might say, with a passion, a passion to produce the best cast steel in all Germany. And because of this, he seldom took time off to mix with people of his own age. When invited by a friend to a carnival, he would reply, "Carnivals are nothing to me." If he was not in his factory, then he was either at his writing-desk or else off on his horse visiting a potential customer. It was no use asking him about the state of European poetry or the name of the latest German nationalist song: "We have no time for reading, politics, and that sort of thing." Even one of his most eulogistic biographers says of Alfred, "The world of the spirit was a closed book to him . . . the question of German unity, which affected the whole world, interested him at most only in so far as it might lead to the collapse of inconvenient Customs barriers . . . he is troubled by no doubts, he does not have to grope or to seek his way, he treads the narrow ridge of his career concerned only with coal and steel, like a sleep-walker." Towards the end of his life, Alfred was to write to a friend, "I have no need to ask Goethe or anyone else in the world what is right, I know the answer myself and I don't consider anyone entitled to know better . . . I always go my own way and never ask anybody what is right." He also once recalled in a letter:

> Forty years ago the cracking of a crucible meant possible ruin. We used to cram the metal into the crucibles as tightly as we could, leaving no cranny unfilled. At that time we had some very thick graphite which used to slip through the fingers like soap. We lived from hand to mouth in those days. Everything simply had to turn out right. There weren't the numerous, constant truck-loads of alumina, nor the three or four barrels of graphite then that we possess in stock now. I began by buying the graphite in Essen at three hundredweights a time. In those days that was quite a big undertaking for me. The counter-jumpers were fairly contemptuous of me, I can tell you! But our present Works have sprung from those small beginnings, when the raw materials were purchased piecemeal and where I acted as my own clerk, letter-writer, cashier, smithy, smelter, coke-pounder, night-watchman . . . and took on many other such jobs as well; where a single horse could cope with our transport quite easily; and where, even ten years later, water for our first steam-engine was brought in buckets from the nearby pond to fill the tanks when they had been pumped dry, since a piped water-system would have been too expensive for us.

Thus began the Krupp legend—the rise from rags to riches—a legend which Alfred himself for the remainder of his life was at pains to promote.

Some of his biographers have tried to make out that he was an inventor, but this is simply another part of the fiction rather than of the fact about Alfred Krupp. He was claimed for instance to have originated a rolling-machine device for mass-producing spoons and forks which hitherto had always been made individually by hand. Yet the truth was that it had been invented in the first place by a former customer of Krupp's who had merely got Alfred to manufacture the specially engraved rollers. While the originals were in his works, Alfred took the opportunity to copy them and later,

when the inventor emigrated to Mexico, he was able to
market an improved version of the machine—a manœuvre
that proved immensely profitable. Alfred was rather a
consolidator than an innovator—not that this is necessarily
to be denigrated, except when it involves deception either of
oneself or of others.

After his visit to Britain, during which he had even con-
templated opening up a factory there, Alfred in the summer
of 1839 had gone on to Paris. His quarry were the goldsmiths
and the jewellers of the French capital to whom he hoped to
sell his die-cylinders and his cast-steel rollers. It was while
he was endeavouring to do so that a group of socialists and
republicans attempted to overthrow the monarchy of Louis
Philippe. But in a letter home to his brother, Alfred did not
show where his sympathies lay, merely saying of the incident,
"If it improves business for the citizens to use these methods
then in the devil's name let them go for one another."
Krupp's at this time were not of course producing anything
that was remotely harmful in the hands of either revolution-
aries or reactionaries. However, his remark is significant in
that it represents the first clear statement of what was later
to become axiomatic to the whole approach of the House of
Krupp: namely that of not trying to change the course of
human events, but of swimming instead with the current, the
attitude that was to be summed up a century later in the
phrase, "As Germany goes, Krupp goes".

When his brother complained to him that he had been
away far too long from the factory, Alfred replied, "Even
if there were a bride awaiting me at home, I still could not
return in a greater hurry." His extended English trip had
lasted all of fifteen months and was the major turning-point
in his early career. As a result of it he became resolved to
produce only the highest quality steel—"Krupp steel must
be above suspicion". This was to be the determining factor
in the House of Krupp's later progress and the hall-mark
of their industrial reputation to this day.

Germany in the early 'forties of the last century was just
beginning to experience the first birth-pangs of the Factory
Age. Handicraft workers were being ruined by the competition of the cheaper, machine-made goods coming mostly

from England. Within a few years, many of Alfred's best customers, such as goldsmiths and silversmiths, disappeared as though struck down by a plague—their skills unable to compete with the output of the newer factories. It was a time of transition, when that class of small, independent producers was dying out and before an industrial proletariat had appeared. It was a period too of relative depression, when bankruptcies were frequent and money for spending on luxuries was somewhat scarce.

And so within a mere matter of months of returning from England and France, Alfred was off again. This time his ports of call were Berlin and Vienna, and then on to Warsaw without bothering even to visit Essen in between. Single rollers no longer interested him now but complete rolling mills. In 1840 a Berlin firm gave him an order worth nearly £1,000, while a year later the Vienna Mint bought five complete rolling mills, valued at £6,000. But this Austrian commission was almost his undoing, for they demanded a standard of precision he was unable to reach and which he should never have agreed to in the first place. The wrangling went on for nearly twelve months, took up most of his time and energies, brought him grey hairs and nearly to the brink of bankruptcy before he was thirty. He lost so much money on this particular deal that he thought even of emigrating to Russia—indeed the expedient of using the land of the Czars as a possible bolt-hole became ever more attractive to him over the years, particularly at those moments of intense personal crisis.

But despite the Austrian débâcle, his steel rollers for making spoons and forks were proving highly profitable, so much so that in 1843 he opened a factory near Vienna for producing table-cutlery: the beginnings of the famous Berndorfer steel works. At the same time he branched out at Essen into making steel springs and machine parts. By now the seven workmen of 1826 had grown to a labour-force 100 strong—and although the old foundry still constituted the core of the works, it was already starting to look hemmed in by a number of new constructions, including a boiler-house and a grinding-shop. Alfred was also in the process of building himself a bigger house in which to live—right next-door to the old cottage where his father had died and where his family had been residing ever since.

Alfred maintained the fiction to his dying day that he had been born in this old cottage, when of course his birthplace was Helene Amalie's much grander house in the Flax Market. Indeed, in 1871 when the old cottage was almost on the point of total collapse because of subsidence from the mines beneath, Alfred had it entirely rebuilt and restored although none of the original furniture or fittings had survived. It became a sort of shrine with him; a place to which he would often return when depressed and one where occasionally he would conduct his most important business. He even decorated it with a steel plaque which read: "Fifty years ago this dwelling, originally a workman's house, was the refuge of my parents. May every one of our workmen escape the load of care which the foundation of these Works brought upon us. For twenty-five years doubt remained of the success which has since then gradually, and ultimately in such a marvellous degree, rewarded the privations, the exertions, the confidence, and the perseverance of the past."

When he died his body lay in state there before being taken to the cemetery for burial. Allied bombers destroyed the cottage in 1943, but one of the first things Alfred's great-grandson did on regaining control of Krupp's was to order its rebuilding. When restored it formed the central attraction of the firm's one hundred and fiftieth anniversary celebrations in 1961 just as it had done at the centenary celebrations fifty years before.

But to return to the early troubles of Alfred.

At the end of 1843 he again found himself short of funds. This time he was rescued by a long-standing friend of the family's, Fritz Sölling, who loaned him £12,000 and as a result became a sleeping partner in the firm. Besides being a clever book-keeper with experience of selling overseas Sölling was also a determined critic of Alfred's business methods, particularly of his expensive travelling and perpetual building—criticisms which over the years led to a state of almost continual friction between the two.

Because of the way in which the depression had hit many of the country's newer industries, the Prussian Government now raised the level of Customs dues in an attempt to help protect them from further foreign competition. Naturally such a move benefited Alfred enormously in his endeavours to supplant British steel with his own native German product. Within the year he had increased his labour-force by another twenty-five and could now afford to spread himself a little by taking on his cousin Adalbert Ascherfeld as factory manager. Ascherfeld tyrannised the men who worked for him and quickly became notorious as a stern disciplinarian—passers-by used to taunt Krupp workers hurrying to the factory gate in the early morning with cries of "Run, run, or else old Ascherfeld will get you."

Alfred was a pioneer of industrial public relations and during his whole life never missed an opportunity to publicise his firm. He was also one of the first manufacturers, especially in Germany, to make maximum use of that up-and-coming sales device, the international industrial exhibition. When, for instance, he won the gold medal for his exhibits of cast steel at the Berlin Industrial Fair of 1844 he used the occasion for an intensive publicity campaign for his factory.

While visiting England and France again in 1846 and 1847, Alfred managed not only to obtain an English patent on the improved spoon-roller but also to meet James Rothschild in Paris, though there is no record of the House of Krupp having at that time done business with Europe's most famous banking family.

But another of the periodic slumps that characterised the nineteenth century brought him hurrying back to Essen. This latest one seemed to hit Krupp's particularly hard—their sales dropped from £12,000 to £6,000 within the year. For want of further credit, the works were in danger of having to close down altogether. Fritz Sölling, Alfred's partner, was inclined to blame everything on Alfred's mismanagement, particularly his having wasted the profits of previous good years on excessive travelling and over-ambitious building schemes. Alfred in his turn tried to pass the blame off on to his two younger brothers, Hermann and Fritz. Fritz had not been with the firm all that long, but had already distinguished himself with his clever and resourceful refinements of many of Alfred's products, especially the

profitable spoon-roller. He had in addition devised a set of
tubular chimes in steel that had been displayed at the 1844
Berlin Exhibition and he had also done much of the early
work on the Krupp steel springs. Besides all these he had constructed a self-propelled carriage as well as a device that was
a forerunner of the modern vacuum cleaner. All in all, Fritz
Krupp seems to have been a particularly bright young man.
But Alfred argued that because of his other inventions Fritz
could not have been concentrating on his proper work for
the firm. Hermann for his part had been bearing the brunt
of running the Essen works while Alfred was travelling
around. On top of this he had been closely concerned with
establishing the new Austrian factory which was proving an
enormous success.

The truth was that Alfred really wanted the firm for
himself. His mother had intended it to be divided among her
four children after her death, but Alfred persuaded her to
sell him the factory outright now, which she did for the
incredibly low figure of £3,750. By way of compensation,
Hermann got the Austrian factory, while the £3,750 was
divided between Fritz and his sister Ida, though only on the
condition they did not disclose any of the firm's secrets or
set up in competition to Alfred. Fritz did not like this
arrangement and left Essen in high dudgeon. He later tried
to start a business of his own near Bonn, though without
much success.

And so it came to pass that on 24 February 1848, Alfred
Krupp took complete possession of the firm his father had
founded and thus began the one-man ownership that has
characterised the House of Krupp ever since. It so happened
that this was the selfsame day which saw the final extinction
of the French monarchy—the event that began the spate of
revolutionary feeling which spread rapidly across Europe,
from Paris to Austria, Hungary, Poland and even Berlin.
Some Prussian entrepreneurs encouraged their employees
to petition King Frederick William IV for greater political
freedom from the feudal land-owners, the Junkers. One of
Krupp's closest competitors, Johann August Borsig, the
Prussian "Railway King", actually led his factory-hands
in person to seek increased political rights from the monarch

himself. Alfred, on the other hand, dismissed such revolutionary activities as being merely so many hindrances to trade. He even went so far as to order his workers to have nothing whatsoever to do with the dissidents, but instead to help prevent the revolution from spreading. When two of his oldest workmen, one of whom had been with the firm longer than Alfred himself, dared to complain, he summarily dismissed them both. His works manager used to march the men to and from the city every night and morning, for the gates of Essen had been shut at the first whiff of revolution and they had to be specially opened each time for Krupp's employees. Alfred also gave orders for his workmen to be kept fully occupied, hoping thereby to keep them "out of mischief", as he described it.

The Year of Revolutions had partly been prompted by the sharp decline in business throughout Prussia and Germany. Many firms went bankrupt and several finance houses were forced to close their doors. Alfred in 1848 sacked almost half his work-force and had to melt down the family silver to pay the wages of the rest. But a big order for a spoon-rolling factory from Russia, and another from Britain two years later, saved the day for him. From that time onwards Alfred never really looked back. The days of early struggle were now well-nigh over.

The eventual collapse of the revolutionary cause led to Prussia strengthening her position still further within Germany, since in most cases it was Prussian soldiers whom the German princes had called on to put down the disorders within their territories. Many of Prussia's leaders now became determined to possess Germany. To the English historian A. J. P. Taylor, "the failure of the revolution discredited liberal ideas. After it nothing remained but the idea of Force, and this idea stood at the helm of German history from then on."

German capitalists and German industrialists were to become dependent on Prussian militarism—none more so than Alfred Krupp, for by and large the story of how Prussia came to swallow Germany between 1848 and 1871 is also the story of how Alfred Krupp came to dominate German industry.

CHAPTER FOUR

"We will make the English open their eyes"

ALFRED KRUPP had started making armaments in fact as far back as 1843, although only on a very modest scale. In that year he had sent to the Mulheim Small Arms Works near Essen what he boasted was "the first mild-steel musket-barrel ever produced". He had been prompted to branch out in this way by a report he had received from his brother Hermann some years before that the gunsmiths of Munich were becoming more and more dissatisfied with their iron musket-barrels. Twelve months later, the Industrial Fair at Berlin gave him the opportunity of showing off to a wider audience breast-plates as well as musket-barrels made of his cast steel. What is more they helped to bring him the exhibition's Gold Medal.

Elated with this success, he immediately tried to interest the Prussian War Ministry in his steel weapons, but it was to be a long and difficult courtship. The samples he had sent to the French War Ministry met with the same indifference. He had also offered to make rifles and cannons of his new material—and indeed he completed his first cast-steel cannon in 1847. It was a three-pounder. But it languished for two years in Berlin before anyone bothered to test it. Even then, although they could not fault the gun's performance, the Prussian War Ministry told Alfred that "the present method of manufacturing light-guns, and their quality, satisfies all reasonable needs and leaves hardly any room for improvement"—a statement comparing in its lack of fore-sight with that response the Wright brothers received from the British Admiralty in 1908: "With reference to your communication concerning the use of aeroplanes, I have consulted my technical advisers and regret to inform you that the

Admiralty are of the opinion that they cannot be of any value for naval purposes."

Guns hitherto had been made of either bronze or iron, and the generals were not going to change overnight the weapons they had grown accustomed to using. For their part, the bureaucrats were of course horrified at the extra cost of Krupp's steel cannons—though bronze in particular was becoming ever more expensive and was in any case extremely heavy, especially for field artillery.

But, nothing daunted, Alfred pressed on, and straight-away began making a six-pounder, which he finished in time to display at the London Crystal Palace Exhibition of 1851. Intended as it was to vaunt Victorian England's achievements to the vulgar world, it was rather ironical that Alfred should have chosen this particular venue for his international début, especially in view of his spying trips to Sheffield thirteen years before.

Mounted on a mahogany base and set inside an elegant old Prussian war-tent, Alfred's cannon was one of the sensations of that sensational show. Women spectators are said to have found it "quite bewitching". To Victorian England, sub-jugating half the world in the name of *Pax Britannica*, weapons were for putting primitive peoples in their places or else for making sure civilised races like themselves rested safer in their beds at night. Hence guns could be admired for their ornament, since fashionable London ladies did not as yet associate them as possible killers of their own kith and kin.

Alfred also exhibited a gigantic steel casting weighing more than 4,300 pounds, nearly 2,000 pounds heavier than the largest British ingot on display, for which pride of place in the Exhibition Hall had been obtained and whose manufacturer had arrogantly described it in the official catalogue as "the monster block". Queen Victoria for one stopped to admire Alfred's casting, while the Exhibition Council awarded it the Bronze Medal for such exhibits. He had not been mincing his words when earlier that year he had told his workmen, "We will make the English open their eyes".

Krupp's straightaway became famous, accepted at long

last as a serious contender by the narrow world of steel manufacture. England's long domination in steel was coming to
an end, though many more decades were to pass by before
she needed to be rudely awakened from the industrial
lethargy and commercial complacency into which she was
about to lapse after 1851.

Yet despite all the glory and the acclaim, no one bought
Alfred's cannon, and in the end he gave it away to the King
of Prussia. Frederick William first of all had it set up in the
Great Marble Hall of his palace at Potsdam so that the Czar
of Russia might marvel at it, but later moved it to the
Arsenal in Berlin. The cannon never fired a shot in anger.
It stands today in a museum in East Berlin with only a small
plaque to denote its historic significance.

The King of Hanover and the Duke of Brunswick were
both subsequently given twelve-pounders as presents too,
but they never so much as wrote Alfred a bare note of
acknowledgement. Frederick William did at least donate a
bed to Essen's main hospital and in 1853 sent his brother,
Prince William, to visit Alfred's factory to thank him for his
unusual gift. As a piece of public relations, Alfred's generosity paid off handsomely, for it led to Prince William becoming
interested in his works. The future Kaiser William I was to be
an invaluable ally for Alfred in his perennial battles with the
Prussian bureaucracy.

Always mindful of publicity, Alfred again seized the
splendid opportunity of another world fair to display his
industrial brashness—this time the Great Paris Exhibition of
1855, Napoleon III's reply to Victoria's "vulgar offering"
four years before. Krupp despatched to the French capital a
steel casting weighing more than twice the one he had
shown at the Crystal Palace. At 10,000 pounds weight, it was
so heavy that the trucks carrying it there broke down in the
Paris streets—bringing of course yet more publicity to
Alfred's firm. Even when it finally reached its allotted position in the exhibition hall, the massive ingot still crashed
through the floor, so much so that in exasperation the
French officials dubbed Krupp "that curséd German
squarehead" ("La sacrée tête carrée d'Allemand").

But again it was a gun made of cast steel that was the real

centre of attraction on the Krupp stand. It too was twice the size of the one he had shown in London—a giant twelve-pounder modelled on France's latest bronze muzzle-loader, yet more than 200 pounds lighter and able too, to fire 3,000 shots before beginning to buckle. The French generals, along with their Emperor and Empress, flocked to admire it—Napoleon III was so enthusiastic that he made Alfred then and there a Knight of the Legion of Honour, while the Exhibition Committee gave him their Gold Medal. One of the most powerful banks in all France, the Crédit Mobilier, even tried to tempt him to move his works, lock, stock and gun-barrel, to French soil. But however much the gallant Gauls may have liked his gun, they still did not buy it. Although they tested his monster cannon at their Vincennes range and found it excellent in every way, they nevertheless went on ordering bronze ones just as they had always done.

Another two years were to go by before anyone bought Alfred's guns, and even then it was only the Viceroy of Egypt, who ordered thirty-six. It was not until 1859, when he was on the point of giving up gun-manufacture altogether, because, as he put it, "it was not proving particularly remunerative", that Prussia at long last came up with an order for 312 six-pounders. Even so, the Director of Prussia's Ordnance Department tried to cut down the number to seventy-two but was over-ruled by Alfred's protector, Prince William, now Prince Regent following the madness of his elder brother. Alfred had also in the meantime received a few enquiries to buy his gun-barrels from Austria, Switzerland, and Russia—the Russians had fired 4,000 shots from one of his barrels without damaging it, but had then promptly put it into a museum!

Although subsequently they were to give him his notoriety, it was not to guns that Alfred owed his rise to riches, but to the railways. The first railway line in Germany had been opened in Bavaria in 1835, while the Cologne–Minden line serving the Ruhr had been completed twelve years later, a station being built at Essen around 1850. By that year there were already 6,000 miles of track in Germany, a figure that was to multiply tenfold within the next sixty years.

Alfred was one of the first German manufacturers to see the tremendous opportunities for steel in this railway boom. "A different future lies before us", he had told a friend, "we live now in the Steel Age." He had got his first major railway contract as early as 1849. It was from the Cologne and Minden Railway, then the biggest of the German railway undertakings, and was for 500 sets of steel springs and axles. In order to cope he had had to extend his works and increase his labour-force to 300. The Jewish banking house of Salomon Oppenheim at Cologne now backed him and provided him with the necessary wherewithal for his enormous expansion. Even so, for the next two decades at least, he continued to walk a fairly precarious financial tightrope, until the immense profits from his armaments began pouring in during the eighteen-seventies.

He had also started on that series of experiments which were to lead to the weldless steel railway tyre, perhaps the biggest single money-spinner of all time for Krupp, and the one that finally put him in the front rank of European as well as German industrialists. Krupp's trade symbol today is still three interlocking rings representing three interlocking railway tyres.

As speeds of railway locomotives rose, and the loads carried by carriages and waggons increased, so breakdowns became ever more frequent, mainly on account of the iron wheels failing or else seizing-up under the strain. A weakness had been discovered at the point where the outer iron tyre, as it were, of the wheel was welded on to the inner rim. To remove that weakness, Alfred applied the same technique he had been using for years in his fork and spoon machines, namely that of rolling seamless steel rings on to the engraved cylinders while they were still hot. He now rolled seamless steel tyres on to the wheel rims of railway carriages. Since there was no join, no welding was needed, and hence a source of weakness was avoided—besides, steel had a longer life and could stand greater strains better than iron.

Alfred had managed to keep all these developments away

from the eyes of his competitors. His security was so excessive that his workmen had called the part of the factory screened off for the experiments "Siberia". But his secrecy paid off. Such was the demand for the weldless tyre that by 1855 his labour-force had leapt to 700. Two years later it stood at more than 1,200.

Krupp steel now became the rage among the railway companies of the world. As well as being recommended for royal trains, it was used in imperial carriages and viceregal yachts, for he had also gone in for making steel axles and steel crankshafts for steamships. By the end of the eighteen-fifties he had had to add so many extra workshops to keep up with the demand for his products that his factory was now eight times bigger than when he had begun a mere quarter of a century before.

His confidence now knew no bounds. In 1859 he started building a massive power-hammer—nicknamed "Fritz". Designed to be the biggest hammer in the world, it was intended for forging blocks of steel weighing up to 100,000 pounds. When one of his competitors heard about this he exclaimed, "Has Herr Krupp gone mad?" But Alfred needed the new hammer for the enormous crankshafts and giant cannons he was planning to make—even though the noise of the hammer, as he put it, "might startle the Antipodes themselves out of their slumbers". Steamships had been getting steadily bigger as speedy ocean travel became more and more of a viable proposition—and if steamships could get bigger, why not guns? He had already begun designing for the Russians a sixty-pounder coastal battery with a thirteen-inch bore. But as yet his own Government showed scant interest in his intentions on this score. They much preferred to buy their heavy artillery from Britain, in particular from either Messrs. Vickers or Messrs. Armstrong, who between them held a virtual monopoly of making such mammoth weapons at this time.

That most of his business came from outside Prussia was a point Alfred never tired of putting to those Prussian ministers and officials who might bother to listen to him, though there were precious few then who would. He was particularly sore that the Prussian State Railways never bought anything from him, whereas his railway tyres, for instance, had become almost the standard product for nearly every other European network. He tried to blame the lack of Prussian custom on the snootiness towards him of von der Heydt, the Prussian minister in charge of railways and commerce. But the real truth was that few bureaucrats in Berlin could stand Alfred—and his high-handedness and overbearing manner had made him intensely disliked among his fellow industrialists too. Some of them fought bitter battles with him in the courts, or else in the columns of newspapers, over his constant allegations that they were copying his processes. At one time Alfred even tried to claim the phrase "cast steel" purely for his own products! As a result he was virtually friendless in his profession and became more and more isolated.

Even so, by the early eighteen-sixties he was easily the Continent's biggest producer of cast steel. He had resident representatives in all the major European capitals, including London. In his choice of Albert Longsdon as his British agent, he was especially lucky. Besides remaining Alfred's closest friend for the rest of his life, Longsdon was instrumental, through his brother Frederick who was a partner of Henry Bessemer, the great English steel inventor, in getting Krupp the German licence for the new Bessemer process— the process which did so much to revolutionise steel-making in the second half of the nineteenth century. Ironically enough it was this British invention that encouraged Alfred to transform his works radically—to change it from being just another specialised steel concern into a fully-integrated iron and steel complex with its own coke-ovens, collieries, and iron-ore mines. By 1861 Krupp's employees already numbered more than 2,000, a figure that was to double within two years, quadruple within four, and pass the 10,000 mark by 1871.

Alfred's banking acquaintances tried to persuade him to convert his firm into a limited liability company, but this he steadfastly refused to do until his dying day. To him, stocks and shares were devices of the devil, designed to rob the poor manufacturer not only of his profit but also of his proper control over his own business—and to Alfred it was both necessary and fitting to be, as he put it, "master in his own house". Indeed he would not tolerate any criticism of his actions whether from his colleagues or from members of his own family. In this respect he was almost the classic example of the Victorian industrialist: he would have objected with his last living gasp even to the minimal control of an annual general meeting of shareholders such as any business tycoon today takes simply in his stride.

After his mother's death in 1850, Alfred had become increasingly lonely in spite of all his success. He had few friends and his nearest relatives continued to spurn him. In May 1853, just after his forty-first birthday, he married a girl less than half his age: Bertha Eichhoff, the daughter of a Cologne tax-inspector and whose grandfather had been a pastry chef in the household of the Archbishop of Cologne. "I found a heart where I had supposed there was only a lump of cast steel", he told a colleague.

Bertha was not an unattractive girl. She had blue eyes and masses of dark hair, but in most of the contemporary drawings and paintings of her that have survived there seems to be a touch of sadness about her eyes, suggesting perhaps a disappointment or even a yearning. Alfred's tough early years had left their marks on him: his hair had long since receded from his forehead and his face was unusually wrinkled. As was the fashion among most men of his age at that time, he sported a dark bushy beard, but in his case it tended to give him a prematurely haggard look. He had always appeared gaunt, even as a child, and despite his riches he was to remain that way for the rest of his life.

A son and heir was born to the couple on 17 February 1854, whom they baptised Friedrich, though he came to be more commonly known by the pet-name of Fritz. He was, however, to be their only child, for whereas the marriage seems to have worked well enough during the first few years it went quickly adrift shortly afterwards. Bertha in particular hated Essen's rainy weather—nor apparently could she stand the incessant noise and smoke at their house, surrounded as it was by all the furnaces and forges and hammers and machinery-shops of Alfred's great factory. For most of her life, Bertha was in the continual care of doctors, as was their child Fritz too. Soon she became unable to bear the Ruhr at all, and was constantly travelling from one health resort to another, from one watering-place to the next, with periodic trips to Berlin for special medical treatment. Alfred had a nervous breakdown himself two years after their marriage and was forced to spend a few months recuperating at a spa in eastern Germany.

The trouble was that Alfred had been living alone too long and had struggled too hard to have gained the softness and the patience necessary, perhaps, in marriage to one so much younger than himself. Obsessed as he had now become with every detail of his own activities, he proceeded to apply a similarly dogmatic tenacity to every detail of his wife's. He was straightaway laying down the law on Bertha's way of dressing, for instance, and was soon telling her that "travelling clothes are not for ornament; on a journey one wears the plainest dust-like materials, as they are always full of dust, which would be very ugly with taffeta, and to beat the dust off would be very vulgar"—and he went on, "Cuffs, shirt-fronts, and all the flummery that is worn in formal dress, are gladly left off on a journey, just as gold and jewels; one is downright and simple, with the consciousness of wearing a clean shirt underneath." Few young girls even in Victorian times would stand for very long that amount of fussiness and fastidiousness.

In any event, the factory remained for Alfred his one true passion in life. Everything else was subordinated to this. Everything else was kept strictly at a distance, strictly on the fringe of his workaday routine. In this way he was very much the industrial man, the man for whom the sight and smell of factory chimneys belching with smoke gives the same satisfaction as another gets from a view of Chartres Cathedral or a reading of a sonnet by Keats. By purposeful living, Alfred meant the profitable use of his time and resources. By power he meant the opportunity to control other men's destinies and not simply the freedom over his own actions such as a creative soul might crave for. Nor did his rise to spectacular riches ever soften him or make him more aware of the rest of living. Quite the reverse, it turned him even more tetchy than before, even more inconsiderate and even more intolerant of the people around him.

In the same year that Prussia's hidebound generals at last yielded to Krupp cannons, Alfred lost his lifelong friend and financial adviser, Fritz Sölling. Sölling had accompanied him on many of his business trips abroad and had been a partner in the firm for many years. Towards the end they had quarrelled almost incessantly, and "one week he was well, the next he was dead" was the terse way in which Alfred recorded his friend's passing. If he could possibly avoid it, Alfred would never talk about death—it was one of the few things that really frightened him.

Prussia's big order set the seal, of course, on Alfred's position as an armaments manufacturer. But having spurned him for so long, this was no sudden change of heart on the part of the bureaucrats in Berlin. Alfred had come to realise that he would never get very far with them on his own and so had decided to circumvent the civil servants by going direct to the military men—to those very same generals who had hitherto turned down his weapons not because they were expensive but because they preferred the old bronze guns they knew and trusted. In particular he had sought out that set of high-ranking army officers surrounding the heir to the Prussian throne.

Sharing a passion for riding, which he used to describe as his "one luxury", he had become friendly with a certain Master of Horse called Krausnick, on whom he lavished much hospitality and attention, always consulting him whenever he bought new steeds or made alterations to his stables. In time, Alfred met Krausnick's boss, who happened to be a younger brother of the King, one Prince Charles Anthony von Hohenzollern, at that moment Divisional Commander of the Prussian Army in Düsseldorf, though soon to become President of the Prince Regent's Council of State in Berlin. Through Krausnick he also made the acquaintance of General Bernhard von Voigts-Rhetz, A.D.C. to Prince William, and later Director of the General War Department in Berlin. Thus began the spinning of that web of close threads between Essen and Berlin that characterises the Krupp saga—for with allies as powerful as these

Alfred was able to storm the very citadel of Prussian bureau-cracy.

In courting these three soldiers, he used every cunning gambit he knew. For ever taking them into his confidence over his latest industrial exploits, all the time posing as a good friend of the army, constantly flattering them by invit-ing them to secret demonstrations of his most modern weapons; always generous and hospitable towards them, yet discreetly so, knowing the acute abhorrence of the Prussian official even to the very notion of a bribe. And in the end all this soft-soaping paid off handsomely, for through these three soldiers he made even closer contact than before with the heir to the Prussian throne—and when William became Prince Regent in 1858 the way was finally open for Alfred. It was less than a year later that, with von Voigts-Rhetz lobbying among the generals and with William intervening at the War Ministry, Alfred got his big order.

William was evidently a great sucker for patriotic noises about Prussia, and Alfred pulled out every chauvinistic stop when writing or talking to him, claiming even that he was losing money and endangering his workers' continued employment by his constant refusal to accept orders for his weapons from any Great Power other than Prussia—all of which was blatantly untrue, for Alfred at this time was desperately trying to sell his cannon to anyone. The Prince Regent again intervened on Alfred's behalf in 1860 when von der Heydt tried to oppose extending Krupp's railway tyre patent. On that occasion William scrawled over the order confirming the extension, "In recognition of the patriotic sentiments which Commercial Counsellor Alfred Krupp of Essen has frequently displayed particularly in declining foreign orders offered to him for guns, orders which promised him substantial profit."

In October 1861, a month after "Fritz", the giant power-hammer, began operating, the Prince Regent, together with his son and the Prussian War Minister, von Roon, visited the Krupp works to see for themselves "the biggest hammer in the world". When, on his brother's death a few months later, William became King of Prussia, one of his earliest actions was to make Alfred a Privy Councillor—and shortly afterwards he even went so far as to confer on him the Order of the Red Eagle with Oak Leaves, an honour usually given only to victorious Prussian generals.

It was around this time, too, that Alfred was first described in a Berlin newspaper as the "Cannon King", a title of which he was immensely proud and one for which nobody was ever seriously to challenge him, for within a few years of Prussia's big order he had sold guns by the score to Belgium, Holland, Spain, Egypt, Turkey, Sweden, Switzerland, Argentina, Austria, Britain and Russia: the Russian order alone was worth a quarter of a million pounds to Alfred!

The age of competitive armaments was beginning—the age when one weapon order would beget a whole series of weapon orders from every country within gun-shot of the first. The age whose spirit was perhaps best symbolised in that speech of a certain Prussian in 1862—"The solution of the great problems of these days is not to be found in speeches and resolutions—but in blood and iron." The phrase "blood and iron" was to become the slogan of the epoch—and no other person dominated the epoch more than the man who had uttered that phrase originally, Otto von Bismarck, first Prussia's Prime Minister from 1862 onwards and then Germany's Chancellor until 1890. Through Bismarck, Prussia came to dominate Germany, and in dominating Germany to dominate Europe—all of which was grist to Alfred Krupp's mill, for as Prussia grew Krupp's grew along with it.

Bismarck was just three years younger than Alfred and, although operating in very different spheres of human activity, the "Iron Chancellor" and the "Cannon King" were in many ways very similar men. In fact they came to complement one another. Since he considered guns to be the final argument of kings, it would have been difficult for Bismarck to have succeeded in his expansionist policies without the Krupp gun-shops—and but for Bismarck Alfred would certainly have never achieved his world prominence in armaments. Between them, they represented the twin pillars of Prussian militarism: the stern-faced, square-headed, jackbooted Bismarck, clad in stiff, grey, forbidding cavalry officer's uniform, and crowned by the grotesque spike of a

Pickelhaube: and the gaunt, slender Krupp with the sinister, staring eyes, black-bearded, black-coated, black-booted, and framed by the grey, smoking chimneys of the Ruhr.

Like Alfred, Bismarck was outwardly harsh, tenacious, and fearless, yet inwardly hysterical. They were both hypo-chondriacs, and in later life came to share the same physician. Like Alfred, Bismarck was tyrannical and unscrupulous, destroying any rival that dared cross his path. Like Alfred, Bismarck was no stickler for truth, employing any deceit or deception to further his aims. Both were incapable of warm, intimate feelings to another human being, whether a wife or a subordinate, and as a result both tended to take refuge in subhuman things: Bismarck in dogs and trees, Alfred in horses and guns. Both were opportunistic and misanthropic. Both came to suffer from megalomania. A colleague close to Bismarck said of him: "I have never known a man who experienced so little joy. There was never any real merriment in his conversation, except when at someone else's expense." It could equally have been said of Alfred. It is no wild generalisation to say that no two Prussians have been so responsible for the image, in the Anglo-Saxon mind at least, of the Prussian as someone evil, aggressive, belligerent, and destructive, steel-grey rather than sky-blue, *Pickelhaube* rather than Easter-bonnet.

Bismarck was a Junker—a member of that class of militar-istic, predatory land-owners who had won their great estates in the east by force and had held them down by force. He had one lasting aim, and that was to preserve his class. To do this he had to preserve Prussia, and to preserve Prussia he had to diminish both Austria and France, to destroy German liberalism, and to supplant German nationalism with Prussian nationalism. In doing all these things, he enabled Prussia to dominate Germany, and in dominating Germany to dominate Europe. To the wife of Prussia's Crown Prince, Bismarck was always "that wicked man"; even King William admitted to a "secret repugnance" towards him. He came to be the "best hated man in Europe", but to Alfred Krupp he was a godsend.

After 1848, Prussia seemed to lose her chance of dominat-ing Germany, even though most of the German princes owed their retention of power to Prussian soldiers stamping out the revolutions within their states. Perhaps because of this Prussia became even more hated in Germany than before—to German intellectuals Prussia was "the most slave-like country in Europe", "no state is administered more like a factory". Nor equally were many of Prussia's rulers, particularly the Junkers, all that enthusiastic at the prospect of "merging with Germany". Traditionally the Junkers looked to the east to extend their lands, preferring to plunder the more pliant Poles than to try to take on the proud, self-confident burgesses of Baden or Bavaria.

And so, in the face of a concerted comeback from Austria, Prussia dithered—until Austria too lost her chance and managed instead to isolate herself by antagonising Russia with her neutrality during the Crimean War. On top of this she even weakened herself by losing a war to France over northern Italy in 1859. By that time, Prussia had of course a new ruler, William, who was more likely to listen to promises of Prussian grandeur from a Bismarck than his eccentric elder brother ever would have—and hence more likely to back a Krupp than (say) a Schweitzer. Besides, William wanted, and was determined to have, a strong army. The army was his one interest and passion in life. He left in the middle of the first complete performance of *The Ring* at Bayreuth in order to go off on military manœuvres. "In a monarchy like ours," he once told a group of his advisers, "the military point of view must not be subordinated to the financial and economic, for the European position of the State depends on it." His brutal suppression of a revolt among Baden troops in 1849 had already earned for him the soubriquet of "The Grape-Shot Prince".

Prussia was of course rapidly changing as a country. She was beginning to emerge as an industrial power. In the Ruhr valley she had what was fast becoming recognised as the greatest coalfield on the whole Continent—and on this coalfield was rising an iron and steel industry already rivalling, and soon to surpass, the older German industrial centres of Saxony and Silesia. The introduction of the railways had brought great prosperity to the Ruhr by making

Ruhr coal competitive in price with English coal in every part
of Germany, including Berlin and Hamburg. What the
German Customs union had begun the railways were completing. But as well as giving Germany an economic unity,
the railways were also giving Prussia a political backbone
that hitherto she had lacked. They were helping to mould
into a state what had previously been just a bunch of
scattered provinces. Significantly too, it was a Prussian
general, von Moltke, who originated the concept of "strategic
railways", who turned military mobilisation into a mere
matter of trains and timetables.

But William soon ran into trouble in trying to enlarge his
army. The politicians cavilled at the extra expense—indeed,
it was their apparently adamant opposition that made him
appoint Bismarck as his Prime Minister against the advice
of almost everyone around him. Bismarck proceeded to
by-pass Parliament, since the politicians continued to refuse
to vote the King the necessary credits for his bigger army.
He soon found a willing and eager ally in Alfred Krupp,
who promptly offered the Crown long-term loans of up to
£300,000 so long of course as they bought his guns. It
was fortunate for Alfred that the War Minister did not take
him up on his offer, since Krupp did not have that sort of
capital to flaunt around so easily.

Opposition to Bismarck was particularly strong around
Essen, so much so that the city's Burgomaster organised a
petition to the King demanding he change his Prime
Minister. Although every other leading citizen signed it,
Alfred refused. But the Opposition party got a bit of their
own back immediately afterwards by raising in Parliament
the question of Krupp's virtual monopoly of supplying the
army's guns at that time—and to Alfred's fury they won
their point, for the War Ministry was instructed to seek
competitive tenders in future for their orders. However,
once again he played his patriotic trump-card with the
King, saying that he might in future have to sell a new
breech-loading device outside Prussia—and once again it
worked, for William promptly countermanded the War
Minister's instruction. What is more, after Bismarck's
successful war against the Danes in 1864 over the duchies of

Schleswig and Holstein, Krupp's were rewarded with a lucrative order for 300 four-pounder guns.

Bismarck paid his first visit to Alfred at Essen on 28 October 1864. He was *en route* to Berlin from Paris where he had been negotiating with the French Emperor and he evidently saw fit to confide in Alfred concerning those discussions, telling him too of his plans for Prussia. Bismarck had quickly realised how much Alfred's guns might assist in these strategems, while Krupp for his part was already sniffing big profits in the possibility of a new harbour at Kiel, of a canal linking the Baltic with the North Sea, and above all of a Prussian Navy. They also discovered that they shared a mutual interest in horses and big trees. Bismarck once wrote to his wife, "I have more to tell myself when I am with trees than when I am with men." Alfred at this time was creating a stud which would not have disgraced any royal court. He liked the smell of horses so much that he had built his study close to the stables. As the years went by, Alfred and Bismarck drew even closer, and it became quite usual for them to dine together whenever Krupp was in Berlin.

For his part, Alfred never hesitated to seek the help of Bismarck or the King in his ordinary business. Indeed, just a year after Bismarck's trip to Essen, Krupp was trying to buy a group of iron-ore mines from the Crown for £60,000 when news of the deal leaked out to one of his chief rivals, the Bochum Union, who promptly entered the bidding. Alfred only matched their increased offer of £75,000 yet still got the mines. Said one contemporary writer of the transaction, "The Government were disposed to assist a firm which was becoming a 'national institution', as King William called it." What is more, a few months later, when Alfred found himself short of funds, the State came up with a loan of £150,000. It was the beginning of the "special relationship" between the Essen firm and the authorities at Berlin. Krupp's had already come a very long way since Friedrich's bankrupt death forty years before.

Within a matter of weeks of Alfred receiving the loan, Prussia was at war with Austria. Bismarck had been resolved on this war since the beginning of the year and had proceeded to bait the Austrians into making the first move: into mobilising their army and persuading many of the other German states to follow suit, so that Prussia could pose as the aggrieved party. Austria, like most of these German states, had in fact been buying guns galore from Krupp. On 9 April 1866, the day following Bismarck's signing an alliance with Italy which completed Austria's virtual isolation, von Roon, the Prussian War Minister, wrote to Alfred asking him in effect to stop sending any more guns to Austria. Krupp replied that he felt he could not give a formal undertaking which might be interpreted as breaking a contract, since this could prejudice any dealings he might want to have with the Austrians in the future—in other words, that when it came to the crunch he would not stretch his patriotism at the cost of potential Krupp profits. However, he did promise to tell Berlin exactly when he was despatching deliveries so that they could intercept them if they so wished. Meanwhile, Alfred's agent in Vienna went on seeking orders from the Austrians even after von Roon's warning. Krupp in any case had just got a contract worth nearly a quarter of a million pounds out of von Roon for new guns for the Prussian Army.

Prussian soldiers invaded Austria on 16 June 1866 and the war lasted a mere seven weeks. It was really decided in one battle at Königgrätz on 3 July—the first major battle in which Krupp guns fought, and on both sides at that! Six days afterwards, General von Voigts-Rhetz was writing to Alfred from the battlefield, "These children of yours conversed for long hot hours with their Austrian cousins . . . highly memorable and interesting, but also very destructive." Deathly too, for 20,000 Austrians fell in the battle.

In point of fact, however, Krupp guns had formed only one-fifth of the Prussian artillery at Königgrätz, and Prussia's success there was due more to the needle-gun, a gun capable of four times the firing rate of the Austrian infantryman's muzzle-loader, but a weapon for which Alfred was not in the slightest way responsible. Nor was every Prussian general as exuberant as Voigts-Rhetz had been over Krupp's contribution, for later that same month Alfred was writing to War Minister von Roon to apologise for several

Krupp guns having blown up on the battle-field and to offer to replace them immediately. Alfred had also just heard of another Krupp gun having exploded in Russia and of a consignment of Krupp railway tyres to England having been reported faulty on arrival. All along, he had been claiming quality and reliability for his products and here were his weapons proving deficient at their first real testing. Once more some of the older generals trotted out the arguments in favour of bronze, but William brushed them all aside and showed his continuing confidence in Krupp—a confidence no longer shared now by von Roon—by ordering another 700 steel guns from Alfred, a mere matter of four months after Königgrätz.

Although the Austro-Prussian war of 1866 was perhaps the shortest of all European wars, it was certainly the most far-reaching in its long-term consequences. In addition to grabbing the duchies of Schleswig and Holstein, Prussia annexed all the north German states that had not sided with her before Königgrätz—states such as Hanover, Hesse, Nassau and Frankfurt. With Austria humiliated and hence out of the running, Prussia was now undoubtedly the number one power in Germany. Thus Bismarck's mechanism was set in motion that led to Prussia's, and eventually Germany's, hegemony in Europe, and in time too to the clash with the other Great Powers in the two world wars of this century.

One of the least-sung results, however, of the Austro-Prussian war was a cholera epidemic, brought back by the demobilised soldiers. It hit Essen with particular virulence, most probably because the city had become terribly over-crowded, her population having doubled during the previous six years, largely on account of the boom in the Krupp factories, and her sanitary facilities had not yet caught up with this expansion.

Only the day before his head groom died of the dreaded disease, Alfred fled from Essen. Never a very healthy man, the tensions of the last few weeks, particularly the failure of his guns at Königgrätz, had taken their toll on him. He had grown increasingly irritable of late and now practically every minor vexation would prostrate him for perhaps weeks on end. During the next two years he hardly returned to his works at all, though he never ceased to bombard his managers with memoranda. For much of this "exile" his wife and son stayed with him, for Fritz was seriously ill again too. Together they travelled first to Koblenz, and then to Heidelberg. Dissatisfied, they moved on to Karlsruhe and then to Basle. Again Alfred still could not settle. They tried both Berne and Geneva, living for quite a long time by the lake there, before finally ending up on the French Riviera. A description of Alfred during the first winter at Nice has been left by the family doctor who accompanied them throughout the whole of the travels:

> He was an odd-looking specimen, who attracted attention everywhere on account of his unusual height and striking leanness. At one time his features had been very regular and handsome. But they had aged rapidly. His face was lifeless, pallid, and full of wrinkles. A paltry trace of grey hair, crowned by a wig, topped his head. He seldom smiled. More often than not his features remained stony and motionless. . . . He took scant interest in anything divorced from his professional work. Accordingly, he deemed a relative of his wife's, Max Bruch, afterwards a famous conductor, to be utterly wasting his time in devoting himself to a life of music. If he had been a technician, Krupp observed in all seriousness, he would have been of some use to himself and to mankind, but as a musician he was leading a totally pointless existence. This narrow-mindedness was, however, compensated by his admirable energy. There was nothing he considered unattainable once he had convinced himself that it was worth while. His own career had brought his self-confidence to such a pitch that his behaviour at times bordered on megalomania.

It was a busy trip for the doctor. Not only did he have to cope with the ever-sickening Fritz, but Alfred, too, often used to stay in bed for days, refusing to get up even though the doctor could diagnose nothing wrong with him other than, as he put it, "hypochondria bordering on insanity". There were times also when Alfred would suddenly explode with fury over some relatively unimportant letter from the works and would then summon all his managers the 600 or so miles from Essen to his bedside—this in an age long before fast jet-travel! And when his executives did finally reach whichever Riviera resort he happened to be frequenting, for the family were constantly hopping about from hotel to hotel along the coast, the news they brought invariably only made his moods worse. Krupp's were no longer pre-eminent as steel-producers, for other firms were coming along to invade those spheres, such as railway-tyre manufacture, where Alfred had fondly thought he had a monopoly for all eternity. Competition was getting keener as markets were becoming saturated through over-production. In order to retain their share of the declining business, Krupp's bosses had had to reduce their prices, which meant of course lower profits going Alfred's way.

But once again an international exhibition provided a welcome diversion. In 1867, Napoleon III, ever on the lookout for opportunities to gild his Second Empire with a little of the lustre of his immortal uncle's First Empire, decided on another world fair for Paris: to be greater and more daring than anything Europe had so far experienced. To a background of Offenbach's gently mocking melodies, the bare Champ de Mars was transformed into an enormous pleasure-park in which a huge fifty-ton Krupp cannon ("a monster such as the world has never seen") out-sized every other exhibit. It fired a 1,000-pound shell and had cost Alfred £22,500 to make. Once again he also showed a massive steel ingot—on this occasion one weighing 80,000 pounds, eight times heavier than that casting exhibited by him at the previous Paris Exhibition twelve years before. As usual too he took away the main prizes, Emperor Napoleon elevating him to an officer in the Legion of Honour. But even so no one bought his gun and he presented it to King William.

It was the news, however, that Prussia was intending to start a navy that brought Alfred hurrying out of his exile, particularly when he heard that the Berlin bureaucrats were favouring British guns. Furious, and even alarmed, Alfred immediately went to see the King to persuade him to hold comparative tests between his guns and the British.

His in point of fact came out much worse, though he argued
with William that the trials had not been altogether fair
since Messrs. Vickers and Messrs. Armstrong had fired
their guns with British powder which he claimed was far
superior to the Prussian powder with which *his* guns had
been fired! Nor did he give up. It so happened that he had
made some similar naval guns only a short time before for
the Russians, with whom his relations were excellent, they
having only recently repeated their offer to him to take
over their State-supported steelworks and armaments
industries for them. What is more, right from Alfred's very
first Russian order there had been a constant two-way
traffic between Essen and St. Petersburg of leading Russian
gun-designers and senior Krupp officials. Trading on this
goodwill, he managed to persuade one of their top artillery
experts to intercede on his behalf with the King—and it
worked, for William once more saw to it that the Prussian
armed services bought only Krupp-made weapons. In
September 1868 the new navy placed an order with Alfred
to buy forty-one heavy guns for their three new ironclads.
This was a crucial victory for Alfred, since it largely determined Prussian, and hence German, naval policy for a long
time to come and was a further stage in his securing a total
monopoly of all Prussian armaments.

Just as Bismarck had a secret bounty, money he had confiscated from Hanover in 1866, which he used mostly for
bribing journalists and politicians, so Alfred had instituted
his own personal propaganda fund for promoting his
interests, particularly in Russia. On top of this he entertained
lavishly—among his guests at Essen in a single typical
year were the Crown Prince of Sweden, a son of the Emperor
of Japan, the Russian General Todleben, Prince Charles
and Prince Alexander of Prussia, together with their families
and full retinues. As others might give away cigarette-
lighters or ash-trays, Alfred bestowed teams of thoroughbred
horses or, more usually, elegantly mounted ceremonial-guns,
"Gala Guns" as they were sometimes called. And it all paid
off handsomely, for Krupp weapons were known the world
over and were being sought by nearly every nation.

But there was one country where Alfred had had conspicuously little success to date—and that, despite all the gold medals and the imperial honours, was France. The French armament-manufacturers like Schneider-Creusot saw to it that the door was kept securely closed on Alfred by outplaying him at his own game of constantly harping on the patriotic duty of buying a country's own products, particularly its own guns. The chauvinistic "Buy British" and "Buy American" sales-drives of the nineteen-sixties had their forerunners in those bitterly-contested business campaigns of the eighteen-sixties between Schneider's and Krupp's. Like the Essen firm, the Creusot concern had their friends in high places: General le Boeuf, the Head of the French Ordnance Board at this time and the strongest opponent of France ever buying Krupp weapons, was a relative of the Schneider family—while the President of the Paris Chamber of Commerce, always an influential body with the French Government of the day, was none other than Eugène Schneider himself. But Alfred never gave up trying, and was still soliciting orders from the French even on the eve of the Franco-Prussian War of 1870. Although it might have been good for Schneider's that the French Army was not equipped with Krupp guns, it was certainly bad for the future of France, and in particular for Napoleon III, that they had spurned Alfred's wares.

That war of course was just another stage in Bismarck's grand scheme of Prussian expansionism. As cunningly as he had isolated Austria four years earlier before baiting her into attacking first, so Bismarck pursued precisely the same tactic with France. Whereas it had been traditional French policy to keep a divided, tame, or at least friendly Germany on her eastern border, Napoleon III had antagonised Austria and most of the southern German states by conniving in Prussia's victory over them in 1866—a victory, which, as we have seen, materially helped Prussia in bringing the larger part of Germany within her orbit. France's inept Emperor had then increased his isolation by allowing a friendship to spring up between Prussia and Russia, ancient foes, without securing a compensatory alliance for himself with Britain, the only other Great Power capable of deterring Bismarck. Napoleon III for his part wanted to impress

public opinion in France, and thus strengthen his claim to
be a true descendant of the great Napoleon I, by restoring
France's frontiers to what they had been before his uncle's
last defeats. He thought he had secured Bismarck's agreement to such a restoration as the reward for France's
neutrality in 1866, but as Prussia grew stronger so Bismarck
turned an increasingly deaf ear to all such entreaties. In
the end, exasperated and outwitted, Napoleon III declared
war on Prussia.

On the day Prussia mobilised, Alfred offered von Roon
£150,000 worth of guns as his contribution towards the
expenses of the war. The gift was declined, but the Government immediately increased their orders for Krupp armaments to such an extent that Alfred had to take on 3,000
extra workers. It meant too that Prussia for the first time was
buying more guns from Alfred than anyone else. Once again
when the War Minister asked him to sell them some of the
weapons he was about to deliver to Russia, Alfred withheld
his consent until he had consulted the Czar—he was not
going to allow any temporary patriotism damage his future
relations with such a good, regular, buyer of Krupp guns as
the Russian Government.

When the worry arose that perhaps the French might cross
the Rhine, some of his senior executives favoured distribut-
ing rifles to the workmen. On hearing the proposal, Alfred
became almost hysterical. "It would be a stupid thing to
do", he told his managers. "If the French come to Essen
we will offer them roast veal and red wine, in that way they
might not destroy the factory."

But it was an idle threat, because, equipped only with
their old-fashioned bronze muzzle-loaders, the French
soldiers were no match for the Prussians. The new Krupp
steel breech-loaders and the new Krupp steel heavy mortars
pulverised the forts of Metz and Sedan in no time at all,
and thus blasted a hole through to the outskirts of Paris
itself. Although most Prussian generals opposed bombarding the French capital, Alfred, along with Bismarck, argued
strongly in favour of it, even rushing to put his old-fashioned
2,000-pounder at the army's disposal. He followed up this
offer by straightaway beginning to devise giant siege guns

capable of casting 1,000-pound shells from great distances into the centre of Paris. Though they were never built in time, they did come to form the basis of the later giant Krupp siege-guns that so horrified the world. When news reached him of Gambetta's daring escape by balloon from the beleaguered city, instead of joining the rest of Europe in rejoicing at such incredible courage, Alfred immediately set about constructing a high-angle anti-balloon gun, the forerunner of today's anti-aircraft guns. Its arrival outside Paris certainly deterred any more escapes by balloon—during daylight at least.

Whether Prussia owed her victory exclusively to Alfred's guns, as some Krupp historians would have us believe, or whether it was due more to her superiority in numbers, strategy, and organisation, coupled with the latter-day Napoleon's inane diplomacy, are questions better put perhaps to professional military historians. What is certain, however, is that, in the French mind at least, Krupp's became indissolubly linked with Prussia's crushing military success. From this moment onwards the name of Krupp, along of course with that of Bismarck and Kaiser William, became among the most hated in all France. It ceased to be identified with anything personal, but came to signify purely and simply a particular implement of destruction.

1871, then, marks the beginning of the Krupp notoriety which Germany's, as well as the family's, conduct during two world wars served only to swell. From being hated by just one nation, Krupp's over the next seventy-four years were to become an object of loathing on an international scale such as perhaps no other industrial organisation has ever attracted.

But for Alfred himself, Prussia's triumph over France in 1871 was the best advertisement he could possibly have wished for his guns. Thereafter the flood-gates were breached and the orders for his weapons came pouring in. Everyone it seemed was scrambling to buy Krupp: his guns defended fortresses from the Yucatan to the Yangtse, from the Bosphorus to Bogota. To own a Krupp cannon was for monarchs and megalomaniacs the status symbol of the age. Alfred Krupp, the "Cannon King", had really mounted his throne —and Essen was in its seventh heaven.

CHAPTER FIVE

"All the rest is gas"

WHEN PRUSSIA by her victory over France set the seal on her hegemony in Germany, Alfred was entering his sixtieth year. Although he was to live for another sixteen and was to become the wealthiest man in all Europe, these were years of personal decline for him—years of megalomania and acute unhappiness.

He had in fact spent most of the war engaged on something totally removed from the blood-letting of battle. In April 1870, just three months before the first shot was fired in anger and while the succession of diplomatic crises was putting almost everyone else off making such firm decisions about the future, Alfred had laid the foundation-stone of his dream-castle on the hill—the monstrous Villa Hügel, that great, graceless, 200-roomed "lumpen" and lugubrious pile still standing today amid parkland near Essen. An arrogantly sprawling place, with cathedral-like halls and steeple-high staircases, it was just such a folly an Orson Welles might have fashioned for a Citizen Kane. Here in suitable splendour, successive Krupps have entertained kings and kaisers, presidents and princes—and of course a führer.

Hügel was the fourth house Alfred had designed and constructed for himself. After moving out of the minuscule four-room wooden cottage with its slanting roof and tiny windows, in which his father had died and in which his mother had brought up her four children, Alfred had built next to it a grander, three-storeyed affair. But this had soon become dwarfed as the factory spread and engulfed it.

Then in 1859, the year of Prussia's first big order for his guns, he had put up, again within the Works, a much more sumptuous and grandiose residence, styled *The*

Garden House. It boasted a vast winter-garden and orangery entirely enclosed in glass, as well as lavishly laid lawns and specially transplanted trees, flowers, and bushes; peacocks, rustic bridges, fountains, even miniature grottoes, made up the bizarre ensemble. But Bertha hated it, for ever complaining of the smoke and the noise from Alfred's great factory close by; for ever complaining of the vibration from his power-hammers which cracked the glasses in her sideboards. Less than four years after they moved in, Krupp's doctor advised them all to move out as fast as possible.

And so once more Alfred went big-house hunting. Most of the neighbouring nobility loathed him, however, and would not allow him even to view their properties, let alone to put in a bid for them. In the end he secretly bought some parkland overlooking the river Ruhr to the south of Essen in the suburb of Bredeney. There he built himself a temporary "mansion house" while he set about designing a castle fit for a king—fit of course for a cannon king. He chose the site where the views were best by getting some of his workmen to move him around on top of a wooden scaffolding—a manœuvre which caused great amusement among the local people.

Because he liked big trees and could not wait to see saplings grow, he bought up entire avenues from neighbouring estates and transplanted them around the vast terraces of his hill.

Hügel was really two castles, one of 160 rooms linked by a pillared gallery in neo-Classic style to another castle of a mere sixty rooms—or, as one writer has preferred to describe it, "a Victorian opera-house to which a Victorian railway-station has been attached". It had originally been planned as a faithful copy of an Italianate Renaissance-type palace, but Alfred's dickering with the designs had produced a monstrosity that was only matched in its solid ugliness and massive tastelessness by some of the other miserable mausoleums Bismarck's Germany was erecting in Berlin at this time. There were no pictures, no tapestries, not even a library. The windows did not open, because Alfred was afraid of draughts. Not a single piece of wood went into the construction. Everything was built of steel and stone.

No gas mains were laid to the house. Instead, the cheerless parlours were illumined by candles and oil-lamps—because, in the most poignant irony of all, the man whose fame and fortune were founded on forges and furnaces was himself afraid of fire.

Alfred had devised a complex heating and ventilating plant, the pipes of which poked peculiarly from the roof of the Hügel in such an extraordinary Emmet-like fashion that they reminded most visitors of some early steam-locomotive. Unfortunately the system never worked properly, for even after numerous modifications the luckless people who had to live there still shivered in winter and sweltered in summer, so that in the end it had to be removed altogether.

Nor was the house itself erected without a struggle. A hurricane tore down the scaffolding, torrential rain flooded the foundations, while cracks soon began appearing in many of the walls on account of subsidence from an iron-mine beneath the site. The building material, ten-ton blocks of limestone, came from quarries near Chantilly in France and were delivered by rail to the foot of the hill. Just three months after work began, war broke out between Prussia and France. Even so, this still did not stop deliveries of the stone—instead they were re-routed to Essen through Belgium, while Alfred for his part went on supplying his customers in France with their railway tyres and steel through England. The two-way traffic was only halted when the final animosities aroused by the siege of Paris forced his agent there to quit the country. Several of the French stonemasons stayed on in Essen throughout the war and Alfred saw to it that they came to no harm. Begun in April 1870, the Villa Hügel was not ready for the family to move in until January 1873. No one ever calculated its exact cost, but it could not have been much under £1 million.

Meantime, Alfred had started work on another monument —a detailed constitution for the House of Krupp. It was to be a sort of "Standing Orders" for his regiment of workers and managers. "As the hart pants for cooling streams, so do I for regulation", he had once told a correspondent. Curiously enough he began this typically teutonic task in the Victorian Englishness of Torquay, the seaside resort to which he had been recommended to go for a health cure during the winter of 1871 and 1872, because another trip to Nice was now out of the question in view of the animosity towards Alfred raised by the Franco-Prussian War. The enterprise took him over a year, of which six months were spent in Torquay, though in the end he was compelled to seek the help of experienced Prussian lawyers.

Called by some "the Magna Carta of the House of Krupp", and by others "a cross between the laws of an absolute monarchy and the rules of a Prussian army barracks", Alfred's *General Regulations* were completed on 13 September 1872, a copy being given immediately to every Krupp employee. In commending the seventy-two paragraphs to his senior executives, Alfred declared: "No case should occur for many years—for a century even—which has not been foreseen in this collection of laws. No post should exist, from that of general-manager to workman, as to the duties of which this collection of rules does not give precise information."

Everyone employed by Krupp was "under obligation" to give himself totally and exclusively to Krupp. If occasionally a workman's job "does not take up all of his time and energies, then he must find some other way to use them in the interest of the firm". In his dotage Alfred even designed uniforms for his workmen to wear at home as well as in the factory. Just before his death, paying what turned out to be his final visit to the foundries, in the spring of 1887, he had noticed that some of his men had erected hutches next to their cottages in which they were keeping goats. Immediately he had ordered the animals to be driven away, arguing with his managers that it was clear that the goats were feeding on *his* grass and *his* clover and pointing out to them that goats had "actually gnawed Greece bare"!

Alfred had always had what can charitably be only described as a psychotic fear of being diddled by his workers. As early as 1838 he had drawn up a set of punishments within the works: when to be five minutes late was to lose a whole hour's wages, when to run up debts in bars and shops was a sufficient reason for instant dismissal ("how else could they repay their debts except by robbing me", he had written to a member of the firm), when to infringe his elaborate set of rules meant fines which went into a fund from which more dutiful workers were "rewarded". These "rewards" were not, however, paid straightaway but were kept until retirement or death—so that there was always that extra stick to brandish over a recalcitrant employee's head. "Regardless of the cost, all workers must be supervised all the time by experienced, energetic men who will be paid a premium for everybody they catch", he instructed his management. From his first days in the firm he had yearned for what he described as "precautions that would protect it from laxness for all eternity".

Like many other industrialists of his time, whether British, French, American or German, Alfred was adamantly opposed to trade unionism. In 1870 for instance when a group of workers struck at a near-by engine factory in Essen, Alfred commanded his executives never to employ these strikers under any circumstances and that if one of his workmen, no matter how skilled or whether even a foreman, should show the slightest objection to the way the firm was run then he was to be instantly dismissed. Later, when one of his own coal-mines in June 1872 joined the first mass coal-strike in Germany, Alfred was so furious that he wanted to sever all connection with that particular mine then and there. "I expect and demand complete trust", he told his managers, and he immediately sent off a letter to every one of his workers inviting them to leave the firm "the sooner the better" if they were dissatisfied with their lot there, for he intended, as he put it, "to be and to remain master in my own house". The patriarchal idea of the lord's castle as his kingdom was being transferred to the industrial scene. Employers such as Krupp regarded themselves as absolute monarchs in their business. Unionisation was seen by them as an infringement of well-established property rights.

It goes without saying that Alfred was also a bitter opponent of socialism and indeed of any suggestion that workers should have a bigger say in the running of the nation's affairs. He was a firm supporter of Bismarck's repressive legislation banning socialist organisations and propaganda, and he even stood for election against Essen's socialist deputy in 1878. To their credit the electors rejected him, though many were his own workmen and it had been an open, unsecret ballot with his foremen taking careful note of which way everyone voted. The year before entering the hustings he had declared to his employees, in a document pinned to every notice-board in every one of his factories, that "issues of high policy require more free time and more knowledge of circumstances for their decision than the workman has at his command". Earlier, he had ordered his senior executives to root out any socialist sympathisers among the workmen and to dismiss them instantly "without giving any reasons except that there is no longer any work for them". He wrote constantly of "exorcising the spirit of socialism" and went out of his way to boast how he had once broken a Ruhr coal-miners' strike by getting blackleg coal from Saarbrücken. As a result, along with Bismarck, he came to be one of the men German socialists most hated.

Alfred might act like an autocrat in his own kingdom, but he was shrewd enough—shrewder than a great many of his industrial contemporaries—to realise that he had everything to gain from creating a contented, loyal, long-serving, highly-skilled, secure labour-force, and so in his despotic way he was a pioneer of what today we term the Welfare State. Even as early as 1844, when he was just thirty-two years old, he was writing to a friend, "Our nominal wage here is nine silver groschen but we increase that figure by one in every case to make sure of keeping our employees". By that time a works' sickness fund and burial fund had been in existence eight years. A workers' pension fund was founded in 1858 and three years later the first houses and hostels were built for his men. Dull, dreary places to mid-twentieth-century eyes, despite the occasional fountains and grassy courtyards, yet they were better than nothing, better than what most other German industrialists were doing, or rather were not doing. On the other hand, if any of his workers were sacked then they were immediately evicted from their homes—and so long as they occupied a Krupp abode they were of course subject to Krupp rules and Krupp regulations. Alfred had what were described as "supervision officers" to see that the tenants of his colonies and settlements obeyed—and it was said that they even checked the rubbish bins for socialist leaflets.

But Alfred was really forced to provide this housing by the startling manner in which Essen had outgrown itself and by the extortionate rentals that were resulting from this over-crowding. From a little more than 4,000 inhabitants at the beginning of the century, it had leapt to nearly 10,000 in 1850, to over 20,000 in 1860, had passed the 50,000 mark in 1870, and was to reach 70,000 by 1890. Krupp's expansion had of course been the major factor in this dramatic growth—for instance, when 7,000 extra workmen were taken on by Krupp within a decade, as they were between 1860 and 1870, it meant the immigration of 25,000 to 30,000 men, women, and children. Many of the newcomers were from the rural areas of eastern Germany and Poland.

By the end of the eighteen-eighties, about one Krupp worker in three was renting accommodation from the firm. Alfred meanwhile had established schools, hospitals, can-teens, bars, public baths, skittle-alleys, even a church and a cemetery. He was not one for frills and fancies, however—for instance he instructed his executives to build the schools "with the greatest simplicity, with light and air, and no luxuries". Nor was his welfare pursued in a spirit of phil-anthropy: if a worker left his employ before the normal retiring age then he automatically forfeited all his con-tributions to the Krupp pension and sickness funds. The fact of the matter was that Alfred thought of welfare as simply just another weapon to wield against an enemy—the enemy this time being the worker who, in Krupp's estimation, had to be both cajoled and coddled into con-tinuing to create for him the profits he considered his proper due. In appearance his paternalism may have seemed almost revolutionary for the age, but in purpose it was old, even by that time archaic. His welfare schemes were a form of latter-day feudalism, a demonstration of his utter disdain for democracy.

The German proletariat, like that of nearly every other nation at this time, was a prey to rapacious shop-owners and bar-keepers. To protect his employees, Alfred set up his own soup kitchens and grocery stores. But some of them preferred to join the profit-sharing co-operatives that had recently sprung up in Essen. This smacked too much of self-reliance to Alfred. "We must make certain that every worker's immediate thought is of the firm and the interests of the factory, and that he is not tempted to mull over speculations in coffee, tobacco, sugar, and raisins", Alfred told his management.

As soon as the opportunity presented itself, he bought out these co-operatives and turned them into branches of his own grocery shops, though offering discounts. Apart from being a shrewd welfare gesture, they proved to be immensely profitable and today form the basis of Krupp's booming retail and supermarket business in the Ruhr. In time too, Alfred came to add a bakery, a butcher's shop, a soft-drinks factory, and a wine store. Already, his firm was beginning to be described as "a state within a state" and his work-people were being called Kruppians, as though they were a separate tribe of Germans.

Dictatorial and disagreeable though he undoubtedly was, Alfred nevertheless managed to instil into everyone who worked for him a pride in their House—and this so-called *Kruppianer* spirit, which stems from Alfred's day, is as unique to Krupp's as is its great size or its notoriety for having made guns. At the turn of the century, for instance, a Krupp worker was considered a very desirable husband because he was almost bound to be steady and his job was immensely secure. Even today, Krupp employees argue that there is a feeling of "belonging" about the firm. Unlike other German firms, Krupp's have never had any trouble in finding apprentices, and once employed there workers tend to stay for life. Indeed when the one hundred and fiftieth anniversary of the firm was celebrated in 1961, there were more than 500 workers present who had participated in the centenary festivities in 1912. The Allies, particularly the British, certainly underestimated this *Kruppianer* spirit after both world wars. The paternalistic way in which the Krupps look after their employees was repaid by the workers tending to regard the head of the family very much as a father-figure, to be relied upon in times of difficulty, to be looked up to always. In a nation of father-figures, the Krupps became the father-figures *par excellence*.

The new German Empire which emerged from the victory of 1871 was a Prussian empire. William, the Prussian King, became the new German Emperor—and Bismarck, the Prussian Prime Minister, became the new German Chancellor. Prussia not only took over the whole of Germany, except for Austria, but also obtained a part of France as well: the two provinces of Alsace and Lorraine, rich in coal and iron-ore. Steel men at that time did not rate Lorraine's ore very highly, because of its considerable phosphorus content. But within a few years the British steel inventors Thomas and Gilchrist were to come up with a way of utilising such ores, and ironically it was their process that gave Germany its immense advantage in steel production over the rest of Europe.

Germany was without doubt now the most powerful State on the continent of Europe. Two questions remained to be resolved however: firstly, whether she would be satisfied with her present borders or would instead seek to extend them farther, and secondly, whether or not France would want some form of revenge. Both Bismarck and Krupp were to play on the possibility of a French war of revenge, each for their own individual ends: Bismarck, because the threat of an enemy at the gates enabled him to pose as being indispensable and thus to keep in power; Alfred, because it sold his guns.

The victors of 1871 also imposed an indemnity of five milliards of francs (about £200 million) on the defeated French—and it was partly the speed with which this immense indemnity was paid off, a mere matter of thirty months, that produced the extraordinary boom Germany experienced immediately after the war. As fast as the francs poured in, the new Imperial German Government spent them on armaments or else on repaying their debts to individual Germans, most of whom suddenly finding themselves possessed of great capital felt prompted to re-invest straightaway. As many new iron-works, blast-furnaces, and machine-producing factories sprang up in Germany during the three years after 1871 as had risen during the whole of the previous seventy. Only about eighteen new companies on the average had been registered each year during the quarter of a century before the war, but in 1871 alone there were over 200 such new registrations, and in 1872 over 500.

The boom benefited Krupp as it did of course every other established manufacturer in the new Germany. His labour-force leapt from 10,000 in 1871 to 16,000 in 1873, by which time he was producing 2,000 more guns a year than at the height of the Franco-Prussian War. Nearly every nation in the world was scrambling to buy them: Austria, Turkey, Egypt, Chile, Brazil, China, Japan and, as usual, Russia.

Krupp's relations with the Russians had always been close. Unlike the Prussian War Ministry, the Czar's men preferred to be involved with the details of gun design. Accordingly over the years there had grown up a considerable two-way flow of ballistic experts and artillery officers between Essen and St. Petersburg. Russian generals were frequent guests of Alfred's at the Villa Hügel and they had tried on many an occasion to tempt him to emigrate to Russia, offering him all sorts of high official positions in the empire.

As the demand grew for bigger and better guns, so weapons became quickly obsolete. Napoleon III for instance lost the Battle of Sedan in 1870 using the same guns with which he had won the Battle of Solferino eleven years before. Since faster obsolescence meant in effect more orders more frequently, it could only bring still more profits to armament manufacturers like Alfred Krupp. Alfred for his part pressed his luck even further by arguing with the Kaiser and Bismarck that in order to keep Germany's stock of weaponry up to date he needed to maintain large and expensive research and development departments, to finance which he demanded yet more orders more often. He was also not above using the plea that the wage bill of his large labour-force could only be met if still further weapons contracts were placed with him by the Imperial Government. Attempts to insist on open tender particularly infuriated him and once a demand from the Admiralty for guarantees of the quality of his guns almost deranged him. He had arrogated unto himself the monopolistic mantle of "the nation's armourer" and he expected extra privileges thereby.

In January 1874, when France had finally paid off her war indemnity and the fear was beginning to mount that she might possibly be plotting a war of revenge, Alfred got an order from the Kaiser for 2,350 field-guns, which even by his standards was pretty huge. It came at a time of great crisis for the House of Krupp—and it came too late. Alfred once again had overreached himself, affected perhaps by the spending spree which had swept Germany during the post-war boom. In just one year, 1872, he had bought over 300 iron-ore mines and collieries, paying up to £130,000 and £200,000 apiece for individual companies. On top of this, he had purchased two big iron-works complete with brand-new blast-furnaces and had built a fleet of four marine transporters to ship the new iron-ore deposits he had recently acquired in Spain.

His profligacy was by no means unique in Germany, and indeed in Europe, as manufacturers everywhere vied with each other in extending their equipment and their factories—until in the end the bubble burst, signalled first by a crash on the Vienna Stock Exchange. Overnight, hundreds of undertakings became bankrupt, prices of stocks and shares plummeted, many firms like Krupp's suddenly found themselves short of money as financiers called in their loans. In Alfred's case he was a million and a half pounds short!

He appealed to the Kaiser and to Bismarck, but the treasury bureaucrats opposed their giving him any help. At last the situation had occurred which he had always dreaded—for the only people who had the vast sums he required were the banks. Their conditions were stiff, as he knew they would be. They insisted on controlling the finances of his firm from top to bottom, and appointed their own man to do so. It meant that the House of Krupp was no longer at Alfred's sole discretion; for the moment at least he would not be master in his own mansion—though as it turned out it was not to harm in any way his standard of living.

Short of Germany's subsequent defeat in two world wars, this was the biggest crisis the firm ever had to face. But the blow was eased somewhat in that the bankers chose as their man at Krupp's Alfred's old business acquaintance, Karl Meyer, the former Berlin bookseller, who had also for a long time been Krupp's representative in the capital, though that did not mean they had always seen eye-to-eye with each other over the administering of the firm.

The banks discovered that the House of Krupp was in fact in an even worse state than they had been led to believe. Alfred was appalled. From now until his death thirteen years later he had little to do with the day-to-day running of the firm. He retired to his hill-top retreat, hardly ever setting foot again inside the works except to receive important visitors. The House of Krupp only paid off its last penny of debt to the banks in the year Alfred died.

So far, Krupp's reputation as a gun-manufacturer had rested on his production of small and medium-sized guns— the British firm of Armstrong still led the world in making heavy guns, particularly the 40 cm. guns of their *Inflexible* class weighing eighty tons apiece. Alfred had long been determined to topple the British from this particular pinnacle. America, Holland, Norway and Switzerland had already been sold 35·5 cm. guns, but Krupp's were without a suitable shooting-range on which to test any bigger weapons.

As soon as the Franco-Prussian War was over, Alfred had begun looking for his own testing-site so as to make himself fully independent of the German ordnance author-ities. In 1874 he secured a range at Dolmen, some forty-five miles from Essen, but within hardly any time at all it proved far too short. A few years later he opened another and bigger one at Meppen, near Osnabruck, having had to persuade over a hundred farmers to give up their land to do so. Complete with huge cranes, concrete gun-emplacements, and shell-proof shelters for visitors, it was easily the best-equipped range in the world—even the German Army sought Alfred's permission to hold their tests on his range.

But Alfred turned his gunnery tests into great social occasions. His gala shooting exhibition of August 1879— termed by Alfred the "Bombardment of Nations"—was a case in point. Representatives from eighteen different

countries were invited, though since armament makers had
to be particularly zealous of diplomatic niceties both France
and Turkey (for Russia's sake) were left off the guest list.
More than twelve different guns were fired, including the
seventeen inch so-called "built-up" gun, then the most
powerful piece of ordnance in the world. Krupp paid for the
expenses of all the hundred or so senior naval and military
officers who attended. He was renowned for his hospitality
and had acquired a private hotel in Essen especially for this
purpose. However, it was also well known that he usually
expected something in return. Indeed, one German War
Minister once warned his staff, "Better not go to Essen, for
manufacturers are apt to get around people with good
dinners, in order that their tongues may be loosened by the
wine."

The Russians had bought £1 million worth of guns from
him in 1876 and by way of thanks Alfred threw in for good
measure the big fourteen-inch cannon capable of firing
1,000-pound shells that the Americans had nicknamed "the
killing machine" when he had shown it at the Philadelphia
Centennial Exhibition. Despite not being invited to his
shooting shows, the Turks nevertheless purchased more than
1,000 guns from him during the eighteen-seventies, and the
Chinese about 500. The giant guns ordered by Italy had to
be shipped the long way round by sea as few of the Swiss
mountain bridges could have withstood their massive
weight.

In 1877, on the anniversary of the Battle of Sedan, Kaiser
William visited the Villa Hügel in great state—with him
were nearly a score of princes and generals. It was his fourth
visit, and relations between William and Alfred remained
close until Alfred's death. Krupp often called on the Kaiser
in Berlin and always felt he could approach him direct
whenever he had a problem. On the occasion of the 1877
visit he gave William two expensively decorated guns for
the new Imperial yacht, *Hohenzollern*. He could afford to be
generous that year because Krupp's had just made a
particularly good "killing" by supplying guns to both sides
in the Russo-Turkish War—a fact of which he boasted
in a memorandum he circulated among British M.P.'s

two years later when he was lobbying for business in London.

This was also the period of the great railway expansions in America: between 1860 and 1880 the mileage of track there nearly trebled. Vast quantities of steel rails were bought from Krupp by such famous American railway names as the Atchison, Topeka and Santa Fe, as well as the Union Pacific and the New York Central. Indeed, it was largely his exports of 170,000 tons of rails and rolling stock a year to the United States during the late eighteen-seventies that enabled him to pay off his great bank debts before they were due. Alfred had made his first American sale as early as 1849; two steel carriage axles to the Pennsylvania Railroad. But the market began to slip away from him during the 1880's with the emergence of a domestic steel industry in the United States. By the end of the century America had of course outstripped the rest of the world in steel production.

It was the loss of important overseas markets like the United States that encouraged Bismarck to raise Custom Tariffs on imported steel—a move which enabled established steel manufacturers like Krupp to impose a virtual stranglehold on German output in the later 1880's. Hitherto as much as two-thirds and occasionally three-quarters of Krupp's production had been exported, but from now on the proportion swung the other way and he became ever more dependent on home sales.

Steel producers everywhere had begun to benefit enormously from the new processes for making steel, such as the Bessemer and the Siemens-Martin "Open Hearth", but it was Thomas and Gilchrist's so-called "basic method" which allowed the vast ore deposits of Lorraine close to the Ruhr to be utilised and which thereby led to Germany's and the Ruhr's ascendancy in European steel production. Ironically, Alfred resisted bitterly the introduction of the Thomas-Gilchrist process because he feared it would make redundant the non-phosphorus iron-ores he had recently bought in Spain, but other Ruhr steel producers were only too anxious to score a point over Krupp and it was left to Alfred's son to try to make up the lost leeway when he eventually took over the running of the firm.

Right up to the end of his life Alfred poured forth a daily

deluge of written commands and complaints to his managers, but since he refused to see them in person they took little notice of his tirades—and mercifully for them the telephone had not then been invented. He had become known simply as "that grumpy old fellow on the Hill". His wife tried on many an occasion to intervene in his disputes but he quarrelled bitterly with her too and in the end in 1882 she left him for ever. Shortly after this he ordered all her personal possessions to be removed from her rooms on the pretext that he needed the space to store his papers.

From now on he filled his time with devising ever more fantastic weapons. One was for a single gun set on a small armoured boat which could fire in opposite directions simultaneously: while the first shot was fired at the enemy the other, meant merely to absorb the recoil, was aimed into the sea behind. Another scheme was for a raft with guns mounted on it and made unsinkable by means of watertight compartments, but as it did not have any method of propulsion of its own it would have had to be towed into action!

When people came to stay at the Villa Hügel he used to pin up rules of behaviour in their rooms, and would leave notes of complaint if they did things he disliked. He would often invite acquaintances and then entirely ignore them for the duration of their stay. Even the black stockings worn by the serving maids sent him into a rage since he thought they should have kept to the white ones of his childhood. Rather late in the day he tried to make up for his long and total lack of interest in music by hiring a pianist to play for him while he took his meals—for a brief time it was Humperdinck, the composer of *Hänsel and Gretel*. He even invested a little money in the local theatre, though it might have been less a sudden concern for the state of drama in Essen and more that he perhaps saw a reflection of his former self in the manager who browbeat him into doing so.

The richest man in all Germany, perhaps in all Europe, he became more and more bored with life. No one would deign to play a game of dominoes or even skat with him because he was such a bad loser. Fewer and fewer people visited him. He had outlived both his brother Hermann and his sister Ida, while his only correspondence with his remaining brother Fritz was through the works management. He retired increasingly into himself: a lonely, pathetic figure moving restlessly from room to room inside his forbidding castle lest the ventilation might fail and cause him to faint. Renounced by his wife and reviled by his only son, Alfred would take to his bed for long periods although suffering no illness. Towards the end he became very conscious of his own physical decay, which appalled him—and death, of which he had always been afraid, now really terrified him. "All I am now is a shadow with a few bones", he told one of his doctors, "all the rest is gas." His final days to a remarkable degree mirror those of such other megalomaniacs, such other misanthropic millionaires as Randolph Hearst and Lord Northcliffe.

Attended only by his valet, Alfred Krupp died, apparently of a heart attack, on Bastille Day, 14 July 1887. He was then seventy-five.

More lasting and more shattering changes in the pace and appearance of living happened in the lifetime of Alfred Krupp than in that of any other Krupp before or since. When he had been born, not a single mile of railway track existed in the whole of Germany, and to travel across Europe took as long as it had a thousand years before. The area now called Germany was then simply another agricultural community, but by the time of his death the country of the kaisers and the cannon kings had become the foremost industrial power on the Europe continent, covered by a railway network of well over 40,000 miles. For at least the first forty years of his life, English steel had dominated world markets, but long before his final decay he had seen Sheffield's pre-eminence supplanted by the products of his own blast-furnaces. The pay-roll of seven that his father had bequeathed to him he had turned into a huge labour-force 21,000 strong. The Krupp workshops had proliferated around Essen until they occupied several thousands of acres and had spread to other parts of Germany as well.

From being a debtor he had grown into the richest man in Europe, worth every penny of £10,000,000 it was said. Many nations had honoured him in some way: from

Portugal's Order of Christ to Japan's Order of the Rising
Sun, from Brazil's Grande Dignitario to Sweden's Order of
Vasa. Emperor Francis Joseph of Austria had given him a
golden snuff-box, Russia's Grand Duke Michael had
presented him with a diamond ring, while Viceroy Li Hung
Chang of China had bestowed on him a 2,000-year-old vase.

Whereas his father had been buried in a pauper's grave,
the great of many nations came to Alfred's funeral. Once
just another unsung, undistinguished Essen firm, Krupp's
had become not only a "national institution" inside Germany, but also a name meriting intense hatred or deep
admiration outside. Even the Kaiser had once quipped to a
fellow monarch, "Krupp's tell governments what they must
buy".

Although it was Friedrich who founded the firm, it was
Alfred who really formed it—and it has stayed in Alfred's
mould ever since. He directed in his will that its ownership
should never be divided but should pass in its entirety to a
single heir—a principle which has been faithfully followed
ever since. It has meant that unlike other great family
fortunes, such as those of the Rockefellers or the Rothschilds,
the Krupp wealth and the Krupp industrial empire has been
kept intact and not carved up among a great number of
heirs.

The year before Alfred died, his first grandchild, Bertha,
had been born, after whom the big gun that demolished
the Belgian forts in 1914 was to be named. The year following Alfred's death, old Kaiser William passed away too—
and within two years of the new Kaiser William's accession
Bismarck had been banished from the chancellorship. An
old era was very much giving way to a new one, but one in
which Krupp's were destined to play an even more fateful
and vigorous role than hitherto.

CHAPTER SIX

"You will be coming in melancholy circumstances"

THE MAN who now inherited Alfred's multi-million-pound
cannon-kingdom was as different from him as Alfred had
been from his own father—and knowing Alfred, as we now
do, it can be no shock to learn that his son should have
burgeoned into a very bizarre fellow indeed!

Fritz Krupp even *looked* unlike his father. A black, bushy
moustache adorned, somewhat incongruously, his round,
dumpy face. He was short and fat, with prematurely
greying hair, and stooped a little as he walked, peering
shortsightedly through gold-rimmed spectacles. When he
was only in his early forties, an English visitor mistook him
for an old man of at least sixty. In fact Fritz was really rather
ugly, whereas Alfred on the other hand, with his tall, slender
figure and fine-boned, bearded face had been considered
quite handsome by many people in his day.

But Fritz had been a delicate child from birth, suffering
first from asthma and then articular rheumatism. His
mother's health had been permanently damaged in bearing
him. Until he was well into his teens the pair of them used to
wander from health-resort to health-resort, from spa to spa,
in search of the sun and the hundred and one other so-called
"cures" of nineteenth-century Europe. As a result, he never
went to school with other children, but was entirely educated
by tutors. Thus he grew up to be a shy, highly sensitive
creature, thoroughly unused to the company of boys and
girls of his own age. His father had thought he would never
be fit enough to take on the task of running the firm and had
begun looking elsewhere in the family for a possible successor.
It was only when Fritz was almost twenty that Alfred became
convinced of his son's suitability and strength. Then with

typical thoroughness and tenacity he had promptly set
about moulding him in his own image.

Father and son had come closest together in the months
immediately following the Prussian victory of 1871, when
Alfred was compiling his Constitution for the House of
Krupp. But the bond between the two was only finally
confirmed by Fritz's tactful handling of his father's moods of
deep gloom and despondency after the firm's financial
crisis in 1874. From then onwards, Fritz became one of
Alfred's few friends. Apart from Albert Longsdon, the
veteran Krupp man in London, he was the only other person
in whom his father would confide during the years of
retreat and decline.

By this time Fritz was acting as Alfred's confidential
secretary, faithfully taking down in his numerous notebooks
the thousands of words of advice his father dictated to him
daily. He had wanted to study the natural sciences, for
which he appeared to have a genuine interest and gift, but
Alfred had vetoed the notion, arguing that science like
technical matters was better left to employees while employers should concern themselves with the mysteries of
management. Alfred even went so far as to tell some of his
business acquaintances that he thought Fritz's exposure to
an academic training might hold dangers for him when it
came to running the firm. All his life, he resisted promoting
technical men to executive positions.

Perhaps it was in preparing his successor that Alfred
betrayed most his megalomania, for he enjoined his son to
read every note and letter he had ever written: "You will
thus be led progressively to absorb the spirit and aspirations
of my career and so save yourself much thought and worry on
your own." Young Fritz must surely have blenched though
when he saw the plethora of paper in his father's cabinets.
Alfred's main preoccupation was to keep his heir in the
closest possible contact with him, short of carrying him
around kangaroo-like in his pouch, for he was determined
that his successor should be a "mirror-image" of him. Only
in this way, he argued to his acquaintances, could the
continuity of the firm be assured. Perhaps this was his most
supreme vanity of all!

A bizarre, almost tragi-comic incident in their relationship occurred in 1874 when Fritz was just twenty years old. A particularly bad attack of rheumatism had laid him low. As a convalescence his doctors had advised a long trip to Egypt. At first the suggestion had angered Alfred since he was depressed himself over having had to mortgage the firm to the banks, but then he had become quite enthusiastic about his son's proposed trip when it had been pointed out to him that perhaps Fritz could combine a little business with his holiday.

Egypt at that time was believed to be contemplating building a railway southwards down the Nile from Cairo to Khartoum, so Alfred thought that a personal visit from Krupp's heir might sway the Egyptians into buying Krupp rails and Krupp springs and Krupp axles. But Fritz soon discovered after his arrival in Cairo that the reports were grossly exaggerated. Therefore, after writing to tell his father this he continued his convalescence by boat down the Nile. As usual, however, Alfred was not prepared to take a simple "no" for an answer and immediately began bombarding his son with further instructions and proposals, none of which reached him until many months had passed, since there were no deliveries of mail on board the steamer as it made its way slowly along the Nile. Alfred interpreted the long silence as at best laziness or at worst hurt pride, and promptly increased the deluge of *obiter dicta*, so much so that when Fritz finally returned to Cairo his doctor-companion felt obliged to hasten back to Essen to explain. Fritz for his part stayed behind enjoying the sun, yet still endeavouring to satisfy his father's strictures to pursue "all possible selling opportunities" among the patently disinterested Egyptians.

After this, Fritz became a sort of filial A.D.C. to Alfred, often having to pass on in person to the managers of the firm his father's complaints and criticisms of their conduct—and over the years he would seem to have grown quite adept at filtering such outbursts and at translating them into more meaningful and perhaps even practical suggestions. When he was twenty-five he acted as host instead of Alfred at the great Meppen "Bombardment of the Nations", but even so it was to be another three years before his father

gave him an income of his own. Fritz's one really rebellious
act in his whole life was his volunteering for a year's service
with the Baden Dragoons at Karlsruhe, though his father
soon put a stop to it. There were people of course who were
quick to point out that whereas Alfred might not mind other
fellows' sons being blown to bits by guns he was apparently
reluctant to let his own son run that risk.

It was also when he was twenty-five that Fritz told Alfred
he wanted to marry Margarethe von Ende, the daughter of a
Prussian Government official. Margarethe and Fritz by
that time had known each other for seven years, but still
Alfred would not agree to their marrying, and went on
saying "no" for another three years despite the pleas of
Fritz's mother. Whether it was because of his inveterate
hatred of Prussian bureaucrats, or whether he had hoped
for a more aristocratic match for his son, Alfred's refusal
was certainly the last straw so far as his own marriage was
concerned—for after a final quarrel in 1882 over his continuing refusal, Bertha packed her bags and never entered
the Villa Hügel again. Yet within a few weeks Alfred had
given Fritz and Margarethe his consent, though not his
blessing. Later that same year they were wed—in Bertha's
presence, but not Alfred's. The young couple went to live
in the "little" castle next door to Alfred, which in the end
had been his only proviso for letting them marry.

Margarethe was the same age as Fritz. After a comfortable
though far from luxurious childhood, she had rebelled
against her prim and puritanical mother by taking a job as
governess to an English admiral's family living in North
Wales. But her mother had her revenge by insisting whenever
Margarethe visited them that she sleep in one of the servants'
bedrooms since "as a paid employee she did not deserve any
better accommodation". It was shortly after this, while
Margarethe was working as tutor at the court of a minor
German prince, that she met Fritz.

Neither plain nor beautiful, her harsh, unhappy early
life had left its mark on Margarethe—which perhaps was
just as well, for it could be said to have groomed her for her
battles with Fritz's father, who seemed to delight in humiliat-
ing and hurting her. If, for instance, a carriage that had been

ordered to take Fritz and her off to some engagement or
other was kept waiting outside for only a short while, Alfred
would send a servant every five minutes or so to enquire
whether Margarethe needed any assistance in her dressing.
Furthermore, he used to chide her for buying vegetables in
the town when they had such vast vegetable gardens of their
own—except that he had ordered his gardeners never to
supply her. At times even the dress and behaviour of the
young couple's guests came in for a blast or two of complaint
from him—and on occasion he would lecture Fritz and his
wife in the presence of others on their responsibilities as
heirs of the House of Krupp.

For with his marriage Fritz became formally accepted as
the "Cannon King's" Crown Prince. He was given 20 per
cent of the profits and a seat on the Committee of Management, though without any particular responsibilities. In
March 1886, when Margarethe and Fritz were both thirty-
two, their first child, Bertha, was born. There is no record
of Fritz having discussed the name with his father, nor is it a
connection with Alfred's wife that eulogisers of the Krupp
saga sing about. However, Alfred had died within the year
—and only a few months later Fritz's mother passed away
too.

Immediately after moving into the main part of the Hügel,
Fritz and Margarethe began desperately trying to make it
into a family house, something that Alfred had never even
attempted. Although they opened the windows, put in a
modern heating and ventilating system, and stocked the
place with books and pictures, they failed—nor was anyone
after them to succeed. To at least one later inhabitant of the
Villa Hügel it was always a "tomb" and Fritz's younger
daughter's abiding memory of it was that it was "for ever
cold".

Whereas Fritz had hitherto struck his managers as being a
somewhat timid, self-effacing kind of chap, once he was boss
he straightaway showed them that he intended ruling not
reigning. He resisted all their attempts to increase their
powers at his expense. Indeed, as if to show the world that
while one cannon king might have died another was certainly
taking his place, Fritz almost indecently soon after his father's

death was setting off on a sort of "Royal Tour". Complete
with large retinue of directors, personal physicians, and
gunnery experts—and of course bearing such suitable gifts as
steel ingots and ceremonial cannons—he visited first of all
the old Kaiser in Berlin, then the King of the Belgians in
Brussels, the King of Saxony in Dresden, the King of
Rumania in Bucharest, finally ending up with the Turkish
Sultan in Constantinople. They for their part responded as
though they were greeting a monarch of sorts by bestowing
on Fritz a profusion of honours and decorations—the Sultan
of Turkey even entrusted him with an important diplomatic
message for Bismarck concerning Germany's policy in the
Balkans. It was only a few days' after Fritz's triumphant
return that his second daughter was born—Barbara, named
after the patroness of gunners of course.

Although Fritz was not as domineering or as ruthless or as
intolerant as his father, the House of Krupp continued to
grow, aided once more by contemporary developments. The
new Kaiser, William II, proclaimed what he described as a
"new direction" for Germany—a direction aimed, he said, at
producing even greater victories than those of the previous
quarter of a century. Within a couple of years he had
dropped the old pilot of the old direction. But the new
direction, as it turned out, was really a collision course, for
it could only be interpreted as a concerted attempt by
Germany to end England's long naval and economic
supremacy.

The new Kaiser wanted a navy because Britain had one,
because he considered it the sign of a Great Power to possess
one, and because it would draw the world's attention to
his Germany. Naturally such a policy could only bring yet
greater profits to Krupp's, and so it was perhaps inevitable
that Fritz should back William to the hilt, even though the
Kaiser was alarming the rest of Europe with such remarks
as that rather than lose "a single stone" of its conquests of
1870, Germany was prepared to leave 42,000,000 people
dead on the battle-field. The new Kaiser could count on
the new "Cannon King". Once again Krupp's and Prussian
Germany's aims and ambitions were indissolubly linked—
and just as Alfred had courted old William so Fritz came

more and more to rely on new William to help him get preferential treatment from officialdom.

It was on William the Second's suggestion that Fritz branched out into shipbuilding, for instance, with his purchase of the decaying Germania shipyards at Kiel in 1896. Again, it was through the new Kaiser that he was able to acquire sufficient land along the waterfront there for him quickly to extend the yards and so make berths big enough for building battleships. Only the year before, William had invited Fritz to be his personal guest at the opening of the Kiel Canal. It was also largely at the Kaiser's prompting that he entered politics in 1893 as the representative for Essen. Fritz fought that election entirely on the need for a larger navy and a bigger army. He had already stood at the polls twice before and had each time been defeated. As it turned out he only just scraped home in 1893, largely because his opponents had been unable to agree on a single candidate to put up against him.

But Fritz was no parliamentarian. He never actually spoke in the Reichstag and rarely pronounced even on the hustings. On the night of his 1893 victory his supporters marched in a torchlight procession to the Villa Hügel, but when they got there he could only splutter out one or two platitudes in greeting that the crowd could barely hear.

Instead, Fritz preferred more subtle methods of putting his point across. In the same year as his election to the Reichstag he acquired his own newspaper, the *Berliner Neueste Nachrichten*. He also began subsidising a press service that provided, so he told the Kaiser, "stories on the activities of Your Majesty and of Your Majesty's Army and Navy", which was his way of saying that it was a propaganda organ on behalf of the military. Along with other leading German manufacturers he financed the German Navy League and the German Colonial League to the tune of hundreds of thousands of pounds.

Founded in 1898, the year after von Tirpitz had been appointed Naval Secretary, the Navy League was unashamedly devoted to securing support in the country for the enormous battle-fleet the Kaiser and his armament manufacturers wanted to build. It so happened that the League's organiser was none other than the editor of Fritz's Berlin newspaper—so perhaps it was no accident that in selling the notion of a fleet to the German industrial proletariat the League emphasised the increased jobs it would bring to armament workers, particularly to those who happened to be on the Krupp pay-roll.

And it worked. The first Navy Act of 1898 authorising seven battleships and nine cruisers was quickly followed two years later by the Second Navy Act outlining a twenty-year programme for laying down at least three new battleships every year. Within fifteen years Krupp's had built nine battleships, five light-cruisers, thirty-three destroyers, and ten submarines. As well as supplying most of the armour-plating to the rest of the new fleet, they were selling the licence to manufacture it to all the major shipbuilding countries of the world, including Britain. In the United States, for instance, Bethlehem Steel and Carnegie were each paying royalties to Fritz of about £9 a ton for the armour-plating they were producing according to his patent— although ironically the famous Krupp Armour was based on an earlier American process for making a nickel-alloy gun-steel.

Fritz's personal income as head of the firm trebled between 1895 and 1902. Before his death it was running at over a million pounds a year, while his private fortune stood at nearly £10 million. These figures were the subject of a bitterly contested Reichstag enquiry at the turn of the century when allegations of over-pricing and excessive profiteering were levelled at the House of Krupp. Even von Tirpitz was made to admit that, until his Ministry had been able to improve its own system of accounting, the navy had been steadily overcharged by Fritz and others for its war-ships. There were also accusations, never adequately disproved, that armament manufacturers such as Krupp and Stumm-Halberg were operating a monopolistic ring that was keeping prices artificially high.

But whether or not every detail of these various allegations was true or not, what *was* certain was that Fritz was easily Germany's richest individual. As well as owning the Villa Hügel, he now had a lavish shooting-lodge at Sayneck on the Rhine together with a magnificent mansion at Baden-Baden. The Kaiser had made him an Excellency and had nominated him to both the Prussian and the German Upper Chambers of Parliament. Berlin saw him more often than Essen. A frequent and regular guest at ministerial dinner parties and court receptions, he also became renowned for his own extensive entertaining. In February 1898, for instance, the *Volkszeitung* newspaper reported that:

> Deputy Krupp gave a luncheon to some 250 people at the Hotel Bristol. . . . Almost every Minister and most members of parliament, were present. Each place laid but with yet more violets and other flowers. Once the meal was finished a special entertainment took place, given by actors and actresses from the Central Theatre and the Winter Garden, together with Tyrolean singers, nigger minstrels, and an Italian concert party.

Whereas nearly all his life Alfred had had to do battle with the Prussian bureaucracy, Fritz now worked in close cooperation, it seemed at times like collaboration, with the new German officials. That web of close threads spun between Berlin and Essen in Alfred's day Fritz now proceeded year by year to draw ever more tightly. As well as the Kaiser himself, almost every German minister, German general, German admiral worth his salt took it upon himself to become a regular visitor to Krupp's. William used to say to his wife that he was going down to Essen "to be shown a bit of shooting". Fritz had no shortage of friends in high places: the Minister of Labour, Major-General Budde, was a former director of one of Krupp's associated firms, the Karlsruhe Arms and Munitions Works. Budde's brother was still a senior executive at Essen, as was the younger brother of von Bülow, the Secretary of State and future Chancellor. Fritz also employed the son of the President of the Ordnance Board and made him responsible for placing the army's weapons contracts with industry.

Krupp's, apparently with the Kaiser's blessing, came to look upon German ambassadors and ministers in places like Constantinople, Tokio, and Peking, as being mere extensions of their international sales force. Indeed Fritz's agents in the field never hesitated to use the diplomatic bag for their business correspondence. On occasion, the interests of the firm could even sway diplomatic decisions. China, for instance, had long been a good customer of Krupp's, buying guns, rails, and warships from them for years, and it is extremely likely that this was a deciding factor in Germany's opposing Japan's demands for extra Chinese territory at the Peace of Shimonoseki—the diplomatic decision which Bismarck dubbed "a leap in the dark". On the other hand when Japan had attacked China in April 1895, and Russia and France had proposed to Germany that they all intervene, the Kaiser had refused. An official German document of this time, across which William had scrawled his approval, declared, "Our manufacturers, exporters, and shippers have been afforded a good opportunity to do business by deliveries and transport of war materials". It later transpired that Krupp's had in fact been supplying guns to Japan as well as to China. Furthermore, during the discussions at The Hague in 1899 when attempts were being made to secure an agreement to limit armaments, William had written in the margin of one of the briefing documents, "But how is Krupp to pay his men?" And Krupp's could also override the actions of German diplomats on the spot: in one instance, again in China, Fritz secured the recall of the Kaiser's senior representative there when he opposed the local Krupp agent.

Apart from the dispute between China and Japan that led to the war of 1895, Krupp's through their indiscriminate selling of weapons to all-comers invariably helped to exacerbate one diplomatic crisis after another. They sold to both sides in the conflict between Austria and Russia over the Balkans and in that between Russia and Turkey over the Bosphorus. Nearly every South American tin-pot dictatorship got its weapons from Fritz whose men on the spot were unmerciful in misleading their customers so long as it meant increased order-books.

When Britain looked around for guns to buy during the Boer War, Krupp's despite a declaration of strict neutrality by the German Government supplied the British Army with the weapons they needed through agents in Italy.

However, such business had its ironies too. During the so-called Boxer Rebellion of 1900, for example, a German gun-boat trying to rescue some German citizens was fired on by a group of Chinese forts along the Yangtse with considerable loss of life among the crew. Later, in his report to Berlin, the gun-boat's commander complained that the shells that had killed his men were Krupp-made!

But there was another side to Fritz Krupp, armament tycoon. Until 1898 he had usually spent his autumns and winters among the fashionable spas of southern Germany or else in one of the newer resorts along the French and Italian Riviera. In that year, however, when he was forty-four years old, he began going instead to Capri. He had never enjoyed good health, and his childhood ailments of asthma and articular rheumatism stayed with him all his life.

Even so, it was not just for the sake of his health that his visits to the Italian island became more and more frequent, and his sojourns there grew longer and longer.

Fritz Krupp was homosexual. While it was not a crime to be homosexual in Italy it was in Germany. Nor as it turned out had Fritz confined his amours to Capri—though the full facts on that score were not to be revealed until after 1919, when it came to light that a member of the Berlin C.I.D. had for many years been compiling a secret dossier of known homosexual blackmail cases among prominent people in the German capital. The list included the Kaiser's A.D.C., the military commandant of Berlin, the private secretary to the Kaiser's wife, a younger brother of the Kaiser, the Court Chamberlain, a Counsellor at the French Embassy— and Fritz Krupp. Apparently Fritz had installed a number of young waiters from Capri at the Hotel Bristol where he used to stay while in Berlin—and a footman, employed at one time by him, when picked up by the police had said of an exceedingly expensive diamond ring discovered on his person that it had been given to him by Krupp, because, as he put it, "Fritz was my friend".

Although prevented by his father from taking a formal training in the natural sciences, Fritz had persisted in his biological studies as an amateur. In particular he had become interested in oceanography and had had his luxurious steam-yacht *Puritan* fitted out for deep-sea research. He liked to fish in it around the shores of Capri for some of the tiny organisms living on the ocean-bed. But he had also bought a grotto in the southern part of the island, a grotto that had one time been the home of a religious recluse called Fra Felice. Hitherto unapproachable, except by sea, Fritz had had a private road cut to it which the local people came to call Strada Krupp. In addition he had transformed the place with terraces, pillars, statues, flowers, and bushes, and had had golden keys specially made to fit the lock of the gate leading to it—keys which he distributed among his closest companions on the island, most of whom appear to have been young fishermen, waiters, barbers, and so on. Fritz used to refer to the grotto as the holy place of a secret fraternity of devout mystics, which he had created and whose membership he alone controlled. But these merry pranks came to the ears of certain Neapolitan newsmen who began publishing in the Italian press lurid stories of so-called orgies and perversions, together with lewd snapshots allegedly featuring Fritz. Inevitably the reports eventually found their way into German newspapers.

As the scandal broke, Fritz quickly and quietly left Capri —it has been said, though never documented, that the Italian Government demanded his departure. On hearing the stories, Margarethe evidently sought the help of the Kaiser, but William merely shrugged her off. Fritz, however, got to know about her action and when he returned to Germany "persuaded" Margarethe to enter a private nursing home for a medical check-up—some critics of Krupp have preferred to describe the manœuvre as that of committing her to a lunatic asylum. Little is known in fact of how their marriage had been faring, though since even the most eulogistic of the family's chroniclers make no mention of it, it would seem fairly evident that husband and wife, like Alfred and Bertha before them, had been going their separate ways for some time.

At first all the stories appearing in the German press were merely insinuations without naming names—simply referring to a "a big industrialist of the highest reputation and enjoying the friendship of the Kaiser and his court". But then on 15 November 1902, two weeks after Margarethe's mysterious disappearance with her doctors, the Social Democrat newspaper in Berlin, *Vorwärts*, published a report headlined "Krupp in Capri" repeating the accusations already made, though this time of course mentioning names. Within a few hours of the story hitting the Berlin streets, Fritz had issued a writ for libel against the paper's editor. The Berlin authorities followed this up by confiscating as many copies of the offending edition as they could find.

Six days later, Fritz asked to see the Kaiser, but on the morning of his appointment was discovered lying unconscious in his room at the Hügel. He died that same day, 22 November 1902, without regaining his senses. His body was immediately committed to a coffin and the lid straightaway sealed—nor was it opened again, even on the day of the funeral. The Kaiser came to the burial, as indeed did most of the members of the Imperial court as well as all the top generals and admirals. Addressing the mourners, William tried to put the blame for Fritz's death on the Social Democrats, who, he said, "had murdered his friend". But no sooner had the Kaiser returned to Berlin than the libel suit against the newspaper editor was promptly dropped— and although some Krupp biographers to this day still persist in talking of Fritz dying from a stroke brought on by worry over the scandal, the evidence would seem surely to indicate no natural end but rather that of a suicide. Indeed just before his death, Fritz had written to a close friend who had asked to visit the Villa Hügel warning him "you will be coming in melancholy circumstances".

Despite the shortness of his time at the helm—just fifteen years in all—the House of Krupp had continued on its spectacular upward course. Fritz had started with 21,000 workers and had left behind 43,000. Under his direction, Krupp's had moved into new fields of activity, such as building warships and making armour-plating, and had quickly attained world prominence in both. They had acquired fresh iron-ore deposits in Sweden and new coal-mines in Lorraine. The old steelworks at Essen had been totally rebuilt and reorganised. To date, these had been the most prosperous days the firm had ever known, but they had also been the most squalid—but then the graph in the fortunes of the House of Krupp during the next forty years was to show a sharp and uncannily pronounced correlation between moral meanness and material success, none more so perhaps than in the period from Fritz's death up to the beginning of the First World War.

CHAPTER SEVEN

"As Germany goes, Krupp goes"

PRECISELY AS his father would have wished, Fritz willed that the House of Krupp should pass undivided to a single heir —since he had no sons it went to his elder daughter, Bertha, who was then just sixteen years old. But there was one surprise in Fritz's will, namely that the firm should at long last become a limited liability company, though admittedly only a private company, not a public one, and the shares were still to be held principally by the head of the family. Indeed, of the 160,000 shares eventually floated, all except four were assigned to Bertha! The four, incidentally, in accordance with the law were divided among members of the Board of Directors, but as most of them were close friends of the family there was hardly any risk being run on that score.

Without doubt Bertha was the richest heiress in Germany, if not in Europe. Her inheritance had been valued at nearly £20 million, while her income was said to amount to more than £1 million a year. With her tall, slender figure, her thin face and her cold, staring eyes, Bertha was nearer in appearance to her grandfather than her own father. Like her younger sister Barbara, Bertha had spent little time in fact with Fritz, and the austere Margarethe would appear to have had an inordinately strong influence on them both: "Our mother seemed infallible to us in every respect, and we clung to her in deepest devotion, not quite without certain feelings of inferiority, since we children as well as our whole entourage were always scared that we might not completely satisfy her demands."

Bertha received her schooling in Baden-Baden, at a fashionable boarding-school for the daughters of upper-class parents—the sort of establishment where the emphasis is on horse-riding and learning to administer large staffs of servants, where the closest the girls ever get to a serious education is in being taught a "genteel" language like French. It was a school for gracious hostesses rather than proficient housewives.

Soon after her husband's death, Margarethe Krupp, as the nominal head of the firm until her daughter came of age, was signing the contract to complete the building of the world's biggest and most modern steelworks at Rheinhausen on the west bank of the Rhine near to its junction with the Ruhr. The project had begun in Fritz's day, for it had become increasingly obvious that Krupp's had outgrown their old Essen site. Indeed, from now on much of the firm's expansion was to happen away from Essen—at Kiel, at Annen, and at Magdeburg. By 1906, with the seven great blast-furnaces of Rheinhausen, named the Friedrich-Alfred works, in full operation using the very latest Thomas "basic process", Krupp's were once more making a bid to outstrip the rest of Europe in steel production.

"I was but little prepared for the tasks awaiting me after my husband's death," Margarethe was to say much later, "since he had held to the principle that business affairs were a man's domain." In fact, during her four years interregnum she concerned herself very little with the business side of Krupp's, preferring to leave the day-to-day administration to its directors. Instead she concentrated on the firm's welfare schemes, partly because it was nearer her own interests and inclinations—and of course more becoming a dowager than having to deal with production lines and gun-tests—but mainly because the directors wanted her to. Krupp's, for once, were under fire themselves, not just on account of the Capri Affair, but more especially through the charges that were being bandied about in the Reichstag and by Berlin gossips of scandalous over-pricing for armour-plating and other war material.

Margarethe's directors wanted to counter all the talk of greedy merchants of death by projecting the House of Krupp's châtelaine-head as an angel of charity. And to a large extent they succeeded, certainly inside Germany itself. This was perhaps the first really effective industrial public relations campaign ever—and it was one that was to continue over the years right up to the present day. If the torrent of pamphlets, glossy brochures, commissioned biographies, official histories, anniversary monographs, and other stuff, that have poured off the firm's presses since 1902, is to be believed, then Krupp's have never had very much to do with forging weapons of war but have been a philanthropic institution devoted simply and disinterestedly to improving the lot of the people "chosen" to work for them. Even a brochure put out as recently as 1963 purporting to list the thirty-four main "milestones" of Krupp history does not mention the production of a single gun, but instead concentrates solely on detailing the introduction of the firm's welfare schemes and "tools of peace"

Under Fritz's régime, Krupp's welfare schemes had certainly been extended, so that by his death they even embraced almshouses for the old. The range and rate of sickness benefits had also been improved—even to building garden suburbs of better-quality, better-designed dwellings. More schools, another hospital, a library, and everything from a chess club and a literary society to an amateur orchestra and a mixed choir had been added to the already impressive list of Krupp extra-mural activities. Through her regular visits to the homes of Krupp workers, Margarethe became better known to them than ever Alfred's wife had been, or indeed any member of the family since—and when she died in 1931 the newspapers of the day estimated that over 150,000 people turned out to watch her funeral cortège go by.

But the thinking behind the welfare had not changed of course. As under Alfred, Krupp's were prepared to rain all manner of benefits on their workers provided they did what they were told—this was the real basis of the industrial paternalism of Imperial Germany which succeeded the military feudalism of old Brandenburg-Prussia. Industrialists were not prepared to encourage self-reliance—nor was the State, as witness Bismarck's schemes of *non*-contributory insurance against accident or sickness. The State, or the State's chosen instrument, whether he be a Krupp or a Kirdorf, a Thyssen or a Stumm-Halberg, was to be the source of all bounty. In that way, argued the new Germany's rulers, the old, tried Prussian dogma of unquestioning deference to authority could be adapted to the modern age: workers would obey the industrialists, and the industrialists would obey the State. As events were to show, few people were in fact more orderly or more submissive than the average German worker and, equally, few were more slavishly devoted to the wishes of a Kaiser or a Führer than German industrial families such as Krupp. Like most rich people the world over, as their possessions multiplied, they rallied to the established order, for they saw in furthering the mystique of the men in power a way of warding off their workers ever having a greater say in the nation's affairs and therefore demanding a greater say in the running of their factory or workshop.

One of the side effects of all this widening of welfare within Krupp's was that the firm came closer and closer to fitting Jerome Bonaparte's description of it as "a state within a state". Even the titles used by the company's principal agents overseas had an ambassadorial ring about them—"Plenipotentiary Representatives of the House of Krupp". And these agents were often men whose standing in the country was equal, if not actually superior, to many ambassadors. The Krupp agent in Vienna, for instance, was a close friend of the Rothschilds; the one in New York was a relative of John Pierpont Morgan, the American financier; Krupp's man in Denmark became in time his country's Minister of War. What is more, because of the closeness of the Krupps to the Kaisers, courting the local Krupp representative was worth the while of any ambitious diplomat —indeed many a German Ambassador came to rely on the local Krupp agent for his information not only as to what was happening in the country where they both were, but more importantly as to what was happening back in Berlin. Krupp's in their turn came to use the local embassies almost as extensions of their own enterprise and to expect the local German ambassador to help them root up business. This was particularly true of Constantinople, Tokio and Peking— for instance, the house of the local Krupp man in Constantinople was right next door to the German Embassy, and the German Ambassador there was largely instrumental in Krupp's cornering of the Turkish market. To win orders from the King of Rumania, Krupp's preferred to work on their own Kaiser first, knowing that a word from one monarch to another meant a lot in their line of business. And they became so adept at it that even their German competitors found it more often than not better to hide from the local German Ambassador exactly what they were up to, since such information would invariably find its way back to Essen.

Selling arms across international borders at the turn of the century was an extremely competitive and hazardous business, resembling more the speakeasy and bootlegging rivalries of Chicago in the 'twenties than the somewhat gentlemanly Anglo-American detergent wars of the 1960's. At times they reminded people even of the early days of the Wild West when competitors bribed the railway companies to refuse to carry each other's weapons and when so-called comparative gunnery tests degenerated into near-riots with opponents' powder-stores "mysteriously" going up in smoke.

The bitterest battles of all were fought between Krupp's and Schneider-Creusot, the French armament people. In 1904, for instance, when Schneider's and the Essen firm were competing for a lucrative Brazilian order, the local Krupp man started a scare that Peru was on the point of attacking her neighbour, which panicked the Brazilians into buying whatever guns were immediately available—it just so happened that Krupp's had a few hundred or so already on their way there. Again, this time in Argentina, Krupp's tipped the scales in their favour by spreading stories, later found to be totally untrue, of a serious accident to some Schneider guns on board a French warship.

Not only was little attention paid to the purposes for which weapons were being purchased, but even to the practicality of the transactions: the tiny state of Andorra was once sold a practice gun by Krupp's that could not be fired without its shell landing on neighbouring French territory, and Krupp salesmen used to delight in dumping expensive though obsolete weapons on such unsuspecting customers as the Turks and the Chinese. The stakes were of course very high —for instance, after Russia's overwhelming defeat by the

Japanese in 1905 she spent about £100 million on re-equipping her navy and army.

But already by Fritz's death most other German armament manufacturers had given up competing with Krupp's, particularly inside Germany itself. The Essen firm had taken a virtual stranglehold on all military deliveries, in so far as the army and navy tended to turn down offers by other German industrial concerns to provide the same weapons even at lower prices. On top of this, the German armed services seemed to go out of their way to discourage any competition against Krupp's. The Admiralty, for instance, insisted on all would-be suppliers furnishing their own testing-ranges—this condition alone was above the means of most competitors, especially new ones. On another occasion, when Rheinmetall underbid Krupp's by a considerable margin for some Turkish orders, yet still lost the contract, it was discovered afterwards that the German Ambassador had advised the Turks to buy Krupp because, according to the Secretary of State, "it was perfectly natural that the older firm, better known abroad, should be recommended".

Krupp's did not bother to load their Board of Directors with back-bench politicians as some British firms do today, hoping thereby to benefit from the contacts these M.P.s may have had with people in high places. Instead, Krupp's preferred to go direct to the men at the top—among their directors at this time were a previous Minister of Railways, the Kaiser's banker, a retired admiral who was known to be a close friend of the Kaiser's, as well as seven former high Government officials. It was a common complaint among Krupp's competitors that the German official machine from the Kaiser downwards was closely identified with the House of Krupp.

At no time more than at the turn of the century was the name of Krupp so intimately associated with the power and prestige of Germany itself. The growth of German industry was considered to have its most convincing expression in the rise of the House of Krupp—indeed when foreigners thought of German industry they thought principally of Krupp—as do many of them still to this day.

Germany had taken a mere thirty years or so to become a

great industrial power. After a slow start, she had quickly from 1871 onwards begun to catch up with the leading European industrial nations such as Britain and France. By the turn of the century she was already expanding at a much faster rate than either of them. As often happens, the imitator moved more rapidly than the pioneer, though Germany was helped in her industrial "take-off", since by this time the key "growth" industries were no longer textiles and iron in which Britain had long been supreme, but were steel, chemicals, electricity, and optical goods, in which Germany had the edge over Britain—German steel production, for instance, mostly centred in the Ruhr, increased twelvefold between 1880 and 1913 and on the eve of the First World War amounted to three times the British figure. In addition, Germany's share of world trade during the same period rose from 17 per cent to 22 per cent, whereas Britain's declined from 38 per cent to 27 per cent.

To Kaiser William, it was particularly galling that the new Germany's strength should not be appreciated more overseas—and playing on his petty conceits and puerile yearnings were the propagandists of such pressure groups as the German Navy League and the German Colonial League with their demands for expansion, always expansion. All of which meant still more business for arms manufacturers like Krupp's, who had of course been contributing handsomely to the German Navy League and the German Colonial League.

Although the aims and interests of the House of Krupp and the House of Hohenzollern had if anything grown closer during Margarethe's stewardship, William had not set foot on Essen soil since the 1902 scandal, despite his frequent and regular visits there while Fritz had been still alive. In August 1906, however, he once more descended on the home of Krupp's, the occasion being the official opening of the new multi-million-pound Rheinhausen steelworks. As though to show that all was now forgiven the Kaiser presented Margarethe with the new Order of William, and to the firm's chairman and managing director he gave each the Order of the Red Eagle. But perhaps the real reason for his reaffirming his regard for the House of Krupp at that time was that, just three months before, Margarethe had announced Bertha's engagement to a hitherto obscure and somewhat undistinguished Prussian diplomat by the name of Gustav von Bohlen und Halbach. Indeed it would seem likely that the Kaiser had had a hand in choosing this consort for Germany's richest heiress.

William in fact went back to Essen only a few weeks later for Bertha and Gustav's wedding. In his speech at the reception, he described Margarethe's husband as having been his "valued and beloved friend", called the bride "my dear Bertha", and somewhat ominously for the future of mankind enjoined her and her husband "to be successful in maintaining the works at the high standard of efficiency which they have attained and in continuing to supply our German Fatherland with offensive and defensive weapons of a quality and performance unapproached by those of any other nation".

The wedding would seem to have been anything but a jolly occasion, because Kaiser William, evidently carried away by his oration, stood talking to some of the guests for several hours—and since according to the strict protocol of the day all other people in the Imperial Presence had to remain on their feet so long as he stayed on his, Bertha's wedding ball was chiefly remembered for the distinct foot-weariness among most of the ladies present!

Before returning to Berlin the next morning, William decreed that henceforth Gustav could add Krupp to his name—that he could call himself in fact Krupp von Bohlen und Halbach, and could pass this name on to his eldest son and all subsequent eldest sons of eldest sons in the cannon kingdom. This action of the Kaiser's was interpreted throughout Europe as yet one more indication of the House of Krupp's unique position in German affairs—and further evidence was forthcoming only a year later when William became godfather to Bertha and Gustav's first-born Alfried, the present head of the House of Krupp.

Although Gustav would seem to have been an intolerably dull choice of husband for Germany's most eligible heiress, so far as William was concerned he was an ideal consort, a man who could be relied upon to carry out to the letter the particular mission his master had in mind for him—and the one thing that can be certainly said of Gustav von Bohlen is that he proved to be a willing and faithful servant of his Kaiser, and later of his Führer.

Despite the double-barreled name, Gustav could not claim noble descent. The Halbachs had settled in the little town of Remscheid, not far from Essen, at the beginning of the sixteenth century, the same century of course that had seen Arndt Krupe's first mention in Essen's archives. They would appear to have been ironsmiths, and indeed there is a record of a licence having been granted in 1666 to a Peter Halbach to operate an iron-mine and to make iron shot for cannons. By the end of the eighteenth century, the Halbachs had become fairly successful manufacturers of scythes and other farming implements, though around the third or fourth decade of the nineteenth century one Arnold Halbach emigrated to America. He settled in Pennsylvania and was soon owning a few coal-mines and iron-works at Scranton. He had married the daughter of Bohl Bohlen who together with a younger brother had emigrated from Germany at about the same time as Arnold and had opened an import business in Philadelphia.

Bohl Bohlen's son Henry became a soldier of fortune, fighting first for America against the Mexicans, and then hiring himself out to the French against the Russians in the Crimea. But it was in the American Civil War that Colonel Henry Bohlen distinguished himself most. When he was finally killed in action at Bull Run, his native city of Philadelphia promptly proclaimed him a hero and decreed thirty days of public mourning for him.

Colonel Bohlen had left a wife and thirteen children, one of whom, a daughter Sophie, in time married her cousin Gustav Halbach, Arnold's son, who now added the Bohlen name to his own to become Gustav Bohlen-Halbach. For reasons that have never been recorded, Gustav returned to Germany with his wife and secured a post on the staff of the Archduke of Baden, eventually becoming Baden's envoy to Holland in the year of Prussia's victory over France. In keeping with his new job he was allowed to change his name to von Bohlen und Halbach, and it was while living

in The Hague that a son was born to the young couple on
7 August 1870 to whom they gave his father's name of
Gustav.

Bertha's husband-to-be served for a year with the Second
Baden Dragoons and then studied law at Heidelberg,
Strasbourg, and Lausanne, before joining the Prussian
Foreign Service at the age of twenty-eight. His first diplomatic posts were minor ones in Washington and Peking,
until in 1903 he was appointed Counsellor with the German
Legation to the Vatican. It was here that he met Bertha
while she was visiting Rome with her mother at the end of
her schooling. When they wed, she was twenty and he
thirty-six.

Once installed in the Villa Hügel, Gustav straightaway set
about familiarising himself with the history of the House of
Krupp, studying in particular the notes and memoranda
left behind by Alfred—an activity that would have surely
endeared him to the old "Cannon King". He had of course
been used to receiving and to obeying instructions, for his
diplomatic duties had required little imagination or initiative
—nor is there evidence that he was of a questioning nature or
intellectually inclined—so perhaps it was a relief to him to
find such a rich vein of rules and regulations as were contained in Alfred's writings. Indeed, the old "Cannon King's"
obiter dicta became a sort of Bible with Gustav and in time
he came to see himself as the only true guardian of the
Krupp traditions as laid down by Alfred.

He also carried over into his new life his old love as a
diplomat for protocol and routine, measuring out his day
precisely, allotting exact times for exercise and for leisure,
for visiting the works, for seeing people, for writing letters,
even for being with his wife and family. Gustav allowed
himself one whole hour per week for playing with his
children, usually with an elaborate toy electric train-set.
Nor when he was not playing with them did his children's
day escape his passion for organisation.

Punctuality was everything to him, and transgressions
were suffered even less than when Alfred was alive. Each
morning on the dot his steed stood at the main door of the
Hügel waiting to take him to the factory. When eventually

the animal was replaced by a motor-car, Gustav's chauffeur had strict instructions to warm up the engine beforehand so as to be ready to drive off the instant his master gave the word. Each evening at 9.45 p.m. Bertha's butler entered the drawing room to signify to every guest that it was time to go, for Gustav retired to his bed at 10.15 p.m. no matter who was present.

With ruthless determination and singleness of purpose, he toured and re-toured the factories, notebook in hand, for he meant to uphold rigidly the interests of the firm into which he had married. Like Alfred he had a passion for documents and liked nothing better than to pore over contracts for hours on end with his lawyers and directors. He could remember the smallest details of the firm's administration: no doubt if he had been living today we would have called him "computer-brained"

Gustav liked cold rooms—and kept the temperature down inside the Villa Hügel to a mere 18°C even in the depths of winter. At his office in the works it was never allowed to rise above 13°C. In this way, he maintained, all argument could be discouraged and every discussion kept short. Quick service was also the rule at table in the Villa. It was usual, regardless of whether anyone else had finished, for the plates of each course to be cleared away as soon as Gustav had had his fill. Bertha's husband had no small talk whatsoever and never encouraged others to indulge in light-hearted bantering either. Meals in any case were frugal affairs, for luxuries were absolutely taboo. His meanness indeed had an air of madness about it, for he would invariably check with his own watch the length of each of his trunk calls against the time charged by the telephone operator—and before going to bed each night he got his valet to calculate to the nearest penny his personal expenses for the day.

A man of merely average ability, his outward appearance belied the petty despot he undoubtedly aspired to be. Only slight of build, thin-lipped, with piercing eyes, he looked far from sturdy, and even his apparently stiff Prussian spine was in fact supported by a body-corset. But it was in his attitude to people and the world around him that Gustav's meagreness was most marked. One of his most eulogistic biographers says of him, "Politics he considered were best left to the professional politicians; he would abide by the decisions of the latter." That of course was to be his trouble. Also, like many of his generation in Germany, he had that "faith in His Majesty" which most democrats today, in Britain and America at least, find difficult if not impossible to comprehend properly—the feeling that the Kaiser would always be the equal of every situation. Whereas to most outside observers Prussia's victories in 1866 and 1870 were seen as the product of superior political dexterity and superb military organisation, to people of Gustav's ilk these successes came to be interpreted as evidence of the inevitability of Prussian Germany's hegemony over the rest of the world. Their country's military and economic strength was construed as proof that their culture and morals must be superior, too, to all others and from this it was deduced that they not only had the right to dominate but that they were *bound* to dominate. "Gustav was so far from taking a critical view of the age that he soon came to regard any attempt to do so as improper", says that same biographer, who presumably thought he was making a praiseworthy point about his employer.

Gustav had inherited from his father a great love of pomp and ceremony. He never passed up the chance for a ritual. Whether it was at the works when records had been achieved or long service was to be rewarded, or whether it was a family occasion such as a christening, he would always delight in compiling detailed printed programmes prescribing the exact order of procedure—and since Bertha produced eight children for him there were plenty of opportunities for Gustav's social graces on that score at least.

But it was the one hundredth anniversary in 1912 of Alfred Krupp's birth that gave Gustav his most splendid majordomo moment. He planned three days of almost continuous celebrations before an exalted guest list that embraced the Kaiser and his court, most of his ministers, the heads of the army and navy, and nearly every foreign diplomat, banker, and industrial tycoon of any standing. In welcoming them, Alfred Hugenberg, at that time a Krupp director but later to be intimately associated with Hitler's rise to power, spoke in language typical of that bizarre affair: "Your Kaiser's eye gazes once more upon us, and proudly follows the victorious course of our industrial enterprise . . . to the virtues of our people, which must be preserved if it is to remain young and energetic, belong also the old Germanic valour and love of arms."

The festivities were due to culminate in a vast mediaeval procession and jousting tournament. Like old Alfred, Gustav had a passion for horses and for everything to do with horses, so on this occasion he took a great delight in arranging the equipping and clothing of the scores of "knights", not to mention the hundreds of "ladies of honour" complete with their blonde tresses reaching down to their thighs. About a thousand people were to take part, and every two-bit actor and actress for miles around had jumped to the bait. The purpose of all this pageantry was to point what Gustav considered was the natural development of modern armaments from mediaeval chivalry—a ludicrous, and for a Krupp frightening, thought. Even the apparent absurdity of staging all this ancient costumed junketing against a backcloth of belching chimneys and flaming blast-furnaces did not deter Gustav, who replied to every suggestion that he drop the whole idea, with the single phrase, "But the Kaiser will love it"—which was perfectly true, for these boyish pranks fitted in all too well with William's puerile notions of Germany's "ancient destinies", and indeed Gustav's gambollings on this occasion have come to be considered by many historians as one of the most apt examples of that incredible pre-war epoch in Germany now known as the Age of William. News, however, of a pit disaster killing 800 Ruhr coal-miners brought the festivities to an abrupt end.

Bertha's consort had reason of course to want to pander to the dreams and fantasies of his Kaiser, because it was William's dreams and fantasies that were providing Krupp's with much of their profits. One of the least-sung consequences of industrialisation is that it transformed the scale and speed of warfare, increasing the efficiency with which an enemy could be slaughtered and causing weapons to become outmoded much more often and much more quickly. It meant too that, whereas a feudal Prussian king going to war needed to rely only on his Junkers to provide the necessary peasant armies, a modern German Emperor bent on battle was almost totally dependent on a Krupp.

In the same year that Bertha and Gustav got wed, Krupp's Germania shipyards built their first U-boat—the basis for the design being the small submarines Krupp's had produced for Russia some years before. Luckily for Germany's future enemies, the Kaiser's naval chiefs did not greet this development with much enthusiasm and had only ordered another eight by the outbreak of war—though, as some cynics have pointed out, because a U-boat cost only about one-twentieth of a dreadnought Krupp's may have themselves preferred not to push too many submarines on the Navy.

By the time Gustav joined the firm, Krupp's had secured for themselves virtually a monopoly in supplying guns and armour-plating to the German Navy—a monopoly that they were to resist bitterly all attempts to break. Gustav's methods of combating such competition were revealed all too clearly in the so-called Brandt Scandal of 1912.

Brandt, a member of Krupp's Berlin office, was convicted of obtaining confidential information for his employers from official sources—though the shortness of his sentence, merely four months, was viewed by most Krupp critics of the day as yet another instance of the Kaiser coming to the rescue of the "nation's armourer", as Gustav was now delighting in describing himself. What emerged from this first Krupp Trial was the now alas all-too-familiar tactics of military officers being lavishly junketed by private business firms, of information concerning rivals' plans and prices being bought from relatively minor service personnel, of friends of the firm being planted in Government departments, of jobs in the firm being obtained for the relatives of high officials, as well as for retired army and navy chiefs, so that they in their turn could court their former colleagues, and so on.

But while revelations like these seemed to put a damper for the moment on their less-direct techniques of dealing with competition, Krupp's, not to be outdone, effectively removed in 1913 their most persistent rival, the Düsseldorf firm of Rheinmetall, by surreptitiously buying a controlling interest in it. Two years before, Gustav had acquired in the same way the biggest wireworks in Germany, to which in the summer of 1914 he added two other major wire-producers, thus securing for himself almost a monopoly in this particular line of manufacture in good time for the biggest boom ever in barbed-wire!

When war finally broke out, Krupp's were employing some 83,000 people, nearly twice as many as at Fritz's death and four times as many as at Alfred's death. Their consumption of gas exceeded that of the rest of the city of Essen, while Germany's capital, Berlin, barely used as much electricity as Krupp's even. Gustav's and Bertha's private fortunes stood at more than twice that of the Kaiser's, while the profits from the firm during the last three years of peace amounted to well over £3 million. Krupp's were now not only the biggest industrial enterprise on the continent of Europe, they were also the foremost machine for making weapons of war that the world had yet known. Like Imperial Germany they were at the zenith of their power and prosperity, but like Imperial Germany their nadir was only four years away—but four very bloody years away. "As Germany goes, Krupp goes", was Gustav's fondest boast. Germany was to go down to disaster and was to take Krupp's with her.

CHAPTER EIGHT

"Never to rise again"

PERHAPS KRUPP's biggest legacy of all to the First World War was in the new sounds they brought to the battle-field —for the war that began in August 1914 was a war after the heart of Alfred Krupp and all the cannon kings who succeeded him. It was a war of guns, particularly of big guns. For her first winter campaign in Champagne France, for instance, mustered 2,000 guns, while the Germans gathered 1,500 for their successful breakthrough of the Russian defences before Gorlice-Tarnow in May 1915. At Verdun in February 1916 General Falkenhayn pitted 600 heavy guns against General Petain's 250—and by the spring of 1918 both sides had something like 10,000 big guns in operation on the Western Front between them. Guns that were churning up northern France and were converting living communities into wastelands of pock-marked fields and bruised hills, guns that were reducing Polish villages to simple piles of rubble, guns that with their shattering impact on ears and nerves were turning thinking soldiers into bewildered animals, guns that were maiming men grotesquely as they had never been maimed before, guns whose stench still clung within the nostrils long after the last shot had been fired. This was the form of warfare that was the logical outcome of all the technical expertise Krupp's had been putting into their weapons over the years. Shortly after hostilities began, H. G. Wells had written, "At the very core of all this evil that has burst at last in world disaster lies this *Kruppism*, this sordid, enormous trade in the instruments of death."

Everyone had thought it was going to be a short, sharp war. "All over by Christmas" had been the sentiment on the

Allied side, while von Tirpitz visiting Krupp's shipyards at Kiel in February 1915 had said of the submarines under construction there, "Well, you know these are going to be much too late for this war." It was assumed too that the armies would win or lose with the weapons they had at the outset—but after the first four weeks of quick movement the war settled down into four years of slow attrition, four years of massive bombardments as both sides tried to blast a hole through the other's front lines. The artillery barrages got bigger and heavier, the guns noisier and greedier. Expenditure on munitions seemed boundless. Krupp's alone were turning out 9,000,000 shells and 3,000 field-guns a month at the height of the struggle. Their work-force of 83,000 on the day of mobilisation had become 165,000 long before the Armistice. Older workshops were torn down to make room for newer, ever large ones. The factories spread around Essen and into other parts of Germany too. It was a war to suit only an armament tycoon: Krupp's total profits for the four years between 1914 and 1918 amounted to something like £40 million.

The First World War was indeed the first "war of materials", the first industrialised slaughter on an international scale—for just as the machine had come to dominate the worker so now munitions came to dominate the soldier. The intensity of the flames within the great steel furnaces along the Ruhr, the Rhône, and the Don, were just as much an indication of which way the war was going as the lists of casualties emanating from London, Paris and Berlin. It was just as much a battle for supremacy between Krupp's and Schneider-Creusot or between Skoda and Vickers, as between Foch and Hindenburg or between Haig and Ludendorff.

Of all the guns that Krupp's supplied to the German armed forces between 1914 and 1918, none has passed more into the folklore of war than Big Bertha, the huge seventeen-inch mobile mortar nicknamed after Gustav's wife—it was even specifically mentioned in the prosecution's indictment of Gustav's son Alfried, the present head of the firm, at his Nuremburg trial for war crimes in 1947 and 1948. The monster gun fired a projectile weighing almost a ton a

distance of nine miles and was a crucial ingredient in the
German General Staff's so-called "Schlieffen Plan" to
knock out France in the opening months of the war before
the Russian "steam-roller" could get under way to compel
the Central Powers to fight on two fronts. According to this
stratagem the German armies needed to move quickly
through Belgium and northern France so as to encircle the
bulk of the French forces facing them in Alsace-Lorraine.
Their path, however, was blocked by a ring of supposedly
impregnable forts in front of Liège. Big Bertha's task was to
remove these obstacles—which she did with astonishing
ease and rapidity in the first few days of the war. Her
enormous shells rushing through the air with the accumu-
lative power of five 250-ton express trains each travelling at
sixty-five m.p.h. crushed these steel fortresses as though they
were merely so many blackbeetles. The swiftness of it all
struck terror into the Belgian soldiers and increased the
dread of the name of Krupp among Frenchmen. For his
part, the Kaiser was so pleased that he gave Gustav the Iron
Cross, while Bonn University, hitherto renowned for its
contributions to creative thinking, promptly made the man
responsible for this terrible weapon of destruction an
honorary Doctor of Philosophy.

But if Big Bertha was the most infamous gun Krupp's
have ever made, then their most incredible one must surely
be 'Long Max', the gun that shelled Paris from a distance
of seventy-five miles during the spring and summer of 1918,
and the gun that is very often confused with Big Bertha.
Built more like a giant rifle than a gun—its barrel was some
112 feet long—Long Max needed to be dismantled for
straightening after every round. Each barrel lasted only sixty
or so rounds. The shells of the "telegraph gun", as it was also
sometimes called, weighed from 200 to 230 pounds a piece
and each one took three minutes to reach its target, rising
to a height of twenty-four miles above the French country-
side before doing so. Although the barrel was thirty-nine
inches in diameter, its bore was only eight and a half inches,
which meant that its steel walls were over fifteen inches
thick. The gun alone weighed all of 180 tons and was set in
60 tons of concrete in the middle of a dense wood in the

Laon Salient near Crépy, where the German front line was nearest the French capital. Designed purely for terror, in fact to frighten the citizens of Paris into forcing their Government to surrender, Long Max was an intrinsic part of General Ludendorff's last desperate offensive.

The giant gun had been mounted in great secrecy, special rail tracks having had to be laid for the purpose. Squadrons of aircraft flew constantly overhead and simultaneous salvoes from other batteries in the area accompanied each round so as to make it all the more difficult for the British and French gunners to pinpoint its exact position. Long Max's crew of sixty was bossed by a full admiral, for it had been developed in fact from the fifteen-inch Krupp naval gun that in April 1915 had successfully shelled Dunkirk from twenty-three and a half miles away. By lengthening the barrel and tapering the point of the shell, Krupp's gun designers had managed to extend its range to sixty miles. But then the German Army's retreat from the Somme in 1917 had taken them all by surprise and had necessitated them having to add an extra fifteen miles to Long Max's range. This they did not accomplish until January 1918. Even so, the building of the gun emplacement and the laying of the special rail-tracks had been started as early as September 1917, though the monster weapon itself was not finally in place before the beginning of March 1918.

Long Max's first shell fell in the middle of Paris near the Quai de Seine just after dawn on 23 March, and the bombardment continued at roughly fifteen-minute intervals throughout that opening day, with the Kaiser even popping down in his special train at lunchtime to watch one of the firings. Before the Allies' counter-offensive forced Ludendorff to order its withdrawal on 9 August 1918—just twenty-four hours after the German Army's self-confessed "Black Day"—Long Max had worn out seven barrels with firing 452 shells into the heart of Paris from three different locations. One location was barely fifty-six miles from Notre Dame itself. More than 1,000 French civilians lost their lives as a result of Long Max while the numbers wounded ran into several thousands. One shot falling on a Paris church during a Good Friday service killed eighty-eight worshippers, most of them women and children. The monster gun was in fact the first in a long line of German secret weapons, but it came too late to change the course of the Kaiser's War and served only to make Germany, and hence Krupp, more hated than ever.

For Gustav and his men the Paris bombardment was the pinnacle of their weapon inventiveness so far. It showed Krupp's meticulous precision and wellnigh incredible handling of materials, yet it was really only a development of existing ballistic techniques and by no means such an imaginatively new departure as, say, the tank was. Indeed as regards the tank, although during the Second World War the Essen firm became identified with the terrible destructive power of a particularly heavily armed one, it was only after the British had introduced them during the battle for Cambrai in November 1917 that Krupp's began making any at all. They had still not supplied a single tank to the German High Command even by the end of the war.

In all the recriminations after 1918 one of the issues that was raised most was whether or not Krupp's had actually anticipated the declaration of war. This question came about through the strange affair of the resignation during the spring of 1915 of one of Gustav's directors, Wilhelm Mühlon, and his subsequent flight to neutral Switzerland where he promptly accused Krupp's of having started to prepare for hostilities at least six months before mobilisation and following secret advice from Berlin. Mühlon had been with the firm for four years and had been in charge of the department dealing with foreign contracts. Like Gustav he was a former Prussian Foreign Service official. His charges against the head of the House of Krupp ranged from Gustav having begun to enlarge his works in the spring of 1914 just at the moment when the heat had been taken out, albeit temporarily, of the international crisis, to his having also from then onwards started to lay in extensive stocks of raw materials, in many cases from sources within the territories of Germany's subsequent enemies, such as nickel from French New Caledonia. Gustav did not really deny these charges until 1932, by which time of course the normal democratic processes for checking such statements had ceased to operate in Germany.

Extreme left-wing critics and passionate pacifists have always liked to believe that an international conspiracy exists among armament manufacturers to hold the rest of the world to ransom, that patriotism as we know it has no meaning among weapon-makers, that the profit motive has its most disgusting expression in the selling of guns and munitions. This is the origin of the phrase "merchants of death". Such conspiracies have never been adequately proved or disproved. There were, however, claims, partially substantiated, that throughout the early part of the First World War Krupp's had continued to obtain vital raw materials from enemy sources by way of neutral countries such as Norway and Sweden. Similarly it has been said that some Krupp products continued reaching Allied customers through those same neutral powers during the first twelve months of the war—indeed Krupp officials did later admit that a few contracts signed before hostilities actually began were honoured in this way.

Yet the most bizarre claim of all, and one that has never been satisfactorily cleared up, was that many of the British shells fired against German troops in the First World War bore the patent mark KPz 96/04 denoting that they contained a fuse made under licence from Krupp's by British armament manufacturers such as Vickers! a licence which usually earned the Essen firm about 1s. 3d. per fuse and against which they allegedly made a financial claim after the war that, so the story goes, was eventually settled substantially in their favour. Furthermore, some of the armour-plating of the British warships was also said to have been made under licence from Krupp's, so that when after the stalemate naval Battle of Jutland in 1916 the Kaiser sent Gustav a telegram telling him it was "a day of triumph for the Krupp works" because of the excellent showing of the Krupp naval guns and the Krupp armour-plating in the German fleet, Admiral Jellicoe too might well have felt inclined, as some cynics have already pointed out, to congratulate Krupp for their efforts in helping protect the British sailors!

It was also in 1916 that Gustav in association with other

Ruhr tycoons like Stinnes, Thyssen, and Haniel, took over
the running of Belgian industry which since Belgium's
occupation in August 1914 had been operated by the German
Army. This of course was merely a foretaste of what was to
happen during the Second World War when Krupp's very
often on their own initiative, though usually encouraged
by the authorities at Berlin, exploited and plundered the
then considerably larger occupied territories of Europe.
Krupp's activities on this score in both world wars have
helped to swell their notoriety.

But so far as the British and the Americans are concerned,
Krupp's notoriety springs for them really from Germany's
declaration of unrestricted submarine warfare in January
1917. This announced intention to sink without warning or
pretext any merchant vessel, whether neutral or enemy,
found within certain restricted waters was meant to bring
Britain to her knees. Instead it helped to bring America into
the war on the Allied side and was the beginning of the end
so far as the Kaiser was concerned. Of the 200 or so U-boats
that Germany possessed at that time, nearly half of them
had been made by Krupp's—and so the terrible, murderous
exploits of these German submarines, particularly their
sinking of unarmed passenger liners like the *Lusitania* and
the *Leinster*, has come to be associated with Krupp in the
minds of ordinary people. Even today the very name *U-boat*
still conjures up something sinister and ruthless among
citizens and sailors alike in the former Allied powers—and
this infamy has rubbed off on the manufacturers of U-boats,
of which by far and away the biggest and the best-known
were Krupp's.

Although many Krupp directors and senior executives
enthusiastically backed continuing the war right up until
the bitter end, and were members of various pressure
groups lobbying the Kaiser to insist on annexing parts of
Poland and Belgium as minimum conditions for an armistice
even as late as January 1918, the workers at Krupp's on the
other hand were among the first to show their disaffection
with the hunger and the other hardships of the long struggle.
Indeed when the Kaiser visited Krupp's for what was to be
the last time in September 1918, just a month after Long

Max had been somewhat ignominiously bundled back to Essen, he was greeted coldly by the workers. Rather pathetically, he had wanted to address a large gathering of them from the top of a coal dump until it had been pointed out to him that only the front few rows would be able to hear him. Instead he spoke to a select band in a corner of one of the big gun-shops. "Be strong as steel", he implored them, "and the unity of the German people, welded into a single block of steel, shall show the enemy its strength." But this essay into home-front propaganda by the Kaiser proved a total failure and instead of noisy enthusiasm, as on previous visits, his speech now met with stony silence. There were even one or two isolated cries, complaining about the lack of food and the shortage of coal. Within two months, the war was over and the House of Hohenzollern with it. The old German prophecy that "a one-armed man would ruin the Empire" had been fulfilled.

On 9 November 1918 all work stopped at Krupp's. The German Revolution which had begun in the fleet eleven days earlier had quickly spread. People everywhere marched in anger, demanding food. Field-Marshal von Hindenburg had advised the Kaiser to quit and to go into exile in Holland. Only the previous day, Krupp machines had been operating at full blast as usual, turning out guns and shells and U-boats and armour-plating for the war effort. But now they fell silent—something that had not happened for nearly a hundred years—their products no longer needed, no longer relevant.

A Social-Democratic Republic had been proclaimed in Berlin. Gustav's avowed enemies were now in power—indeed, one of the planks of their party's platform was to nationalise the armament industry. For their part too the victorious Allies had announced their intention of destroying Krupp's "never to rise again". Gustav found himself confronted with soldiers' and workers' committees on the Soviet model demanding a say in the running of his firm. Fearing the worst, he prepared to defend himself in his castle on the hill against the angry mob—but none came.

Although besought by the new authorities in Berlin not to discharge any of his workers, Gustav was afraid of what such a large body of men might in their idleness do to his plant—of the 165,000 men in his employ at the time of the Armistice, 105,000 were concentrated in Essen alone. He decided to keep only those who had been with him at the outset of the war and to sack the others as quickly as possible —he even offered to pay their train fare to any point inside Germany if they left within three days. More than 52,000 had quit Essen by the end of the month, most of them unable to take advantage of the free rail-ticket offer because there were not enough trains. Instead they travelled by horse or on foot. Essen soon became a ghost town and the great Krupp factory there nothing but a morgue. Food was scarce and coal almost unobtainable. On top of everything, German troops had been straggling back from occupied France and Belgium plundering and pillaging as they passed through the Ruhr.

Along with the Kaiser and 893 other prominent Germans, Gustav was cited as a war criminal by the victors at Versailles, though he was never tried as such—partly through German resistance, but mainly because of doubts among the Allies themselves as to the legality of the notion. He was, however, forbidden to produce arms ever again, except for a mere four guns a year to be used solely for Germany's internal security. What is more, his works were to be opened to Allied inspectors for all time. Nearly 1,000,000 machines, tools, and sheds, were ordered to be scrapped, the warships still being built at Kiel were to be broken up, and half Krupp's steel-making capacity was to be taken away. The responsibility for all this demolition and dismantling rested with Gustav, though Allied Control Commissioners were of course appointed to see that the work was carried out.

The victors at Versailles had singled out Krupp's, arguing that if you annihilated the "nation's armourer" then you had crippled Germany's military might for all time. This argument was to be heard again in 1945. Certainly, as people walked through the empty workshops and watched the labourers smashing the machines and knocking down the sheds, they must have believed that Krupp's were really finished. Yet with a tenacity that one can both admire and dread, Gustav and his directors even in those early days had already started rebuilding their factory-empire. They had of course been left with half their steel-making capacity, which on its own amounted to quite a formidable enterprise, and naturally they had seen to it that it was the older, less efficient half that was destroyed.

Within a few months of the Armistice, Krupp's had to all intents and purposes begun their conversion from "weapons of war" to "tools of peace". Gustav had straightaway offered money prizes to his men for suggestions as to what to produce. Remembering that old Alfred had made a fortune out of railway parts long before he had managed to sell a single cannon, Gustav decided to go in for making complete locomotives himself. The Prussian State Railways backed him by promptly ordering 150 together with 2,000 goods wagons, all for delivery by 1924. In November 1919, just twelve months after the end of hostilities, Gustav handed over to them the first Krupp-made locomotive amid great pomp and ceremony—and with his twelve-year-old heir, suitably sailor-suited, on the foot-plate. A year later he was selling them to Russia, Rumania, India, South Africa and Brazil.

Gustav tried his hand at a whole range of new and unfamiliar products: from cash registers to milk-cans, from locks to lawn-mowers. Some were financial disasters, but others like false teeth and heavy lorries turned out to be all-time winners and remain on the list of Krupp wares even to this day. Although prompted by the shortage of gold and platinum for use in tooth fillings, their manufacture of stainless steel dentures really sprang from their wartime experience of needing to develop a rust-resistant steel alloy for the breech mechanisms of U-boat guns. Nickel- and silver-plating quickly deteriorated in the salt water, but experiments with other alloys had produced a new stainless steel which Krupp's patented as V2A Steel. This new steel soon proved suitable for surgical instruments as well as table cutlery. Some of the stainless steel false teeth were exported to the Soviet Union.

Russia, as we have seen, had always been a good customer of Krupp's, dating back to old Alfred's days, and Gustav had lost no time in making contact with the new régime. Perhaps his most bizarre deal with the Soviets during the immediate post-war years was the agricultural concession which he secured in 1922. The Russians put up the men and the land, some 247,000 acres of it in the Donetz Basin of the Ukraine, while Gustav supplied the capital and the technical know-how. The aim was to transform this virgin land into large wheat-growing, mechanised farms. But although this particular project failed abysmally, it was at least a foot in the Soviet door for Krupp's and one which over the years they were to exploit still further.

The concession had been arranged by a director of the firm, Otto Wiedfeldt, who later that same year, 1922, became German Ambassador to the United States. During Wiedfeldt's four-year term of office in Washington, Krupp's succeeded in securing two important American loans that enabled them to come through the difficult period of inflation in Germany when the value of the paper-mark plummeted daily: in November 1921 40 paper-marks were being exchanged to the £, by the end of July 1922 the figure was already up to 120, by the end of October 1922 to 900, by the end of January 1923 to 10,000, by the end of June 1923 to 30,000, and by the end of September 1923 to 30,000,000!

Gustav's iron-ore deposits in Spain and Latvia had of course been confiscated during the war, while the Peace Settlement had taken away his supplies in Lorraine too. Now he proceeded to secure sources in Sweden and Finland. In addition, when he could not get enough German coal he even imported British coal. He also became part owner of the Spanish Levant Shipping Union and the Brazilian Monteney Coal Company, as well as taking a financial interest in magnesite mines in Styria, Chile, Turkey and South Africa. To do all this, he needed foreign currency, which was hard to come by in inflation-torn Germany. But apart from the Americans a group of Dutch financiers also came to his aid with a loan of £5 million. Indeed his relations with Holland grew closer and closer as he proceeded to channel the whole of his overseas trade through a Dutch firm, the Allgemeene Overzee'sche Handelmaatschappij of The Hague, and as he came to deposit most of his foreign profits with the Dutch financial house of Amsterdamsche

Crediet Maatschappij, one of whose directors was a Krupp appointee, Herr Buschfeld, himself already a director of the Essen firm. In this way Gustav managed to avoid the worst effects of the inflation which ruined many other long-established German firms at this time. He even benefited in a small way from this national misfortune by securing the job of printing for the State a part of the daily rush of new paper money. Indeed, the firm has stayed in printing ever since. With an almost unbelievable resilience, Krupp's were back in business in a big way—and within five or six years of the 1918 disaster. Yet with this precedent on record, it is incredible that Krupp's recovery after the 1945 débâcle should have still come as a surprise to a great many people.

As well as limiting its army to 100,000, restricting its navy to a negligible size, and abolishing its airforce altogether, the Treaty of Versailles also imposed reparations on the new Germany of the Weimar Republic, though the actual figure of £6,500 million worth was only agreed upon in May 1921. By that time the United States for one had opted out of any argument over making Germany pay such a sum, while Britain for her part was merely lukewarm about the idea. It was only France who was really insisting on it—fearing the now probable recovery of her ancestral foe.

On 11 January 1923, claiming that Germany had fallen behind with her reparation payments—she had in fact failed to meet a deadline in delivering 100,000 telegraph poles—France sent troops into the Ruhr to impose all future payments by force. The German President and his ministers appealed successfully to the people of the Ruhr not to co-operate with the French in any way. When the campaign of passive resistance proved extremely effective, the new French authorities there retaliated by punishing harshly, in some cases even with death, those Germans who tried to impede their use of the railways. French soldiers already controlled most of the transport services in the Ruhr and had banned the shipment of coal to the rest of Germany.

Shrewdly, and as later events were to show significantly, Gustav before the French arrived had arranged for all the Krupp papers, files, and blueprints to be shipped to a secret hideout in another part of Germany—though just exactly what he had to conceal was not to emerge until after 1945. When, during the early part of March 1923, the situation in the Ruhr grew intense, Gustav did in fact warn his workers against inciting the French occupiers. But on 31 March a platoon of French *poilus*, attempting to commandeer some cars and some lorries garaged near the Krupp administrative headquarters, were provoked into firing on a crowd of Krupp employees who had been summoned to the scene by the blaring of factory sirens. Thirteen workers were killed and over forty wounded. The men who lost their lives immediately became martyrs in the eyes of the whole of Germany. A massive funeral was arranged for them, with Gustav as the principal mourner. There were torch light processions and ceremonial lyings-in-state. A short time afterwards Gustav, along with seven of his directors and two senior officials, was arrested by the French who charged him with having deliberately instigated the whole incident. The sentences they received before a somewhat hastily assembled military tribunal ranged from six months to twenty years. Gustav himself was given fifteen years and was fined £5 million. Ironically he was imprisoned in the Düsseldorf jail, one of whose walls adjoined a factory he owned.

Within six months, however, after both the Pope and the King of Spain had interceded on their behalf, Gustav and his colleagues were released. But his short stint in jail had served to make him a national hero. When he attended a Privy Council in Berlin a little time later all the members, some of whom had previously been his bitterest political foes, stood up as a mark of respect as he entered. According to Baron Tilo von Wilmowsky, his brother-in-law, who took Bertha to see Gustav in prison, one of the first things he said to his wife was "Well, now I really have a perfect right to call myself a Kruppian, haven't I?"

Gustav found chaos in Essen when he returned. Business was at a standstill. The inflation had run rampant, morale was low, looting was commonplace, everyone was hungry, while passive resistance had long since collapsed. The French were now very much in command, confiscating food, coal, and rail trucks as and when they pleased. They had even commandeered the Villa Hügel as a billet for some of their generals. The new German State seemed to be crumbling. A separate "Republic of the Rhine" had been proclaimed in Aachen with French support. Bavaria too was in open rebellion against Berlin. The Communists had failed with one attempted coup in Hamburg, though they had almost succeeded in Saxony and Thuringia. On 8 November 1923 an obscure Austrian demagogue tried to take over the city of Munich, but within twenty-four hours was forced to flee. His name was Adolf Hitler and he was about ten years too soon.

Fearing bankruptcy, most of Gustav's directors had pleaded with him to close down all the factories—or at least to shut down the Essen foundries so as to concentrate on the newer, more efficient Rheinhausen steel plant. But Gustav would have none of this. He had set out to model himself on the old "Cannon King" and was wont to reply to all such talk of contraction with the remark, "But Alfred would never have dreamt of doing such a thing". Gustav felt it to be his sacred duty to preserve the Krupp empire come what may. Besides, he now had another burning passion—to save the House of Krupp for Germany's sake. Just as Hitler's spell behind bars at Landsberg made *him* more resolute and intransigent, so undoubtedly the time Gustav spent in Düsseldorf jail, together with the tremendous reception accorded him throughout Germany on his release, hardened the man.

It would appear then that it was Gustav's experiences in that fateful year of 1923 which finally encouraged him in the belief that the House of Krupp uniquely held the means and the power to bring Germany out of the "confusion and the darkness" in which she now found herself and to restore her to "a position of glory". It was a belief that was to have fatal results for much of Europe's youth then flowering.

CHAPTER NINE

"Even the Allied snooping commissions were duped"

IF THERE were ever a competition for the most damaging
document a man has written about himself or allowed to be
published about himself, then one of the first prizes would
surely go to Gustav Krupp for his article "Plant Leaders
and Armament Workers" which appeared in his firm's
house magazine for 1 March 1942. Perhaps the incautious
confidence of those early war years went to his head and
tempted him into revealing things which his son Alfried
would certainly have preferred to have remained hidden
for all eternity, especially when the document was used as
evidence against him at his trial for war crimes in 1947 and
1948.

Interestingly enough, no official Krupp biography or
history published since 1945 makes any reference to this
article of Gustav's—Krupp public relations policy since the
end of the war has been of course to pursue the fiction that
Gustav and his merry men had nothing whatsoever to do
with German rearmament until after 1936, the year when
theoretically the Allies withdrew their treaty restrictions on
such rearmament. Moreover, Krupp spokesmen still argue
to this day that Gustav resisted all entreaties of Hitler and his
henchmen to begin rearming before 1936—although the
official Krupp propaganda line during the Nazi era was to
boast of "Krupp preparedness".

Gustav brags in his article of how almost from the very
moment of his country's defeat in November 1918, and even
while the victors at Versailles were squabbling over the
exact terms under which the House of Krupp might be
allowed to survive, he began to prepare in secret for Germany's eventual rearmament. What is more, he argued that

he had to do all this in the face of antagonism from many of
his fellow Krupp directors:

At that time [1919] the situation seemed almost hope-
less . . . the machines were destroyed, the tools were
smashed, but the men remained—the men in the construction offices and workshops, who in happy co-
operation had brought the production of guns to its
last degree of perfection. Their skill had to be maintained by all means, also their vast funds of knowledge
and experience. The decisions I had to make at that
time were perhaps the most difficult ones in my life.
I wanted and had to maintain Krupp, in spite of all
opposition, as an armament plant—although for the
distant future. . . . Without arousing any commotion,
the necessary measures and preparations were undertaken. Thus, to the surprise of many people, Krupp
began to manufacture products which really appeared
to be far distant from the previous work of an armament plant. Even the Allied snooping commissions
were duped. Padlocks, milk-cans, cash registers, track
repair machines, rubbish carts, and similar small things,
appeared really unsuspicious—and even locomotives
and automobiles made an entirely "civilian" impression.
After the assumption of power by Adolf Hitler, I had
the satisfaction of being able to report to the Führer
that Krupp's stood ready after a short warming-up
period to begin the rearmament of the German people
without any gaps of experience. . . . I was often permitted to accompany the Führer through the old and
new workshops and to experience how the workers of
Krupp cheered him in gratitude.

Clearly, Gustav could not have done all this alone, nor
without financial help on a large scale. Indeed, he talks in
the same article of "a very small and intimate circle" being
privy to his thoughts and deeds. Furthermore, there is on
record a letter to Gustav from Joseph Wirth, who was
Chancellor of the German Republic in 1921 and 1922,
in which he says, "considerable sums were released to the firm
by the Reich to preserve German armament technology . . . to

lay new foundations for the technological progress of German weaponry".

According to some calculations, Gustav received up to £15 million from the State before Hitler came to power. The payments were disguised as compensation for armament contracts still in the pipe-line at the time of the Armistice though never deliv~red, for the dismantling of his works and the Allies' confiscation of his interests overseas, and for the damage the French soldiers caused to his property and the interruptions in his output during their occupation of the Ruhr.

Unwittingly, the United States helped too by granting Krupp's credits of £12 million in 1925 and 1926 ostensibly to assist them to combat the inflation. Even British money found its way into the Krupp coffers at this time, when Gustav's claim for Krupp patents used by the Allies during the war, principally his patents on shell fuses, was finally settled in his favour. The amount demanded was said to be £6 million, though the actual sum paid was never disclosed. One cannot help wondering whether anybody during the negotiations considered it at all incongruous that Britain should be paying a German firm for the means whereby her soldiers had defended themselves from German arms during a war they did not start—or for that matter that a German firm should be receiving payment from her country's former enemies for having provided the means whereby thousands of German soldiers had been killed or maimed. It is an incident matched in its cynicism and infamy only by the claim in 1913 of another German armament tycoon, Stumm-Halberg, to be compensated for not being able to mine the pockets of iron-ore lying beneath the graves in the military cemeteries of Metz and St. Privat!

The Treaty of Versailles had two major loopholes. In the first place, although banning the making of weapons inside Germany, except within certain clearly defined limits, it said nothing about German firms producing arms outside the country. Secondly, although the victors were meticulous in demanding the demolition of all the machinery capable of turning out "weapons of war" then and there, they were careless, and in fact carefree, about confiscating the blueprints from which such machinery could be re-built, or of preventing newer weapons from being designed on German drawing-boards.

Significantly, one of Gustav's earliest actions after 1918 was to buy his way into the Swedish armaments firm of Aktiebolaget Bofors by selling them many of his patents, blueprints, and secret processes. Indeed, by 1925 he held 6,000,000 of Bofors' 19,000,000 shares. He then proceeded, in the safety of a country well beyond the jurisdiction of the Allies, and in any case unbeknown to them, to build up a corps of technicians and designers, many of whom he transferred from Essen, to plan, develop, test, and even build the Krupp weapons of the future. Some of the products of these clandestine joint endeavours were sold overseas, with Krupp's and Bofors sharing the profits. As early as 1920 the two partners had begun developing, for instance, the 7·5 cm. mountain gun that was later to be "tested" in the Spanish Civil War. Tank ammunition, as well as a heavy machine-gun and an anti-aircraft gun, were all produced by Krupp's in Sweden long before the Government there became sufficiently anxious and knowledgeable to insist on the two partners parting company in 1935, although the Swedish Socialist Party had first stumbled on the fact of Gustav's shareholding in Bofors six years earlier but had failed to do anything effective about it.

But it was not just Sweden with which Gustav had secret arrangements. Since both Holland and Switzerland had common frontiers with Germany, Krupp personnel and Krupp goods could pass in and out of the two countries without much difficulty. A Krupp anti-aircraft gun for instance was developed in Switzerland near Zürich. But it was in Holland, right on the Ruhr's doorstep, where the most valuable work, from Gustav's point of view, was done. He in fact obtained most of the essential raw materials for all his illicit projects through Dutch associates—indeed, the Netherlands became a sort of central store for those products of his various endeavours that he did not wish the Allies or even some of his own countrymen to know about. France realised as early as 1926 that Gustav was up to something in Holland and tried to bring diplomatic pressure to bear upon the Dutch Government of the day to stop it. This they refused to do, arguing that they did not interfere with "private business"—but it is firmly believed that many influential Dutchmen at this time were involved financially with Krupp's.

Gustav's old team of naval designers were transferred *en bloc* from the Germania shipyards at Kiel to Rotterdam to work on secret projects for the German Navy. The projects included submarine and torpedo components. In 1922 a dummy Dutch company called the Ingenieurskantoor voor Scheepsbouw was established by Krupp's, according to documents captured in Essen in 1945, "for the preservation and further implementation of German U-boat experiences". Two submarines developed in Holland by Krupp's were sold to the Turks in 1925. Others were built in Spain and Finland according to Krupp specifications. Indeed, despite the Allies having confiscated most of his former holdings in Spain, Gustav was soon back there in force. This time he did not stop at just buying iron-ore deposits at Bilbao as before, but extended his interests to engineering at Barcelona and shipping at Cadiz. It was at a Cadiz shipyard that most of the preparatory work was carried out on the new, improved U-boats that were ready to be mass-produced at Kiel after 1936. One such U-boat was in fact built at Cadiz for the German Navy as early as 1929.

Krupp's also had secret agreements with the Japanese for making U-boats. In 1920, with the full approval of the German Admiralty, Gustav entered into partnership with a shipbuilding company near Nagasaki to exchange technical information concerning submarine manufacture. Eventually Krupp's chief submarine-designer, Dr. Techel, went out to Japan to supervise the construction of U-boats at the Kawasaki shipyards.

In April 1922, Germany and Russia surprised the world by apparently reconciling their wartime differences in a treaty of friendship, the so-called "Treaty of Rapallo". But in addition to all the diplomatic bargaining there had also been highly secret top-level military talks in which the head of the German National Defence Force, General Seeckt, and the German Chancellor, Dr. Wirth, had taken part—

talks which led to a secret military pact being signed between the Red Army and the new German Army on 29 July 1922. Although given the bogus title of "Provisional Trade Agreement", its real intention was to involve German armament firms such as Krupp's in the redevelopment of Russia's weapon-making industries. The German Government laid aside virtually unlimited funds to the German generals for this task and even created a cover organisation for their operations called "The Society for the Encouragement of Commercial Enterprises". Its true purpose included Russian manufacture of new Junker bombers, the training of German airmen on Soviet soil, as well as the joint development of a poison gas and a wide range of artillery ammunition. The Steppes became a proving ground for Krupp guns and Krupp tanks. Significantly it was also in 1922 that Gustav got his agricultural concession in the Ukraine.

But not all of Krupp's illicit work on weapon development took place outside Germany. Much of it, as Gustav boasted in his 1942 article, went on right under the very noses of the Allied inspectors in Essen. Although these inspectors had one success in May 1920 when they caught Gustav still producing three-inch field-guns ostensibly for the Reichswehr, Germany's National Defence Force, this was their only victory. After that the Essen firm became more subtle.

France's occupation of the Ruhr disturbed these clandestine activities, though it also supplied an extra stimulus and an additional excuse. For one thing, the Allied disarmament controls lapsed during the occupation, because the French were considered *persona non grata* elsewhere in Germany as a result of their military action in the Ruhr, while the British and the Americans were so embarrassed by the whole affair that they even withdrew their inspectors for a time from Essen. General Seeckt took advantage of the crisis, together with the subsequent hardening of German attitudes towards France, to begin recruitment for his illegal army, the so-called Black Army. At one time nearly half a million strong, its members were armed from the secret caches of weapons which had already been set up all over Germany and which were stocked principally with the guns and ammunition that Krupp's among others should have handed over to the

Allies immediately after 1918 but had quickly smuggled out to Holland instead.

In November 1925 Seeckt spent five days with Gustav in Essen during which the whole strategem of Germany's secret rearmament was discussed in full. Afterwards the general noted in his diary "the readiness of Krupp to oblige the military administration in order to gain experience in designing armaments".

Four months before this meeting, Gustav had set up an artillery-designing office in Berlin under the camouflage of a machine-tool factory called Koch- und Kienzle-Entwicklung. It was here during the next two years that some of Krupp's most intensive and most successful development work was carried out on naval, coastal, and anti-aircraft guns, as well as field-howitzers. The Berlin office was disbanded towards the end of 1927 when the Krupp team of designers and technicians were brought back to Essen, presumably because evading the attentions of the Allies had become that much easier now that the French troops had been withdrawn from the Ruhr and the British disarmament inspectors had returned home for good.

According to the prosecution at Alfried's Nuremberg Trial, Krupp's began producing tanks as early as 1926, though they were referred to then as "agricultural tractors". This was of course in flagrant disregard of the Treaty of Versailles which forbade Germany ever to possess or to make tanks, armoured cars, and heavy guns. Indeed a Krupp document written in 1942 boasts that "with the exception of the hydraulic safety switch, the basic principles of armament and turret design for tanks had already been worked out in 1926".

In 1928 the Ordnance Department of the new German Army asked Krupp's, along with Daimler and Rheinmetall, each to produce two light tanks of seven and a half tons apiece, armed with a 3·75 cm. field-gun and a heavy machine-gun. Within eighteen months Gustav was able to demonstrate this tank to officials of the Reichswehr at his Meppen testing ground. Satisfied with its performance, the German generals then and there commissioned the same three firms to produce a heavier tank to be armed with a

7·5 cm. gun and three heavy machine-guns. Once again within a comparatively short time Gustav came up with the goods—the goods being the prototypes of those tanks with which the German panzer divisions overran Western Europe during 1940, and from which was later developed the dreaded Krupp Tiger tank that decimated the American forces during the battle for the Ardennes in 1944. "I wish to express our thanks for the excellent support which you and your staff have again given us in our development work during the past year," wrote Colonel Zwengauer, deputy chief of the new German Army's Ordnance Inspection Office, to Gustav just before the end of 1932. "The department is convinced that, thanks to your active co-operation and valuable advice, our armament development in 1932 has made considerable progress, which is of great significance to our intent of rearming as a whole."

Gustav boasted in 1942 that all the Krupp guns used in the war up to that date had been fully developed by 1933 —that once Hitler had come to power the problem had been merely one of how to mass-produce them. If that was so— and we have no reason to disbelieve him—then it would appear that during the period when the Versailles ban on German weapon development was still technically operative, Krupp's designed, built, and successfully tested at least eight new types of cannon, field-gun, and howitzer, not to mention a revolutionary self-propelled gun, an improved version of their First World War 21 cm. mortar, a finely sprung gun-carriage, and a heavy howitzer suited for mountain warfare which had first been ordered by the Dutch for use in Indonesia.

Soon after the Treaty of Versailles had been signed, Gustav had set up a special information department in Essen and had arranged for military and technical publications from all over the world to be sent there to be perused for items of interest to his gun-designers—in this way they kept abreast of the latest developments. Some of his other dodges and stratagems appear rather ludicrous, however, forty years after the event—particularly his way of hiding Long Max, the giant gun that had shelled Paris in 1918. He stood the great barrel up on end and surrounded it with a ring of bricks so that it became just another Krupp chimney—the Krupp factories at Essen had scores of chimneys and presumably no one had told the Allied inspectors to count them!

As usual there was a constant stream of private visitors to Krupp's at this time, though not nearly so many as in their days of great prosperity before the First World War. Yet however carefully screened they all were before being allowed anywhere near the Essen works, Gustav still feared that one or two might be tempted to take the odd photograph of some of the goings on there when nobody was looking. To combat this he made sure that all guests after their tours were entertained in a special hospitality room he had made high up in the Krupp administrative building. Allied troops examining this room in 1945 found it contained enough infra-red rays even then to ruin the film of any camera that entered it!

Although the firm's public relations policy today is still to play down Gustav's role in Germany's secret rearmament between the wars, Krupp spokesmen during the Nazi era constantly harped on the great financial sacrifices Bertha and her husband had had to bear in the cause of keeping their country prepared for its eventual rearmament. Said a Krupp document issued after Hitler came to power:

> The firm decided, as the trustee of an historical heritage, to safeguard its irreplaceable knowledge for the armed strength of our nation, and to keep the personnel and shops in readiness for later armament orders, if or when the occasion should arise. With this in mind, we tailored our new production programme to a pattern in which our employees could attain and improve their experience of armaments, although the manufacture and sale of some of the products entailed big losses.

Nor was this a plea that went entirely unheeded. Indeed, after a long wrangle over details with the Nazi authorities, Gustav received something like £15 million by way of compensation for the "losses" his patriotism had brought him before 1933.

Once again Krupp's had become a "special case". But

even before Hitler had seized control in 1933 it was clear that Krupp's would never be allowed to go bankrupt. So long as they were conniving in the secret plans and clandestine stratagems of those German generals and politicians who were seeking to thwart the attempts of the victorious Allies to disarm Germany for all eternity, Gustav and his men would never starve.

Whereas much of German industry had a chequered time in the decade between 1923 and 1933, for Gustav's firm it was a period of steady growth. His directors' fears of possible insolvency soon gave way on their part to modest confidence as, backed by massive credits from the United States, Germany stabilised her currency after 1924. Some of this American money found its way into Gustav's hands, while a group of German bankers loaned him a further £3 million in January 1927. Once more Krupp's prospered and grew: from employing 48,760 people in 1926, Gustav's labour-force steadily climbed to 80,000 in 1928.

With the country's economy apparently resurgent, and unemployment certainly declining, the Communists as well as right-wing parties like Hitler's National Socialists were losing much of their appeal and hence their strength. Germany's admission to the League of Nations, on top of the adoption of the so-called "Young Plan" for staggering reparation payments over a period of at least sixty years, all seemed to spell the removal of much of the tension on the diplomatic front too.

But then in 1929, the bottom fell out of everything. The Great Depression hit Germany far worse than most other countries, principally because her economy was still relatively shaky, but also because the bulk of the American loans were only of short duration and were immediately recalled when the spectacular American stock-exchange boom came to an abrupt end in the October of that year. Germans had unfortunately invested this short-term money in long-term projects. There was a run on the banks and several big businesses went bankrupt—though not of course Krupp's.

In the traditional manner of the firm, Gustav had quietly and steadily been building up reserves. Thus he could withstand a shock such as 1929 better than most. Also, being a family concern, Krupp's did not really have to bother about dividends, which in theory they had not been paying since the Armistice—in any case dividends for them were merely like transferring money from one pocket to another in the same pair of trousers.

Despite all the assistance and encouragement he was getting from the Government, Gustav still did not like the young German Republic that had been established in 1918. Although the Social Democrat proposals for nationalising the armaments industry, and for taxing tycoons like Krupp out of existence, had long since disappeared into thin air, Gustav still did not find Germany's new political leaders to his taste. He looked to some form of dictatorship by the generals, or at least to some sort of re-establishment of the old régime —indeed he had kept in touch with Kaiser William, writing to him every year on his birthday. Even Field-Marshal Hindenburg's election to the Presidency in 1925 had not tempered his distaste for the Republic. Like many of his ilk and generation he was inclined to look upon the Weimar Constitution as merely a temporary measure and to long for a "big change" that would produce a more permanent solution—though, as to exactly what shape this permanent solution should take, Gustav again like most of his generation and ilk was vague and ingenuous. In this way of course they were an easy prey to the ready-made, permanent-sounding package deals of demagogues like Adolf Hitler.

CHAPTER TEN

"The evolution of political events corresponds to desires I have long cherished"

YET, EVEN though Gustav readily backed the cause of rearming Germany, he did not throw in his lot with Hitler right from the start. Not that that was entirely unforeseeable, since anyone with von Bohlen's diplomatic background and social attitudes would be expected to disdain the brutish brawling and the brainless demagoguery of the storm-troopers. The Krupps were snobs and, like other German snobs, looked upon Hitler at the beginning as something of a parvenu. Indeed even after the Nazis' seizure of power in 1933, Gustav's wife still went on describing Adolf as "that certain gentleman".

Besides, as their history shows, the Krupps were always proud of their close relations with the army. In a sense they took their cue from the generals—and before 1933, however much the rank and file may have been hobnobbing with the National Socialists, the generals by and large were extremely suspicious of the radicalism and the racialism of Hitler and his henchmen. Gustav's closest ties with the new German Army had been with generals such as Seeckt and von Schleicher, both of whom had kept decidedly aloof from the National Socialists. Indeed, it is on record that as late as March 1932 von Schleicher and the other Reichswehr generals were determined to do everything they could to prevent Hitler gaining power; they had vowed to disobey his orders, if necessary. What is more, when on 27 January 1933 some senior officers went to press their opposition to Hitler on Hindenburg, even the aged field-marshal is said to have replied, "Gentlemen, surely you do not think that I would appoint that Austrian corporal Chancellor of Germany."

Two days later, of course, Hindenburg did precisely that.

Gustav's sympathies were undoubtedly with the right-wing parties. But even after October 1928, when Alfred Hugenberg, Krupp's former managing-director, became Chairman of the German Nationalist Party—the party preaching rearmament and a return to the Reich's former frontiers—Gustav still did not openly commit himself to their cause, though it seems likely that he was not above slipping them the occasional generous cheque towards campaign funds. In October 1931 Hugenberg's party threw in their lot with Hitler to form the so-called "Harzburg Front" to fight the elections together, but there was still silence from Gustav. Fritz Thyssen, the Ruhr industrialist who contributed handsomely to Nazi funds in the early days yet later came to renounce the Führer, states categorically in his memoirs *I Paid Hitler* that "until Hitler's seizure of power, Herr von Krupp was his violent opponent". He goes on, "as late as the day before President von Hindenburg appointed Adolf Hitler chancellor Krupp urgently warned the old field-marshal against such a course".

Along with the other Ruhr magnates, Gustav had resented Chancellor Bruning's purchase for the Government of a substantial holding in the giant Vereinigte Stahlwerke combine—the combine which controlled nearly three-quarters of the Ruhr's steel production at that time. It was this bitter opposition by industrialists such as Krupp to Bruning which, coming on top of that of the Prussian Junker landlords who wanted to bring him down for quite different reasons, spelt the end of the Weimar Republic's "only last hope", as some historians have described him. In Bruning's place, Hindenburg substituted von Papen and his so-called "Cabinet of Barons", one of whom was a director of Krupp's, von Schaeffer, who became Minister of Labour. It was von Papen's irresponsible behaviour that in the end paved the way for Hitler's successive victories at the polls. All too late, Gustav tried to warn Hindenburg against Hitler but by that time the head of the House of Krupp had been instrumental in successfully demoralising all possible rivals to the Nazis.

When on 27 January 1932 Hitler was invited to speak to

the big Ruhr magnates at their club in Düsseldorf, the famous Industrie Club, Gustav did not attend, though he did send a representative. Similarly, in November of that same year, when Hjalmar Schacht, the President of the German Central Bank, was collecting signatures for an appeal to Hindenburg to appoint Hitler as his Chancellor, Gustav refused to pen his name to the petition. The Krupps were always proud of their loyalty to the State, and this State before 1933 was not yet the Nazi State, but when after February 1933 it became the State of Adolf Hitler, then Gustav transferred his loyalty to the new Government of Germany.

But whereas Gustav was perhaps slow in realising that Hitler might be a godsend to him in his declared aim of restoring the firm to the unique position it had held in Germany's affairs before 1919, Adolf for his part had come to the conclusion quite early on that he was going to need all the Krupps of this world for the particular "mission" he had in mind. While their party's platform called for the socialisation of big business, Hitler and his henchmen always went out of their way in their speeches to except from this public take-over "the really great pioneers of our heavy industry, like Krupp's". Indeed on the very eve of his coming to power, Hitler was asked by one of the more radical members of his party, Otto Strasser, whether he would leave Krupp's exactly as it was. "But of course I should leave it alone," he had replied. "Do you think that I should be so mad as to destroy Germany's economy?"

Although Gustav did not by any means "finance the Führer's rise to power" as some have alleged, he certainly did nothing to prevent such a climb, nor to help provide an alternative. Like a lot of the big German industrialists, he saw no danger in the Nazis in their early days of power, thinking perhaps that he could always in the end "manipulate" them in the interests of Big Business. But however gradual, and far from fervent, his conversion to Hitlerism may have been, once the Führer was firmly in the saddle Gustav gave him his enthusiastic, indeed at times almost grovelling, support. In the words of Fritz Thyssen, "after

Hitler was appointed chancellor, Herr von Krupp became a super-Nazi".

On the surface, Gustav and Hitler would appear to have had very little in common—to one the limelight was anathema, to the other an opiate. But in fact they complemented each other. Gustav believed in *economic order*, that is in the suppression of all undue competition and unnecessary hindrances, such as for instance trade unions —while Hitler for his part believed of course in *political order*, that is in the suppression of all undue competition and unnecessary hindrances to the unfettered will of himself. Furthermore, while Gustav considered politics as important only as long as they provided him with the strong and stable framework in which to go about his business, Hitler regarded politics as his primary interest and only concerned himself with economics in so far as they gave him the strength and the stability to go about his political business. Gustav lived for profitable production, whereas Hitler dreamed of glory and grandeur, which could only be based on the profitable production of industrialists such as Gustav.

Gustav met Hitler for the first time on 20 February 1933, just a month after President Hindenburg had appointed Adolf as his Chancellor. Goering had called a conference in Berlin of twenty or so top German businessmen. As Chairman of the Federation of German Industries, to which he had been elected in autumn 1931, Gustav naturally attended. Besides him there were also such people as Schacht, Walter Funk, Albert Voegler, managing director of the giant Vereinigte Stahlwerke, and four directors of IG Farben. It was only two weeks to go to the new elections summoned by Hitler, and the Nazis were seeking funds with which to conduct their campaign. Hitler addressed the gathering and evidently impressed Gustav with his strong remarks about restoring the power of the German Army and helping German industry to recover its former prestige and position in the land. The means, he suggested, were eliminating the Communists and destroying the trade unions.

The Krupps of course had had a long history of opposition to unionisation dating back to old Alfred's days. The changed times of the war and the Weimar Republic had forced employers to recognise the unions. This they had done only reluctantly—and, like Gustav, many of them had been eagerly looking ever since for an opportunity to rescind such recognition. According to Schacht, "after Hitler had made his speech, Krupp answered and expressed the unanimous feeling of the industrialists in support of the Führer". Said Gustav, "only in a politically strong and fully independent State could industry and business develop and flourish". That Hitler had struck the right chord in him can be judged perhaps by the alacrity with which Gustav concluded his remarks by pledging the Nazis £150,000 towards their campaign fund.

In time-honoured fashion the Krupps, after fifteen years in which there had been a power vacuum, were climbing on to the new political band-wagon. Indeed, as we have already pointed out, once Hitler was firmly in control there was no holding Gustav in his ardour for the Nazi cause. Without consulting the other members of the Federation of German Industries, he decreed in April 1933 that Jews could no longer remain on its roll and forthwith suspended the Federation's Jewish executive director, replacing him with two Nazis. He also sent off a letter to Hitler in which he declared that "the evolution of political events corresponds to desires I have long cherished". By August of that year he was issuing the order introducing the Hitler salute into all German factories, not just his own. Already he was signing his letters "Heil Hitler" long before it became the general practice throughout German industry. What is more, in the very same month that Goering was founding the Gestapo, Gustav was submitting to the Führer a plan for reorganising German industry so as to make it fit in more closely with Hitler's aims and philosophies. A few weeks later he was instructing Krupp agents overseas to do all in their power to disseminate favourable propaganda of the "new Germany". The head of the House of Krupp had indeed become a super-Nazi.

As the years went by, Gustav's fervour for his Führer began to know no bounds. In letters to Hindenburg as well as to Hitler he expressed his enthusiastic approval of Germany's unilateral withdrawal from the League of Nations—

and he saw to it too that the Krupp sales network overseas helped to spread Nazi propaganda beyond Germany's boundary. When the employers' organisations met again in Berlin on 7 November 1933, Gustav was the instigator of the resolution pledging their united support for Adolf in his fight for "military equality" with every other nation. It was Gustav too who personally negotiated the so-called "Hitler Donation", the *Hitler Spende*, whereby big businessmen contributed to Nazi Party funds and so bought themselves immunity from the attentions of the Gestapo and the violence of the storm-troopers. He remained chairman of it until 1942 when he was succeeded in the post of the Party's chief fund-raiser by his son Alfried.

Gustav spoke at numerous public meetings and conferences in support of the Nazis. When Goebbels asked him for a memorandum in praise of Hitler to be used in the so-called "Plebiscite" of November 1933, Gustav willingly complied. Hitler rewarded him for this loyalty by making him "Economic Führer" in the spring of 1934 and by placing the first seven groups of the new economic organisation under his single control. Said Gustav on his appointment, "our aim is to effect a co-ordination of the totalitarian State and the responsible independence of industrial administration".

On 28 June 1934, Hitler paid his first official visit to the Krupp works at Essen. He had tried to visit Gustav's factory as an ordinary sightseer some six years before, but had been turned away at the gates, merely being allowed to sign the visitors' book, which he had done with a great flourish, underlining his signature many times. The page containing it later became a choice memento of Gustav's. But on the 1934 occasion, Bertha's eldest daughter Irmgard greeted him with a curtsey and a bouquet of flowers, while Gustav fussed about making sure that every where the German Führer and his party went they were accorded the correct Nazi salute. Gustav's colleagues recalled later how during those early days he had almost an obsession about saluting correctly. It was just two days before the great "Blood Purge" of 30 June 1934 in which hundreds of Hitler's earliest supporters were brutally massacred. Among them were some former friends of

Alfried Krupp with his General Manager, Berthold Beitz. The painting is
of Alfred Krupp, the old "Cannon King"

Left: Long Max—the monster rifle that shelled Paris in 1918

Right: Fat Gustav—the biggest gun ever made; it besieged Sevastopol in 1942

Below: Big Bertha—the giant mortar that destroyed the Belgian forts in 1914

Above: The earliest Krupp fulling mill, *c.* 1820. *Below:* Alfried, his son Arndt, and his General Manager, Berthold Beitz, together with the Krupp directors and senior executives in front of the Villa Hügel on the occasion of the firm's 150th anniversary in 1961

Above left: Friedrich Krupp, the founder of the firm, 1787–1826; and *right:* Alfred Krupp, the "Cannon King", 1812–1887

Above: Alfried Krupp as a child with his mother, Bertha. *Below left:* Fritz Krupp, 1854–1902; and *right:* Gustav von Bohlen, 1870–1950

Alfried Krupp being sentenced for war crimes at Nuremberg, 1948

Alfried's release from Landsberg Prison, 3rd February 1951: he was met
by his brother Berthold, who brought him a bouquet of tulips

Alfried today in the drawing-room of his modern bungalow at Essen

The main Krupp armament factories at Essen as found by the Allies
in 1945

Below: The Krupp steel-mills at Rheinhausen today

Gustav's, such as General von Schleicher, but there is no record of a single word of complaint from him about their deaths. Nor was there any objection from Gustav when another close acquaintance, Gottfried Treviranus, a one-time Cabinet Minister, was forced to flee the country for fear of his life. Instead, Gustav even welcomed a section of the Gestapo being established within the works, and so far as is known raised no eyebrow when from time to time some of his workers were arrested or murdered. In all some 700 or so Krupp employees were sent to concentration camps by the Nazis prior to the outbreak of hostilities in September 1939. Allied troops after 1945 discovered torture equipment in the basement of Krupp's head office at Essen, including a tiny steel cage in which recalcitrant workers were imprisoned —it was so small the luckless victim must have had to have been bent almost double, and in addition it had a hole at the top through which icy cold water was apparently poured.

Bertha evidently had many misgivings about her husband's newly found political allegiance—and even mentioned it tearfully on occasion to some of her most intimate friends. "See how low we have fallen", she is said to have murmured to one of her serving-maids on the morning the Krupp "house flag" was run down on the flagpoles outside the Villa Hügel and Hitler's swastika banner was raised in its stead. But she did nothing directly to dissuade Gustav. Perhaps it would have been pointless, for by that time he had banished all doubts from his mind. Indeed, once when a fellow industrialist who was dining with him started mildly criticising the Nazis, Gustav promptly got up and left the table. Then again Fritz Thyssen recalls in his memoirs how at a gathering of top Ruhr magnates held during 1938 at the home of one of the IG Farben directors, several of the men present cited cases to each other of corruption within the Nazi Party. "Herr von Krupp rose and said, 'I cannot bear hearing those accusations and I am leaving the meeting.'"

After his first trip to Essen in June 1934, Hitler became a regular visitor to the Krupp works, dropping in at least once or twice a year. Nazi leaders like Goering, Goebbels, Ribbentrop and Hess were more frequent guests of Gustav's, as in time were Mussolini, Himmler and Admiral Raeder.

The workers used to turn out in their tens of thousands to greet them—and the ever-present Reich newsreel cameramen were faithfully on hand to record for posterity their rapturous receptions. Even now, the sight of all those far-gone faces, albeit on film, has a foetid effect on the memory.

27 March 1936 must have been a particularly memorable day for Gustav and his men. It was just twenty days after Hitler had ordered German troops to march into the de-militarised Rhineland in defiance of the Treaty of Versailles—and Adolf had come down in person to speak to the whole works in the huge "Hindenburg Bay", that massive gun-shop erected in 1917 at the height of the First World War to forge the Kaiser's great cannons, and which was already grinding out giant guns by the score for Gustav's Führer. At 4 p.m. precisely the factory hooters all blared out a harsh note, while employees, foremen, and managers alike stopped work temporarily "to hold inner communion with their Führer", as one eyewitness described it. Another bystander remembered seeing "tears streaming from the eyes of Gustav Krupp". The American newspaper writer Mrs. Anne O'Hare McCormick happened to be present too and she recalled "Dr. Gustav Krupp von Bohlen, an anxious little man in a morning coat, in welcoming the Führer to his great plant, looking oddly out of place in that pressing throng of workers and uniforms".

But Gustav could afford to look oddly out of place on that platform alongside his Führer and amid the swirling swastika-banners, for with Hitler at the helm of state Krupp's were experiencing an unprecedented prosperity. During the first three years of Nazi rule in Germany, the firm's profits had doubled: from nearly £6 million in 1933 to just under £12 million in 1935. Straightaway after his initial meeting with Adolf in February 1933, Gustav had begun openly to shift over from "tools of peace" to "weapons of war", although the Allies did not in fact remove their restrictions on German rearmament until the end of 1935.

Compared with the year before, his imports of copper had doubled during the first four months of 1933, while his purchases of scrap-iron rose eightfold and of iron-ore six-fold. Tanks replaced lorries on the assembly lines, and thousands of blocks of steel, cast in earlier years for just such an occasion as this, now began to be moulded into gun-barrels. Behind screens at his Kiel shipyards, Gustav started building U-boats, minesweepers, and destroyers *en masse*. Later that same year, it was reported from China that Krupp agents there were offering vast quantities of cut-price arms— evidently Gustav was clearing the decks for large-scale production of modern weapons by liquidating the stocks of his older lines hitherto held in neutral countries like Holland and Spain. A few months after this, Goering announced the rebirth of the Luftwaffe, while Krupp's publicly tested anti-aircraft guns along the Baltic coast. Once again Essen-made armaments were sold openly overseas: in South America, Turkey, Greece and Soviet Russia.

Relations were not always rosy between the House of Krupp and the authorities of the Third Reich. Occasionally there were disputes over cost and delivery-dates, as Gustav endeavoured to maintain some semblance of commercial sense in the war economy the Nazis were rapidly erecting. But more often than not, Bertha's husband saw eye-to-eye with Hitler and his aides without much effort or compromise on his part. For instance in 1936, following a clash with some Ruhr magnates concerning prices, the State announced its intention of going into steel production on its own, by build-ing the massive "Herman Goering Works" at Salzgitter. Whereas the other steel producers refused to give Goering any assistance in his project, Gustav offered equipment, know-how, and even personnel.

As a result, Nazi honours by the hundred were showered on Gustav. The Minister of Economics made him "German Führer of Economics", while the Minister of Labour gave him the title "Pioneer of Labour". It fell to the Minister of Armaments to award him the "War Cross of Merit", a new order, of which, since it came in two classes, the regular and the commander's cross, Gustav received both at once. But the supreme accolade of all for the head of the House of Krupp came on his seventieth birthday when his Führer motored over in person to the Villa Hügel to bestow on him the Nazis' highest civilian honour, the Golden Party Badge.

On the eve of the Second World War, Krupp's shipyards

were launching U-boats at the rate of one a month. They already had a battleship, an aircraft-carrier, and a number of cruisers and escort-vessels to their name. At Essen, Gustav's gun-shops were turning out field-howitzers and heavy mortars by the score. Mass-production was just beginning to get under way of the multi-purpose 88 mm. anti-aircraft cum anti-tank gun which had been tried out a few years before with devastating effect in the Spanish Civil War, and which later on was to achieve a certain notoriety and even dread among Allied troops fighting in Greece and North Africa. Indeed, one writer has described it as "perhaps the most efficient single weapon supplied to any army during the war". Krupp's had doubled their steel capacity in less than five years, although to extend their plant at Essen they had had to knock down one of their oldest housing schemes of which hitherto they had been extremely boastful. From 35,000 strong in 1932, their labour-force had almost quadrupled to 112,000 by 1938. Gustav had taken advantage of Germany's annexation of Austria in that year to purchase at a knockdown price the old Berndorfer steelworks founded a century before by Alfred Krupp's younger brother Hermann. "A pleasant consequence of the Anschluss" was how the official Krupp family historian in 1943 described the compulsory take-over.

To such a devoted follower of his Führer as Gustav Krupp had become, it must have been ·a particularly hallowed and heady moment on 10 May 1939 when he went to call upon Hitler at Berchtesgaden, his Bavarian mountain retreat. With him he had taken a massive present, for it was Adolf's fiftieth birthday. As was to be expected from the head of the House of Krupp, the gift was both gigantic and grotesque: a titan-like table of dark oak into which had been set various figures and designs made out of Krupp stainless steel. The centre of the "piece" was adorned with two solid steel lions and was removable, for underneath lay a steel model of the house in which Hitler had been born. With it was a tableau of figurines symbolising Germany's industrial achievements—and as if that was not enough, a quotation from the Führer's *Mein Kampf* had been inscribed around the edge of the table's top.

Gustav was now getting on in years and by all accounts his mind was beginning to weaken. Just a year before the Second World War broke out, he had presented to Hitler, during one of the Nazi leader's periodic visits to Krupp's, the latest member of the firm's board of directors. It was his eldest son and designated heir, Alfried von Bohlen, who was then thirty-one years old. A new generation of Krupps was coming along to assume command.

CHAPTER ELEVEN

"Life in the old house was not very personal"

ALFRIED FELIX ALWYN KRUPP von Bohlen und Halbach,
the present head of the House of Krupp, arrived in this
world on 13 August 1907, just ten months after his parents'
marriage. Almost without waiting for breath, Gustav had
telegraphed his colleagues on the board of directors inform-
ing them "that a vigorous boy has just been born to us to
whom in memory of his great ancestor we shall give the name
of Alfried. May he grow up in the midst·of the Krupp
establishment and prepare himself by his practical work
for the important task of taking over those responsible duties,
the high significance of which I realise more and more every
day." It sounded less like the casual trumpeting of a proud
father than the carefully calculated huzza of a prince-consort
flinging down in triumph the gauntlet of a legitimate heir
in the face of a recalcitrant and potentially rebellious
nobility.

Nor when it came to Alfried's christening did Gustav
neglect the opportunity of making it into a great ceremonial
occasion, one befitting an historic House. Like a general
ordering his troops into battle, he allowed no detail of the
day's ritual to escape his dutiful eye. Even the guests were
graded not just as to their permitted nearness to the christening font but also as to in which room they were to be entertained afterwards—while the menu for the baptismal
banquet had been chosen with the number one godparent
firmly in mind. This godfather was Kaiser William II—a
gesture judged by Europe's rulers as yet a further sign of
the fatherly regard the House of Hohenzollern then felt
towards the House of Krupp and of the Essen family's
unparalleled footing in their country's affairs.

Alfried's birthright was worth perhaps some £20 million on the morning he was christened. Today, sixty years later, despite the bombing and the dismantling, his legacy has blossomed into a cool £1,500 million factory-kingdom—a spectacular growth even by the spectacular standards of those extraordinary Essen entrepreneurs.

Gustav's heir was barely one year old when a second brother, Arnold, was born. Arnold lived only a few months, however. But thereafter four brothers and two sisters came in fairly quick succession: Claus was born on 18 September 1910, Irmgard on 31 May 1912, Berthold on 12 December 1913, Harald on 30 May 1916, Waldtraut on 31 August 1920, and finally Eckbert, another 31 August baby, in 1922. Both Claus and Eckbert were to lose their lives in the Second World War, while Harald was to linger eleven years in a Russian prisoner-of-war camp.

When it came to work, Gustav as we know was not wont to spare himself. But he also imposed a life of almost Spartan severity on his offspring too. He brought to their education and their upbringing that mania for routine and for meticulous detail that characterised his own working life. Inefficiency he hated, not only in himself but in others, and so he made out a precise schedule of his children's day: when they were to get up, when they were to eat, when they were to play, and what they were to be taught in their six hours of lessons.

Like old Alfred, whom he came more and more to ape as the years went by, Gustav was dotty about horses and insisted on each of his children not only being painted on horseback but also receiving riding instruction daily. Yet even this was no diversion, for the grooms were obliged to accompany them and to correct every fault immediately. In fact the one hundred or so servants of the Villa Hügel were required to report any child's misbehaviour promptly to its parents. Gustav permitted no boisterousness or high jinks anywhere on the premises, and he was inclined to frown upon the slightest noise. The boys were forbidden to fight and the girls to giggle; to shout or to laugh loudly was to risk instant punishment. Every afternoon, whether or not they really wished to, the children were detailed to call upon their father in his study—while once a week, again whether they wanted to or not, Gustav would play with them *en masse* for exactly one hour only and usually with a toy of his own choosing. More often than not, the toy was the monster model electric train-set he had had specially made for them.

In such circumstances little love or genuine human contact existed between parents and children. Bertha had of course had an austere childhood herself and she certainly made no effort to interfere with her husband's way of bringing up their offspring. Like the Victorian parent of fiction and fact, nothing delighted Gustav more than to trot out his children in front of guests at the Villa—but since Alfried and his brothers and sisters were admonished not to speak unless spoken to, while their father took careful note of their appearance and deportment, these can hardly have been joyful occasions for them. After his release from jail in 1951, Alfried commented to a visitor at his new bungalow in the grounds of the Hügel, "Life in the old house was not very personal". One of his brothers went further and termed the Villa "the tomb of our youth".

Bertha kept a sort of "Krupp Book of Records" into which she got one of her many secretaries to document the family's every progression. To this registry we are indebted for such details as that Alfried measured twenty-two-and-a-half inches at birth, that "when he was only one year old he was already able to stand up in his cot", and that by the time of his twenty-first birthday he was well over six feet tall.

Alfried's early teachers were mainly French governesses, indeed he could speak their language fluently long before he was fully familiar with the grammar of his own native German. Not that this was unusual for scions of upper-class German families at that time, since despite the ancestral animosity between the two cultures French was still looked upon as the language of genteel intercourse—and having been a diplomat Gustav must have been conversant with French too.

Gustav had set out to model himself in every way on the old "Cannon King"—and just as Alfred had enjoined his heir to discipline himself for the heavy responsibilities of inheriting the House of Krupp, by following his pattern of singleness of purpose and self-denying, highminded devotion to duty, so Gustav made the same noxious noises at his own first-born. Life for Alfried was meant to be not a joy but a duty, in particular a duty to his inheritance—and there is little doubt that such a dismal drumming-in of dreary platitudes has left a lasting mark on the make-up of the man who runs the House of Krupp today. As one Krupp biographer has already put it, "There was much, indeed almost incessant, talk of loyalties, but virtually none of love—human feeling was not something to be recorded in the books of Krupp accountancy."

Apart from the bizarre interlude of the firm's one hundredth anniversary celebrations in 1912, when the five-year-old Alfried had been scheduled to ride by his father's side in the mediaeval jousting procession, dressed in a red and brown jerkin, with a crown of little flowers on his head, and mounted on a tiny grey pony—though this awesome and awful entrance never in fact took place—Alfried's first main contact with the works he was to inherit was in 1919, the year after his godfather had fled into exile. Just twelve years old, he had been taken by Gustav on a tour of inspection initially of the steel plant and then, a short time later, down a coal-mine. When a few months afterwards he also visited a group of Krupp iron-ore deposits south of Essen, a senior official of the firm accompanied him to answer his expected questions—though whether or not Alfried asked the ones his father had had in mind was alas never recorded.

It was not until he had passed his fifteenth birthday, however, that Alfried was at last allowed to sample a little of the life beyond the portals of the Villa Hügel and the works. In 1922 his parents sent him to the Realgymnasium in the nearby suburb of Essen-Bredeney. A sort of secondary school with a bias towards science and technical subjects, its establishment had been paid for by the Krupp family. As was only to be expected, Alfried did not take the academy by storm. He did, however, display those traits of dogged determination and self-restraint which had stood his ancestors in such good stead and which he himself was to find particularly invaluable in the years of recovery after 1951. Inevitably, his upbringing, wealth, and name set him apart from the other boys—and it would seem that they in their turn teased him unmercifully, especially when the staff, ever mindful of their promotion prospects in an institution dependent on Krupp funds, tended to court his attentions and to make him something of a teachers' pet. But Alfried stood it all good-naturedly and even on occasion let the boys persuade him to "go out on the town", in other words to visit a few of Essen's bars and night-spots, though by all accounts these ventures were not exactly a feast of fun. On even rarer occasions, he invited one or two school-friends up to the Villa Hügel for a meal—an experiment in co-existence that must have been an ordeal for everyone. "As soon as you get anything on your plate, a lackey comes up and snatches it away", wrote one of these schoolboy visitors to a relative, according to *Der Spiegel*, the German weekly news-magazine. "If you don't want to go hungry, you have to eat so fast that it hurts your teeth."

Alfried spent three years at the school and in time came to captain the rowing team. He achieved some prominence in his studies too, passing out with high marks. Then in 1925, by now a tall, gangling lad of eighteen, he went into his father's factories at Essen to learn the art of steel-making from the bottom. As Gustav delighted in boasting to all and sundry, Alfried received exactly the same pay as any other Krupp apprentice, and like them had to clock in and out of the works every day. He used to have to set out from the Hügel before 6 a.m., though his father had relented enough to buy him a motor-cycle.

But after just six months of this ritual, Gustav changed his mind and decided to send his eldest son to a university after all, albeit only the Munich Polytechnic—he was not going to risk any rarefied heights of liberal learning on an heir to the House of Krupp. Alfried's year at Munich was also his first long spell away from home. It was here that he got his passion for driving fast, open sports-cars—a passion, perhaps his only passion, that has remained with him even to this day.

At Munich he drove a red Simson, which by the time he had moved on to the Polytechnic at Berlin-Charlottenberg in 1927 he had exchanged for an Austro-Daimler. Despite the fast cars, however, Alfried appears to have been a serious student and to have pleased not only his teachers but also his father. After two years at Berlin, Gustav then sent his heir to Aachen Technical College, at that time considered by many to be Germany's finest institution for studying engineering and steel-making.

The period when Alfried was a student, 1926 to 1934, was perhaps the most intensely political period that Germans have ever known. It was a time when myriads of nationalistic groupings and splinter parties were trying to woo the favours, not just of voting adults, but more especially of the unrepresented youth. It was a time of mass rallies and torchlight processions, of vast demonstrations and vengeful demagoguery, of secret passwords and clandestine armies. It was a time too when the moral fibre of the young was being sapped by the violence and the brutality that went unchecked, by the assassinations and the murders that went unpunished, by the confidence-tricksters, the swindlers, and the perjurers who went undenounced.

Gustav did not bother to hide from his son his blatant disregard for the disarmament provisions of the Treaty of Versailles, nor his unashamed scepticism for the continuance of democracy in Germany. In a household where what little talk took place was entirely of guns and generals, of cabals and cartels, of pass-books and place-men, it was hardly surprising that Alfried should grow up to be somewhat less sensitive towards the ideals of liberty and equality, rather less anxious for the promotion of human rights and human dignity than his contemporaries in (say) Britain, France or America. Though just how much of an active part he took in the political huckstering of his student days is not easy to discern, nor is it a subject on which he or any member of his family enjoys to expatiate. What we do know is that in 1931 while at Aachen he joined Hitler's bodyguard, the notorious SS, to whose funds thereafter he contributed ten shillings monthly.

Alfried finally finished his theoretical studies at Aachen in

1934, qualifying as a *Diplomingenieur* or Certificated Engineer. But still his training was not at an end, for his father promptly sent him off to Berlin again, this time to work for six months without salary at the Dresdner Bank, the bank with which the House of Krupp has been most closely associated since the turn of the century. Perhaps Gustav was remembering old Alfred's instruction to *his* son: "The first thing is account-ing, finance, calculation. In these things you must always be completely at home. No one must be able to lead you astray, and only then will you be safe from what I want to warn you against—from self-interested and intriguing persons ever making you abandon the helm and allow yourself to fall into the hands of a joint-stock company."

Back from Berlin, and by now a young, eligible bachelor of twenty-eight, tall, handsome and slim, the heir to untold millions, Alfried during 1935 lived for a time the con-ventional life of the international playboy. While his father was busily rearming Germany and expelling Jews from the Krupp management, Alfried, complete with ever-present fast car, was flashing through the flesh-pots of Europe—an interval of abandon and unabashed pleasure that he was never to repeat. It was during this sort of incontinent con-tinental tour that he met Anneliese Bahr, the daughter of a Hamburg wholesale merchant, to whom after a lightning courtship he became engaged. Blonde, pretty, buxom and thoroughly middle-class, Anneliese had been married once before to another Hamburg wholesale merchant. But as was only to be expected, Alfried's parents adamantly opposed the match. Only a few years earlier, when one of the Krupp senior executives had divorced his wife, Bertha had insisted that he be dismissed immediately. Furthermore, for Gustav with his newly-found Nazi friends, the liaison was perhaps doubly embarrassing since Anneliese's sister had a Jewish husband. But Alfried persisted and, in one of the few rebellious acts of his life, married Anneliese in 1937 against the wishes of his parents. A year later Anneliese bore him a son, his only son, and the present heir to the House of Krupp, Arndt.

Even so, the marriage was permitted to last only four years. Although many friends of the family say that these were the only years when Alfried laughed, Gustav and Bertha won out in the end, insisting that he divorce Anneliese and hinting at possibly disinheriting him if he did not. As well as having a rough time from her parents-in-law, Anneliese had also come in for a fair amount of cold-shouldering and even ridicule from the wives of the other industrial magnates of the Ruhr. So much so that no official Krupp biography or history mentions her or the marriage—so far as they are concerned Anneliese is the wife who never was!

Meantime of course Alfried had joined the works. After his playboy year was over he had first of all spent a few months in each of the various administrative departments of the firm, before becoming deputy-director of the department of raw materials and artillery development on 1 October 1936. With Hitler hastening to put Germany on a wartime footing, this department was easily the busiest and the most crucial in the whole of Krupp's. Only seven months earlier, Adolf had torn up both the Treaty of Versailles and the Treaty of Locarno in sending troops into the demilitarised zones of the Rhineland. In May the League of Nations had capitulated to Mussolini over Abyssinia and now the Führer was about to sign a military agreement with the Italian dictator. He had already committed himself to sending German soldiers and aircraft to support Franco in the Spanish Civil War. Belatedly, though all the more tragically, the Allies chose this occasion to decide to let Germany do legally what she had of course been doing long since illegally, that is to rearm.

Just how much Alfried was an active participant in Gustav's scheming is far from clear, since the present proprietor of the House of Krupp continues to deny that his firm in any way violated the Treaty of Versailles. But knowing Gustav as we now do, it would seem unlikely that he would have taken his son into his confidence over the details of his secret rearming projects—and knowing Alfried as we now do it is equally unlikely that he, if he had been aware fully of what his father was up to, would have done anything either to dissuade him or to prevent him.

Gustav had involved his family as well as his firm with Hitler right up to their necks—and for Alfried to have stood out against his father and his new-found Nazi friends would have required physical courage, and physical courage was something in which the Krupps had hitherto been found lacking. Some people, however, have argued, and indeed continue to argue, that it was a bit much to expect Alfried, not a very strong-willed creature, to have become a martyr. Even so, there were of course many Germans who while not opposing Hitler openly did not at the same time support him enthusiastically. Alfried was not one of those Germans. In fact there is every indication that like Gustav he went out of his way to show his approval of the Nazi cause—and indeed to this day he has never renounced Nazism.

In November 1937 he attended for the first time one of the annual rallies of the Nazi party at Nuremberg. His younger brother Claus went with him. What they both made of this initial encounter with the histrionic side of Nazism, with its massed marching and counter-marching, its torchlight processions and vainglorious speeches, its chauvinistic songs and its Roman-style standard-bearers and swastika banners, we shall never know, for neither of them were men of poetic expression or even of moderate penmanship. What we do know, however, is that shortly afterwards their father wrote to Martin Bormann in Berlin expressing regret that he had been unable to go to the rally himself, but saying that "our two sons both returned from Nuremburg deeply moved. I am very pleased that they have gained these tremendous and lasting impressions. My own experience at Nuremberg was that only there could one fully understand the purpose and the power of the movement, and I am therefore doubly pleased with the foundation that has thus been assured for our sons."

A year later Alfried joined the Nazi Party and was given the number 6989627. At the same time he also became a member of the National Socialist Flying Corps, eventually reaching the rank of full colonel. He had of course met Hitler many times during the Führer's frequent visits to Essen, and had become friendly too with some of the other Nazi leaders, particularly Goering. In October 1938, just a few days after Hitler's triumph at Munich over the British Prime Minister, Neville Chamberlain, Alfried was presented to the Führer again, this time as a full director of the firm, the director in charge of mining and armaments. Alfried was now as totally tied to Nazism and to all its terrible exploits as the most gun-happy Gestapo-man or the most craven concentration-camp chief. His involvement in their guilt was from this day on merely a matter of degree. He had begun to tread that path which was to lead him to the defendants' dock at Nuremberg ten years later.

When war finally came, Alfried was considered far too essential to Hitler and his generals for him to be allowed to go off to fight for his fatherland. Instead he had to remain where he was, at the helm of Krupp's. However, his younger brothers were thought fitting cannon fodder, and, as we have seen, of the four of them two were killed: Claus in an air crash just after the beginning of the war, and Eckbert in Italy just before the end of the war, while Harald ended up in a Russian prisoner-of-war camp where he remained for eleven years before being released in 1955. On receiving the news of Claus' death, Gustav resisted all the attempts of his colleagues and his friends to comfort him, merely remarking, "But my son had the honour to die for his Führer." Ironically, one of his nephews, Kurt von Wilmowsky, who had had the misfortune to have been in England when war was declared, was later drowned when the unarmed British ship carrying him to an internment-camp in Canada was sunk by a Krupp-built U-boat.

At his trial for war crimes in 1948 Alfried's counsel made much of the fact that he did not *formally* become head of the House of Krupp until 1943. But there is little doubt that from the very first day of hostilities, if not even earlier, Alfried occupied a far more active role in Krupp affairs than his ailing father. What emerges clearly from the Nuremberg documents is that by 1939 Gustav was already merely a figurehead in the firm—for one thing he was by then approaching seventy years of age while Alfried was just thirty-two. Furthermore, as many who knew him at that time have since attested, Gustav's faculties had already begun to go. Goebbels, for instance, described him in his diary as being "gaga". Three directors handled the day-to-day running of Krupp's, and Alfried was one of them—the director in charge of mining and armaments. It therefore fell to him to have to deal at first hand with the demands of Hitler and his generals for war material of all kinds. His attendance at gun-trials was particularly assiduous, and as his father withdrew more and more from the firm, Alfried, even before 1943, was acting as host to the scores of VIP visitors to the works: from victorious U-boat commanders to Japanese generals.

The task of preparing the prosecution's case at Alfried's trial was made that much easier by the sheer thoroughness of Krupp's public relations department. No event involving a member of the family with one of their Nazi masters appeared to go unrecorded or unsung. In fact more often than not they were filmed. The Allies captured these cine-dossiers in 1945 and copies of them reside today in the vaults of the Imperial War Museum in London and of the National Archive in Washington. There is film of Alfried and Gustav hobnobbing with Hitler and Hess. There is film of Alfried and Gustav gossiping to Goering and Goebbels. There is film of Alfried and Gustav *Sieg-heil*ing the swastika flag. There is film of Alfried and Gustav receiving Nazi awards and presenting Nazi awards. There is film of Alfried and Gustav unveiling portraits and busts of the German dictator. There is film of tumultuous receptions being accorded the Führer by the workers of Krupp and by the managers of Krupp on his frequent visits to the factories. There is film of Gustav and Bertha standing side by side with Hitler at the launching of the cruiser *Prinz Eugen* from the Krupp shipyards at Kiel in 1938—only to end up ten years later as a target vessel in one of the American nuclear-bomb tests at Bikini atoll. There is film of the Führer saluting a long line of Krupp-made U-boats—and there is seemingly endless footage of Gustav pontificating on the virtues of Nazism. Much of this material I used in a television documentary I made for Associated TeleVision on the House of Krupp in 1965. But what Alfried thinks of it all when he sees those films, if he ever does, we shall probably never know.

CHAPTER TWELVE

"We take great pride in the fact that our products have come up to expectations"

JUST HOW massive a contribution Krupp's Armaments Division made to Hitler's war machine can be judged from an official German military document prepared in February 1942. It extols in particular the Krupp 88 mm. anti-aircraft gun that had already been put through its terrible paces in Spain on behalf of Franco long before the Second World War had even started. But it also lauds Krupp anti-tank guns and Krupp self-propelled guns. It especially praises the Krupp 105 mm. recoil-less gun with which the German paratroopers had been equipped for the invasion of Crete "where it gave an excellent account of itself". It lists too Krupp rocket-assisted shells and Krupp armour-piercing shells. It boasts of the effectiveness of Krupp tanks and Krupp fuse-setting machines. It commends the high quality of the Krupp naval guns and the Krupp armour-plating as fitted to the pride of the German Fleet: the battleships *Bismarck* and *Tirpitz*, the cruisers *Scharnhorst* and *Gneisenau*. And it records of course the contribution of the U-boats Krupp's were building by the score. All of which must have been extremely gratifying to Alfried, the director in charge of armaments. It allowed him to declare in his annual report, "We take great pride in the fact that our products have come up to expectations."

As the German Army overran one country after another, Krupp experts were sent to see that the captured factories were quickly tied into the Nazi military machine. On Berlin's instruction, Alfried himself flew out to the Ukraine in the summer of 1942 to supervise the taking over of the iron and steel industry there, while other directors made certain that the Essen firm got the biggest slice possible in the pickings of machine-tool factories in France, shipbuilding facilities in Holland, metal works in Belgium, nickel mines in Greece, and chromium deposits in Yugoslavia. Even the great Philips electrical complex at Eindhoven in Holland fell into Krupp's grip.

Nor was it always simply a matter of plundering the output on the spot—in many cases Krupp technicians dismantled whatever machines they could lay hands on for transshipping to Krupp sites elsewhere. For example, in 1943 the Russians' modern electro-steel mill at Mariupol was broken down to be re-erected as part of Krupp's new Berthawerke near Breslau in eastern Germany. Towards the end of the war Krupp's despoliation of the occupied countries became quite wilful. In France for instance most of the Austin factory at Liancourt, the Almag plant at Mulhouse, and the Alsthow works at Belfort, were man-handled bodily back to Essen.

In view of such devotion to the Nazi cause, it came as no shock to anyone when in March 1943 Alfried was awarded the Nazi Cross for Meritorious War Service. He had already that same year been made a War Economy Leader by Hitler who had charged him with the main responsibility for mobilising the full resources of the nation's armament industry. To accept this post, which he had done "eagerly and readily", Alfried had had to submit a so-called "declaration of political attitude". He had been required in fact to swear that he stood by "the National-Socialist conception of the State, without any reserve".

His father, as we have pointed out, had already had his share of Hitler honours. Yet another one had come his way in May 1940, when with the German Wehrmacht triumphant on all fronts, thanks to Krupp guns, Krupp tanks, and Krupp U-boats, the Führer recognised his indebtedness to the House of Krupp by designating it "a model enterprise of National Socialism"—and Rudolf Hess, Hitler's deputy, had hurried down to Essen in person to give Gustav his Golden Banner of Industry. According to the official Krupp report of the occasion, Hess delivered a "stirring address" which was "characterised by a most timely political note—

settling final accounts with the Jewish-plutocratic-democratic world". In accepting the diploma, Alfried's father had said that he considered it "a tribute to a social-political attitude which, while having its roots in an age-old tradition, has developed organically so as to fit into the new times in National-Socialist Germany". It could have been Hitler himself speaking!

Just as in the First World War, when they had produced the notorious Big Bertha and the incredible Long Max, so now in the second Krupp's had an equally fantastic and terrifying gun up their sleeves, nicknamed "Fat Gustav". The biggest gun ever made, it could pierce armour-plating five feet thick and concrete eleven feet thick from a distance of twenty-five miles. Each shell weighed seven tons and measured thirty-two inches across, while the crater it caused could be as much as 100 feet deep and 100 feet wide. Intended for the siege of Leningrad, the 1,500-ton gun did not arrive there in time, but it was used with devastating effect at Sevastopol in June 1942.

Work on the giant weapon had begun as far back as 1935, when a member of the German Army Ordnance Office had telephoned Krupp's to ask what weight and speed of projectile would be required to demolish the massive defences of the Maginot Line which the French were then in the process of completing. As a result of this initial enquiry, three teams of Krupp ballistic experts were set the task of compiling preliminary blueprints for siege-guns of 700, 800, and 1,000 mm. calibre respectively. According to the Nuremberg testimony of Dr. Erich Mueller, Krupp's chief gun designer at that time, nothing more was heard from the authorities about the project until Hitler's visit to the works in March 1936. Fresh from his triumph over the reoccupation of the Rhineland, Adolf evidently brought up the question of the giant gun's feasibility during conversations with Gustav, Alfried and Mueller. He was told by them that the difficulties would probably lie in fashioning the large forgings and the extra-heavy castings necessary for such a solid piece of ordnance, but that nevertheless it was theoretically possible. Hitler, however, still did not commission the scheme.

Even so, without waiting for a definite commitment from

the authorities, Gustav gave the go-ahead for detailed work on the gun to begin that summer. By the end of the year, draft plans had been completed and these were discussed with the army's own experts early in 1937. The problem was the date of delivery, for the generals were now extremely impatient to receive their "secret weapon". Let Mueller take up the tale:

> This date of delivery could not be fixed exactly because it was dependent on whether two workshops which were at that time being built as part of the naval programme could be completed in time and whether the various large machines for manufacturing the different mechanical barrel parts and the large cradle could be set up there in time. The workshops were supposed to be completed in 1939. Under the above-mentioned conditions the year 1940 was given as the earliest date for the production of the gun. Moreover, this deadline could be met only by departing from the usual production methods of starting forgings and castings only after the whole construction had been completed. The Army gave its consent to this, and a special contract was drawn up which authorised Krupp to start construction without simultaneous checking by the Army and to begin production immediately after finishing the parts of the construction in question.

Krupp's started making the gun in the spring of 1937. Within twelve months the first shells had been tested on the German Army's artillery range at Hillersleben, when a projectile fired at a concrete bunker whose walls were more than nine feet thick completely demolished it. During the opening weeks of 1939 further trials were held at an ancient fortress near Grulich, again with the same results.

Although production of the monster weapon was well advanced by the time of Germany's invasion of Poland, difficulties arose shortly afterwards and it soon became clear that it was not going to be ready for the drive against the Maginot Line. Accordingly, in the spring of 1940 Hitler called Mueller to a conference at Berchtesgaden to discuss the gun's progress. Dissatisfied with the reasons offered for its slowness he demanded that the completion of the gun be given every possible priority.

Alfried himself now took charge of the project, and later that summer, while the Battle of Britain was at its height, the giant gun-barrel was successfully tested in his presence. By the beginning of 1941 the whole weapon was ready for its first test-firing. Gustav attended, along with Alfried and the other Krupp directors. Later that spring the gun was fired again at Hügenwald, this time before Hitler and the top Nazi leaders.

When Fat Gustav finally saw action at Sevastopol in the summer of 1942, Alfried flew with Mueller to witness the monster gun's brief moment of misspent glory. Since the early spring, carefully selected workers had been slaving to prepare the massive mounting—the outsize cannon could only operate from a specially strengthened twin-track railway. The gun itself was shipped there piece by piece during April and was assembled only just in time for the first fearsome shot to be fired in anger that June. Alfried and Mueller spent five days in all watching the product of their wits strike terror into the hapless Russian city.

Only fifty-three shots were fired from the weapon on that occasion, but the damage it caused was monstrous. However, it proved far too cumbersome and far too expensive ever to be used again, though there was just one more attempt to set it up in front of Leningrad later that same year. Fortunately the Red Army arrived before it and thus prevented that noble city's destruction.

Fat Gustav finished the war lying forlornly in a corner of the vast Essen works, having somehow escaped the attentions of the British and American bombers. Inevitably its 130-feet-long barrel was one of the first objects the Allied break-up men attacked with their pickaxes and oxy-acetylene burners after 1945. Presumably it ended up being melted down to make something like pots and pans in one of the countries ravaged by the Nazis—a fitting conclusion perhaps to a ten-year cycle of Krupp infamy.

As it happened, and despite all the millions spent on its development, Gustav had given the monster gun to Hitler as a present! (Though there is no record of the Führer having physically received it.) Krupp's could of course afford to be generous, since in the first year alone of the war they had made a profit of some £28 million. But Gustav had another motive. He wanted to interest Hitler in changing the House of Krupp's legal status, so as to keep its ownership intact and inside the family for all time. Both the Kaisers in their turn had come to consider Krupp's as something of a "special case". Now Gustav was asking his Führer to make the Essen firm's position even more unique by exempting it from inheritance tax and by letting it pass like a monarch's throne from a single incumbent to a single heir—which had been old Alfred's wish.

After almost a year of legal arguing, Gustav duly got his way, and on 12 November 1943 Hitler promulgated the *Lex Krupp*—in recognition of the family's, as he put it, "incomparable effort to boost the military power of Germany". Three days later, at a cold, cheerless ceremony in the presence of the firm's lawyers, Bertha as the direct descendant of Alfred and Friedrich, and therefore the formal owner of the House of Krupp, renounced her title in favour of her eldest son. Just as the Kaiser had rechristened Gustav von Bohlen, Gustav *Krupp* von Bohlen, so Hitler now did the same with Alfried. Thus Alfried Krupp von Bohlen und Halbach came into his inheritance.

The Führer's decree also meant that the firm was no longer the joint-stock company it had been since Friedrich's death. Instead it reverted to the "single proprietorship" of Alfred's time, which is still its status today. There is just one share in the House of Krupp—and that belongs to Alfried. He is the sole owner of Fried. Krupp of Essen.

In his first proclamation as head of the firm, Alfried boasted of the glorious history of the Krupp weapon forges and pointed with pride to the Krupp workers as strong adherents of the Nazi ideology. He also promised revenge against the Allies. But what intrigued his employees more was his curt announcement that henceforth the old Board of Directors would become a Directorate "though consisting of the same people as before, *with the exception of Herr Loeser, resigned*"—for thereby hung a tale.

Ewald Oskar Ludwig Loeser was one of the three executive

directors, along with Professor Goerens and Alfried himself, who had been responsible for the day-to-day running of the firm after Gustav became merely a figure-head chairman at the outset of the war. Of the three, Loeser and Alfried had failed to hit it off together right from the start. When Alfried had become a director in October 1938, Loeser had already been one for twelve months. What is more, he had quickly assumed a position of prominence and power within the firm. Goerens was more of a boffin than a boss and was certainly no match for the wily, intensely ambitious Loeser. Alfred even alluded to this power struggle during his own evidence at his trial at Nuremburg when he described Loeser's position after joining the board as being "extra-ordinarily strong". It would seem that the rivalry between Alfried and Loeser continued behind the scenes right up until just before the promulgation of the *Lex Krupp*. Indeed Loeser had tried desperately to dissuade Gustav from going ahead with the scheme, arguing that the family might not always produce a scion capable of taking on the heavy responsibilities of administering such a massive and crucially important enterprise as Krupp's—an argument which needless to say cut no ice whatsoever with Alfried in parti-cular, and which the senile Gustav was now past even con-sidering. Therefore with the transfer of ownership duly completed, and Alfried firmly in the saddle, Loeser would appear to have come to the end of the road. But that is not all there is to the story.

Loeser had in fact owed his appointment at Krupp's to one Carl Friedrich Goerdeler, Hitler's Price Commissioner until his conservative economic views clashed with the Nazi's rearmament plans in 1935 and thus forced him to quit the Führer's employ. Before that, Goerdeler had been Lord Mayor of Leipzig when Loeser had been his City Treasurer. Loeser had resigned from this post in 1934, dis-gusted apparently with the way the local Nazi thugs were interfering with his department's affairs.

Goerdeler had the reputation for being something of a financial "whizz-kid", which was why Hitler had singled him out for the Price Commissioner job in the first place. So after he had left that post, his services were sought by many industrial firms, chief among them being Krupp's. Gustav, however, decided to withdraw his offer when he discovered that Hitler would be displeased if Goerdeler were appointed. Goerdeler for his part suggested Loeser in his stead. As well as agreeing to this, Gustav got out of the embarrassing situation as regards Goerdeler himself by taking him on, too, as a sort of roving ambassador for the firm, arranging to pay for the ex-Lord Mayor's foreign travel expenses so long as he kept Krupp's supplied with financial information as to what their competitors were up to abroad. Unbeknown to Gustav of course Goerdeler was already plotting to overthrow Hitler and looked upon Loeser as a likely lieutenant once the coup had taken place. Meantime his Krupp credentials were an excellent guise to keep the Gestapo away.

In the end the *putsch* to establish what Goerdeler referred to as "the new front of decency" did not happen until 20 July 1944, some eight months after the promulgation of the *Lex Krupp*. If it had succeeded Goerdeler was to have been Chancellor and Loeser his Finance Minister. Instead, Goerdeler was one of the thousands of plotters whom the Nazis caught and brutally executed. Loeser too was jailed, but he kept his life. Two other suspects similarly imprisoned were Gustav's brother-in-law, Baron Thilo von Wilmowsky, and his wife Barbara, Bertha's younger sister. They had long been close acquaintances of Loeser, Goerdeler, and many of the other conspirators. Barbara Wilmowsky was soon released, but her husband spent ten months being moved from concentration-camp to concentration-camp before he was set free by the Americans in May 1945. Twenty-two years earlier, in 1923, Baron Wilmowsky had of course visited Gustav in his Düsseldorf jail—but neither Gustav nor Alfried returned the compliment during Thilo's sojourn with the SS. However, Bertha did at least occasionally smuggle some food to Barbara and her husband while they were in custody. Today, Baron Wilmowsky is chairman of Fried. Krupp of Essen and lives with his wife in a house in the grounds of the Villa Hügel.

When Alfried had become head of the House of Krupp in November 1943, the firm was then employing well over

115,000 people in its various shipyards, gun-shops, tank factories, steel plants, and armour-plating works dotted across Germany. What this figure did not include, however, were the thousands of slave labourers whom Krupp's were hiring from the Gestapo for four shillings per pair of hands per day.

At first, Alfried and his directors had been able to cope with the Wehrmacht's apparently insatiable appetite for their products by taking on more German workers or else even commandeering French prisoners of war. But after the Vichy Agreement many of these P.O.W.s were sent back to France. On top of this, once the Eastern Front began to take its terrible toll of human lives, working for Krupp was no longer for the German male a means of escaping the fighting. As more and more of even the unfit workers were despatched to the front, so the problem grew of how to fill their places. In the end, the solution chosen was to impress foreign labourers from some of the countries occupied by the Reich, particularly from the eastern countries—and when that source proved difficult and not always reliable, a few thousand Russian prisoners of war, and even concentration-camp inmates, were thrown in too for good measure.

Just as there were a great many German doctors and nurses employed in the prison camps who would have nothing to do with the horrible inhuman experiments carried out there, so there were a great many German firms and businesses that managed to evade the necessity of employing slave labour at all by hanging on to their existing workers. But Krupp's went out of their way to employ slave labour. They even demanded such workers. And so far as one knows, neither Gustav nor Alfried raised any protest whatsoever against this. If they had, it is almost certain that it would have had some effect, because such was the crucial importance of Krupp's to the Nazi war effort that Hitler could not have afforded to see them without the labour they needed.

Thus began the most infamous chapter in the whole Krupp saga—and one whose abject villainy and base-minded squalor was only truly revealed during the trial of Alfried and his fellow Krupp directors at Nuremberg between December 1947 and July 1948. Even now, case-hardened as we are to stories of atrocity and of man's monumental cruelty to man, the official account of the trial still makes disgusting reading. This record of needless barbarity and odious savagery, of a factory regimen rotten and rancid to the core, of a management meanly apathetic and wantonly neglectful of the condition and needs of a large section of their labour-force, cannot and must not be ignored in making a final assessment of the House of Krupp. This is by far the biggest blemish on the name of Krupp—and one which overrides whatever goodwill had hitherto been attached to Krupp's on account of the welfare schemes for some of their workers. Because of this ignominy, to many people Krupp will always be a distasteful word—and Alfried, as the acknowledged head of the firm during this period, for ever a depressing creature. Krupp's use of slave labour was the prosecution's most incriminating charge against Alfried at his trial after the war—and it is therefore in the chapter dealing with the trial that we will consider the evidence brought forward to substantiate this charge.

With his succession to the ownership of the House of Krupp in November 1943, Alfried would seem to have attained the pinnacle of his ambition. He was then only thirty-six. But his personal victory coincided with his country's slide towards defeat—for by November 1943 the signs of Germany's coming downfall were obvious enough even for the narrow-minded, Nazi-indoctrinated Krupps to have noticed them. Italy had already capitulated, and the German Army's long flight back from Russia had begun. But the clearest indications of all were in the sound of the British and American bombers over Essen.

Essen's first major air-raid of the war had occurred on 5 March 1943. It had been a harsh taste of what lay in store for the people of that Ruhr city. Three hundred and forty-five aircraft had taken part in that initial night-attack, their bombs laying waste 160 acres in the centre of Essen and badly damaging another 450. Hitherto the Ruhr towns had escaped the brunt of the British and American air-raids because their ever-present pall of smoke made accurate bomb-aiming well-nigh impossible. But the introduction of the Royal Air Force's so-called Pathfinder squadrons in the spring of 1943 had put an end to this immunity. The British Mosquito planes pinpointed their targets with flares, while the heavy bombers following up did the rest. Goering's proud boast that the Ruhr, like Berlin, would never be bombed became only a bitter memory to the people who lived and worked there—and the Krupp anti-aircraft guns that vainly tried to keep out the Allied attacks were seen by their makers to be by no means the invincible weapons they had been claimed to be.

Inevitably Essen—and Krupp's in particular—was singled out for special attention. Between March 1943 and April 1945 the Royal Air Force alone made 11,336 individual sorties over the home of Krupp's, and in 186 full-scale air-raids dropped some 36,420 tons of incendiary and high-explosive bombs, most of them on the three square miles of Alfried's factories. By the end of 1944 output in them was down to 30 per cent of capacity. One bomb on 23 October 1944 severed the firm's main water supply from the river and stopped production altogether for a time. In fact no complete gun left the Essen workshops after the autumn of 1944.

The list of the types of bombers used in these raids reads like a roll-call of British history—there were Hampdens, Blenheims, Whitleys, Wellingtons, Lancasters, Halifaxes and Manchesters. Essen was indeed one of R.A.F. Bomber Command's most favoured "targets for tonight". Its seemingly monotonous repetition in B.B.C. newscasts during 1944 and early 1945 has meant that its name will remain firmly implanted in the memory of most British people for all time. My class at school had a wall map of Germany on which we used to pin flags where the big bombing attacks had taken place. Essen, I remember clearly, was well "flagged", as of course were most of the Ruhr cities, particularly Dortmund, Gelsenkirchen, Hamm, and Duisburg. These names, along with that of Essen, became far more familiar to me in my schooldays than either Venice, Cairo, or Constantinople—as indeed they still are. At that time the Dortmund–Ems Canal seemed to flow through our classroom in rather the same way as a dozen years later the Suez Canal was to appear to Lady Eden to be running through her drawing-room! Visiting the Ruhr for the first time during the autumn of 1964 was like stepping back twenty years into my schooldays.

Goebbels wrote in his diary that he considered Essen to be "the city hardest hit by English air-raids"—while just before Christmas 1944 General Heinz Gudcrian reported to Hitler that the city was prostrate. At first the Krupp workers had eagerly repaired every morning the ravages the raids the night before had wrought upon their machines —and more often than not, despite the seemingly impossibility of the task, had in fact got their equipment going again by lunch-time. But their spirit had been sapped even before Essen suffered its final and most ferocious air-raid on 11 March 1945. On that day nearly half the main Krupp factory was totally destroyed and work there ceased completely. It was not to start up again before Allied troops had captured the town a month later.

The Villa Hügel, as well as the administrative wing of the Krupp works where Alfried and the other directors had their offices, both survived the bombing. In any case the executives had seen to it that they were well supplied with shelters —and indeed the voluminous family shelter below the basement of the Villa Hügel became one of the favourite "sights" offered Allied visitors there after the war.

But the forced labourers from the concentration camps fared far worse, for virtually nothing was done to shield them from the Allied rain of death. Huddled as they were in meagre, cold hutments close to the works, the mind boggles at the intense terror they must have experienced during the raids. At the height of the Allied bombing-attacks in late 1944, Krupp's were employing 70,000 such workers, and the casualties among those luckless Poles, Russians, Czechs, Hungarians, Rumanians, and even Italians were needlessly large. Every one of the fifty-seven Krupp prison camps located within the city's precincts was destroyed at least once—some two or three times. What is more, the onus of repairing them fell on the inmates. Since they were denied proper materials other than what was at hand, and since they were weary from their work and painfully under-nourished, in most cases the camps were simply left as they were after the raids, while the poor wretches existed as best they could among the ruins. Of all the evidence produced during the various Nuremberg trials, perhaps none was more damning than the affidavit of a German police official whose task it had been to inspect one of these Krupp camps:

The camp inmates were mostly Jewish women and girls from Hungary and Rumania. They were brought to Essen at the beginning of 1944 and were put to work at Krupp's. The accommodation and feeding of the camp prisoners was beneath all dignity. At first the prisoners were accommodated in simple wooden huts. These huts were burned down during an air-raid and from that time on the prisoners had to sleep in a damp cellar. Their beds were made on the floor and consisted of a straw-filled sack and two blankets. In most cases it was not possible for the prisoners to wash themselves daily as there was no water. There was no possibility of having a bath. I could often observe from the Krupp factory during the lunch-break how the prisoners boiled their underclothing in an old bucket or container over a wood fire and cleaned themselves. . . . A slit trench served as an air-raid shelter, while the SS guards went to the Humboldt shelter which was bombproof.

Reveille was at 5 a.m. There was no coffee or any food served in the morning. . . . They marched for three-quarters of an hour to the factory, poorly clothed and badly shod, some without shoes, and, in rain or snow, covered merely with a blanket. Work began at 6 a.m. Lunch-break was from 12 to 12.30. Only during the break was it at all possible for the prisoners to cook something for themselves from potato peelings and other garbage. The daily working period was one of 10 or 11 hours. Although the prisoners were completely undernourished, their work was very heavy physically. The prisoners were often maltreated at their work-benches by Nazi overseers and female SS guards. At 5 or 6 in the afternoon they were marched back to the camp. The accompanying guards consisted of female SS who, in spite of protests from the civil population, often maltreated the prisoners on the way back with kicks, blows, and scarcely repeatable words. It often, happened that individual women and girls had to be carried back to the camp by their comrades owing to exhaustion.

At 6 or 7 p.m. these exhausted people arrived back in camp. Then the real meal was distributed. This consisted of cabbage soup. This was followed by the evening meal of water soup and a piece of bread which was for the following day. Occasionally the food on Sundays was better. As long as it existed there was never any inspection of the camp by the firm of Krupp.

But by May 1945, for those slave-labourers who had survived that long, their suffering was at an end. "As Germany goes, Krupp goes"—Germany had fallen and so had Krupp.

CHAPTER THIRTEEN

"OK Bud, you're the guy we want—let's go"

On the morning of 11 April 1945, just nineteen days before
Hitler committed suicide in his Berlin bunker, two American
Army officers motored up the long carriage-way to the Villa
Hügel. They were Lieutenant-Colonel Clarence M. Sag-
moen and his adjutant, Captain Benjamin G. Westerveld;
a sergeant and another soldier manning the machine-gun
in the back of their jeep completed the party. Karl Dohr-
mann, Alfried's venerable butler, awaited them at the door
of the main house.

"Herr von Bohlen expects you. Will you please come this
way." But Alfried, clad in a grey lounge-suit and wearing a
blue-and-white striped shirt with a tie of the same colours,
stood already in the hall, holding a black "Anthony Eden"
type hat in his hand.

"Are you Krupp?" asked the captain bluntly.

"I am the owner of this property," replied Alfried in his
usual, perfect, though somewhat halting, English.

"OK Bud, you're the guy we want—let's go." And so,
after barely twenty-two years, a second head of the House
of Krupp went off into custody at the behest of one of
Germany's victors.

Advanced units of the United States 9th Army under
General Simpson had moved into Essen the night before.
They had met little resistance and had quickly taken possession of what few major buildings still remained standing
there. Krupp's administrative headquarters had been
surrendered to them by a tall, bespectacled, so far unnamed,
Krupp employee who told the American soldiers, "It's a
relief that those awful days and nights of bombing have
come to an end." Said another, "I think about 2,000 work-
people were killed in that last big raid."

Alfried was taken after his arrest to a drab little kitchen in the third-floor flat of a bomb-scarred block of workmen's homes in the centre of Essen which curiously enough was serving as the Americans' advanced base. War correspondents with the U.S. 9th Army were allowed to view the Lieutenant-Colonel's prize and even to question him as he sat at a cheap wooden table covered with a paltry stained square of so-called "American cloth". The journalists present were to record later how Alfried appeared "coldly self-possessed", even "faintly disdainful", though with "a rather uneasy mannerism of frequently passing his tongue across his thin lips". When asked by one what he expected to be manufacturing after the war, Krupp is said to have replied, "That all depends on the market."

But most of this early interrogation was about the last days of the struggle in the Ruhr and the effects of the Allied bombing on his own works. Apparently he shirked nothing, testifying to how production had ceased totally after the last raid on 11 March, how in fact trains had stopped operating through Essen three days before that, how the most damaging attacks of all had occurred during October 1944 when a single "block-buster" had severed the works' main water-supplies and had thus held up war production at a critical time in Hitler's counter-efforts against the Allies' rapid push across Europe.

It emerged too from the questioning that Goebbels had last visited Essen just before Christmas 1944 to deliver a "pep-talk" to the Krupp workers, rather on the style of the Kaiser's attempt in September 1918, and with the same paltry effect. Shortly afterwards, the Nazis' organisation in the Ruhr had rapidly begun to disintegrate. Alfried had preferred to ignore their wilder orders to defend his works to the last man or else to evacuate vital equipment to other parts of Germany in the face of the Allied advance. Even so, he had given instructions for valuable machinery to be dismantled and shipped to Essen from the Austin factory at Liancourt, as well as from the Almag plant at Mulhouse, only days before the Americans had arrived at both those places. For himself he had chosen to sit tight in the Villa Hügel awaiting the Allied troops. His butler vouched to enquiring reporters how Alfried had "slept as peacefully as a child" right up to, and even including, the night before his arrest when he knew that American forces were already in the vicinity.

Evidently, that very morning, on the eve of his capture, although told by his staff at the Hügel that a company of American combat troops had already reached the northern and western outskirts of Essen, Alfried had driven in to take his last look at the wrecked city of the cannon kings. Everywhere was rubble. Groups of dazed, sullen, dispirited Germans picked their way between huge mounds of debris. The most bewildered bystanders of all were those Krupp slave-workers whom the SS had forgotten to ship eastwards to certain death. Others had not been so lucky, but just a few weeks earlier had been sent back to Buchenwald or Belsen, never to be heard of again.

The Americans counted thirty-two dead bodies of forced labourers in the streets of Essen, apparently massacred by the Gestapo shortly before the last German forces had quit the city. Indeed one of their first civilian tasks was to impress some captured German policemen into burying the luckless shot-riddled Poles and Russians. They also quickly found themselves being called on to prevent the stronger of the concentration-camp inmates from taking revenge on their former masters, particularly the Krupp managers.

All told, some 32,000 foreign forced-labourers, 21,000 o them Poles and Russians, had been left behind in Essen. Many of them went insanely wild with excitement at the fact of liberation and thought it only fitting that they should be allowed to plunder and to pillage as they pleased. Again it fell to the American soldiers to prevent the ravaging from getting out of hand. But Essen's citizens not only defended themselves resolutely enough against all such onslaughts, they also took the opportunity of a breakdown in the policing of the city to indulge in a little localised looting themselves. Inevitably, Krupp's survived even this petty despoiling. Many of Alfried's managers and foremen had stayed at their posts. What is more, they had rustled up a small army of loyal workers to protect the more valuable pieces of equipment and machinery from the scrap-scavengers

—and on the very day the American troops marched in they had begun the long struggle to clear the factories of rubble. Even so, for several months more, Essen remained a dangerous as well as a devastated city.

"Shattered beyond description", was how the *Daily Herald*'s war correspondent, Charles Bray, summed up the position at Essen. "Indescribable", said the *News Chronicle*'s Ronald Wilkins. "Essen is just a chaos of burned-out, broken masonry and twisted ironwork", was the verdict of Stanley Nash of *The Star*. To an American reporter, the whole Ruhr was just "a grotesque junk-heap". Even five months after Essen's capture a *Daily Telegraph* writer was telling his British readers that there was not an undamaged house for miles around and that the city proper "had ceased to exist". According to his statistics 365,000 persons out of a pre-war population of 666,000 still eked out a precarious existence there. For the most part, they lived in dank cellars under piles of rubble or else five and six to a room in partly destroyed houses on the city's outskirts, all having to line up at the street pumps for their water-supplies.

A quick check by American troops soon after they arrived brought the estimate that roughly half of Essen's factories and public buildings, together with nearly two-thirds of its private houses and flats, had been either destroyed or damaged beyond repair. Nor had the Krupp-built garden-suburbs and apartment-blocks escaped either. As though symbolising the end of Essen's long association with armaments, the giant statue of Alfred the old "Cannon King" had been toppled by a 1,000 pound bomb from its pedestal in the centre of the city—but significantly, as it turned out, the iron body of the figure had not broken under the impact of the fall and was merely lying intact at the bottom of the bomb-crater!

To at least one British intelligence officer soon on the scene after April 1945, the Ruhr, and Essen especially, "gave one an overwhelming impression of complete devastation and desolation . . . one would have thought that it was quite impossible to restore any form of decent existence there ever again".

Yet the damage to the Ruhr's industry was more apparent

than real. In particular, Krupp's were not the total write-off they at first seemed: an American technical team on the spot found that, contrary to British bombing reports, Alfried's factories at Essen were only 30 per cent damaged. What had really brought his production to a complete standstill was the destruction of the roads, railways, and canals: it was no good producing the stuff if you could not ship it. This was to be the Allies' headache too, once hostilities had ceased in the Ruhr and the whole emphasis there was on getting the coal moving again. Indeed within eleven days of Essen's capture the first trainloads of Krupp coal were steaming out of the city "to aid the Allied war-effort", as the British newspapers at the time put it. By June 1945, less than a month after Germany's surrender, a few factories were going again in the Ruhr, including the Krupp locomotive shops. They were being used to repair the damaged trains and goods-wagons. Others were already making parts to rebuild the shattered bridges and to shore up the collapsed canal banks. But theirs was an immense uphill task, for well over half of Germany's locomotives and rolling-stock had been destroyed in the bombing, and every major canal and river was blocked by broken bridges and sunken barges. It was here on Germany's communications that the Allied bombing had had its greatest impact and biggest success.

By August 1945 the British had got 128 of the Ruhr's 157 coal-mines operating again: with German labour but under Allied supervision. But the problem was to ship the coal. All Western Europe was crying out for it—and the Ruhr seemed to be the obvious source, despite some earlier schemes for destroying every industrial building there and converting the area into one gigantic cow-pasture. The Dutch were especially crying out for Ruhr coal for their power-stations— as were the Belgians for their textile factories and their cement works, the Danes for their food-processing plants, the Norwegians for their fish-canneries, and the French for practically everything.

Within no time at all it seemed, the Ruhr coal-miner was one of the most courted figures on the whole Continent. He was even given bigger rations than the average British worker. Reginald Peck, the *Daily Telegraph*'s correspondent in Germany, recalled to me once how, when Essen miners were fed on British bacon (brought over in great secrecy because of the outcry it would have created back in Britain where bacon was of course still rationed), they complained bitterly that it was not fat enough for them—what the Ruhr coal-miner wanted was not good lean, streaky bacon such as delights the British palate, but bacon that was almost totally fat with no lean at all.

Absenteeism was rife among the miners. Many of them claimed they needed to stay at home to protect their families from the thousands of displaced persons and former forced labourers wandering the Ruhr out for revenge. Others argued they needed to go off into the country to seek food and fuel. Besides, what was the point, they said, in working for money when there was nothing in the shops to spend it on. They even asked at one stage to be paid in coal and food: coal was being strictly denied to Germans for their domestic use, though they were of course benefiting from that Ruhr coal which was finding its way into Ruhr power-stations and Ruhr gas-works. The emphasis, however, was on getting the coal out of the Ruhr and into those countries ravaged by the Third Reich: resuscitating the industries of these nations had a greater priority than repairing and reopening factories in the Ruhr itself, particularly while the great debate went on amongst the Allies as to whether or not Germany was to be allowed to recover at all.

The Villa Hügel, having been first taken over as a billet for American Army officers, including for a time the selfsame two who had arrested Alfried, had by the late summer of 1945 been commandeered as the headquarters of the Allied-run North German Coal Control Commission. Now the nine-foot-high Krupp family portraits looked down on American and British shorthand typists—and even Bertha's bedroom was being used as an office by one of the Allied coal controllers. Hobnailed boots rang out on the polished parquet flooring of the one-hundred-foot-long entrance hall to the Villa. Both the dining-room that could seat sixty-five comfortably and an odd-shaped parlour called "The Chinese Room", yet boasting a couple of billiard tables, had been divided up by beaver-board into cubicles that served as offices. Bermondsey and Brooklyn voices chatted over telephones in what had once been the ball-room and which had many a time resounded to the *Sieg-heils* of a heel-clicking, dutiful Krupp labour-force receiving their long-service medals from Papa Gustav. In some instances the same men and women who barely a few months before had been plotting the Ruhr's ruin were now planning its recovery.

As for Alfried, after his initial interrogation in the Command Post in the centre of town, he was taken back to the Hügel and kept under house-arrest in one of the gardeners' cottages there. Then in June 1945 he was transferred to a prison encampment elsewhere in the Ruhr, along with many other important Nazis and known Hitler-sympathisers. That same month, the British took over from the Americans in Essen, since, as agreed at Potsdam, the Ruhr was to be a part of the British Zone of occupied Germany. In September 1945 they arrested all the Krupp directors they could lay their hands on—two even attempted suicide to evade capture. Later that autumn it was announced that a forty-nine-year-old chartered accountant from North Harrow, Ernest Douglas Fowles, had been put in charge of Alfried's empire.

Fowles had worked for twelve years for an English firm in Germany before the war. He had won the Croix de Guerre in the First World War, though for much of the second he had been a voluntary fire-watcher at St. Paul's Cathedral and a member of the 11th Middlesex Battalion of the Home Guard. His deputy, Major Jack Trefusis, had in fact held a post with Krupp's in their foreign trade department for two years between 1937 and 1939.

On the very day that troops of the Cheshire Regiment occupied the Krupp works and raised the Union Jack for the first time above the eight-storey-high Krupp administrative building, Fowles and Trefusis called all the remaining Krupp managers and senior workmen to a meeting in the board-room high up in the tall office-tower. Somewhat melodramatically, though perhaps thinking that it was the most poignant and pertinent way to put across the Allied policy for the Ruhr to these former Nazi stalwarts, Fowles waved his hand towards the skyline of ruined smokestacks and broken-down blast-furnaces. "Not one of those chimneys will ever smoke again", he exclaimed. "Krupp's as you knew it, gentlemen, is finished for ever."

Alas for poor Ernest Douglas Fowles, his well-intentioned sortie into rhetoric was to go down in the ribald annals of Essen, and indeed of Western Germany: to be repeated with ridicule, to be scoffed at, and to be sniggered over. Yet who, looking out over the scene of desolation and devastation presenting itself from that eighth-floor window on that damp November afternoon in 1945, could have doubted Fowles' words—save perhaps for those who remembered only too well that when the victors at Versailles had pronounced a similar sentence on Krupp's more than a quarter of a century earlier the Essen firm had been back in business within a matter of months.

This time, however, the fall of the House of Krupp did look complete. Hardly a single building, no matter how small, was undamaged. The cast steel works, the *Gussstahl-fabrik*, the core of the Krupp empire, was merely a drunken tracery of twisted struts and torn girders: open to the skies and revealing below a chaos of tottering masonry and crushed machinery. This time too the victors seemed more resolved than before to put Krupp's, and indeed the whole of the Ruhr, out of action once and for all; just three days before Christmas 1945 the British Government announced that all Krupp properties had been expropriated and would henceforth be held in trust by Britain pending a final decision by the Allies as to their future. "Krupp's would cease to exist", said the official statement; "there will be an end for all time to the traditions and influences so long associated with it"—and again who could have disbelieved the British Government's spokesman then?

When the "Big Three" Allied leaders had met at Yalta in February of that same year, 1945—when there could be no doubt about the final outcome of the war—one of the trickiest questions discussed but not resolved was that of possible reparations. Stalin demanded 10,000 million dollars in money-recompense from Germany, but to this both Churchill and Roosevelt were adamantly opposed. Instead, they argued that if their defeated foe was to be made to make any amends at all for his terrible deeds then it should take the form of machinery and factories: either to be shipped whole or else to be broken up into manageable pieces and sent to those countries that had suffered most under the Nazi yoke. And they were still debating the issue when the conference broke up.

What the Allies *were* agreed on, however, was that the former Reich should be disarmed and shorn of its military potential—which meant, so far as Krupp's were concerned, that their armament factories would be razed to the ground. The French, together with a group of Roosevelt's advisers centred around Henry Morgenthau Jr., the American Secretary of the Treasury, wanted to go further and to strip the Ruhr of all its industries. They were anxious even to turn the Germans out of the area altogether, to internationalise the Ruhr, and to keep it solely for farmland in which no factory, however small, would be permitted.

As well as Roosevelt, Churchill too for a time went along with this so-called Morgenthau Plan. But already by the war's end most of the Allies, particularly the Russians, were against the total destruction and dismemberment of industrial Germany. General Eisenhower, for one, wanted the Ruhr restored, not dismantled (though without its armament factories of course), so that Germany would not be too much of a burden on the American taxpayer.

As was perhaps only to be expected, the French, in the person of Charles de Gaulle, took the toughest line of all on this question of possibly separating the Ruhr politically from the rest of Germany—Germany after all was their traditional foe, and the Ruhr was Germany's arsenal-cum-powerhouse. But Churchill, for another, was by this time gloomily alarmed at the growing Communist menace—and as well as wishing to keep some German troops still in arms, he was also arguing in favour of a strong, undivided Germany (but a Germany none the less firmly under Allied control) that might cushion Western Europe from Stalinist Russia and might even perhaps deter the Soviets from spreading any farther. Already world events were beginning to move inexorably in Germany's—and hence Krupp's—favour.

No sooner had the war been won than the former Allies quickly began falling out among themselves. This was particularly visible at the Potsdam Conference called in the summer of 1945 to decide in detail what to do with Germany. It was relatively easy to secure agreement on broad aims such as that Germany should be prevented from ever again being in a position to support aggression and that her industry should be organised in such a fashion as to benefit Europe as a whole—the devil of course was in the details. Stalin, for his part, was mainly concerned with securing as much booty as possible and in making conditions in continental Europe as ripe as possible for an eventual Communist take-over. The Western Allies for their part did not perhaps pay close enough attention to the details of the dismantling of the Ruhr factories that the Russians were proposing. Instead, they were inclined to squabble among themselves over forms of control and over degrees of what came to be known as "decartelisation": that is, into just how small a unit German industry should be divided.

The feeling was strong then within the West that it was the big Ruhr industrialists who had played *the* crucial role in Hitler's rise to power. Said Ernest Bevin, for instance, soon after the war, "The Ruhr industries were in the hands of magnates who were closely allied to the German military machine, who financed Hitler, and who in two world wars were part and parcel of German aggressive policy"—and Britain's Labour Foreign Secretary went on, "We have no desire to see these gentlemen or their like return to a position which they have abused with such tragic results". Declared he on another occasion, "I do not believe in giving a warlike race, uncontrolled by anyone, another arsenal of that character; if a fellow has shot at me three times, I don't see why I should give him a pistol to make sure the fourth time".

Everyone seemed agreed that the great coal and steel empires of the Ruhr, such as Krupp's, should be broken up—the question at issue was how, and how small. The Americans, perhaps infected by their New Deal enthusiasm for "trust-busting", wanted the units to be very small—no more than 3,000 employees per concern. This, to the British, appeared too small to be economic. Moreover, Churchill's wartime coalition had given way in the summer of 1945—in the middle of the Potsdam Conference in fact—to a Labour Government intent on socialist solutions to the great problems of the day, not just at home but in Britain's relations overseas too. Nationalisation of key industries had taken pride of place in the party's election programme—and what better, said some of the British labour leaders, than to export these ideas to defeated Germany. Ernest Bevin, the great trade unionist now turned diplomat, argued strongly in favour of nationalising the Ruhr's industries, particularly its coal and steel. But to this the Americans were adamantly opposed. Besides, there was the unfortunate snag that there was no German Government in existence at that time—and, with no government to hand it over to, it seemed difficult, if not actually impossible, to nationalise an industry.

The French persisted in their demand that the Ruhr-Saar industrial complex be separated politically as well as economically from the rest of Germany and that it should be subjected to some form of international control for all time. But the Russians, the Americans, and to a certain extent even the British, continued to be lukewarm towards this idea. Bevin and his Foreign Office colleagues might well have gone along with international *economic* control of the Ruhr, but remained unconvinced of the need for long-term *political* control. As a result of the frosty reception to their plan for the Ruhr, the French became increasingly estranged from their former Allies. They were inclined at times to be petulant and unhelpful over policies for Germany—as witness the files of the inter-Allied coal control for the Ruhr which are full of British and American complaints to the French for not returning empty goods-wagons that had been sent to France filled with coal. This was a situation that not only the Soviets found to their liking, but which the Germans, and particularly some of the former Ruhr industrial magnates like Krupp's, were able all too easily to exploit in their favour too.

Meantime of course, the Russians with the approval and physical help of the British and the Americans, were ravaging the Ruhr under the guise of "dismantling". One of the factories so chosen for this "reparations-in-kind" was the big Krupp steel foundry at Borbeck, close to Essen. This, perhaps the most modern plant of its type anywhere in the world, had escaped the brunt of the bombing, although it had been making parts for Tiger tanks throughout the war. By and large it was still intact and without much difficulty could have been got working again to supply much-needed steel to Western Europe. Instead, a joint British and Russian demolition team descended on it in the summer of 1946 and began the lengthy, laborious, and costly task of breaking it down for shipment to Russia.

Twenty-eight hundred men, most of them previously employed at Krupp's, worked for nearly three years dismembering the machines: packing them piece by piece into crates before loading them into barges and railway trucks for the long journey eastwards to Georgia via Hamburg and the Black Sea. Ninety-one thousand tons were shipped in this way from Borbeck alone, together with valuable blueprints and precious production formulas—though it was estimated that only about one-sixth of the parts sent were in the end able to be re-used and that the cost of the whole operation was roughly about three times their eventual value.

Other complete units from the Ruhr, such as rolling-mills and heavy tools, went to Yugoslavia, France, Belgium, and Czechoslovakia—in fact to most of the countries ravaged by the Nazis. In some instances, valuable machines were broken down for scrap or else despatched where they were scarcely ever used. A 15,000-ton forge, sent in segments to Yugoslavia, when unpacked several years later was discovered virtually to have corroded away. There were even cases reported of giant girders, largely unused and clearly undamaged, being cut up by oxy-acetylene burners and shipped as scrap to the selfsame blast-furnaces in France and Britain from which new girders were being ordered for the Ruhr. Some of the machines which British engineers had got working again soon after the war, in order to turn out locomotives and goods-wagons needed for transporting the Ruhr coal everone was crying out for, were eventually ordered to be broken up for scrap too.

The detailed operation of the dismantling stemmed from decisions taken—or rather not taken—at Potsdam. As such, it was completely inflexible, since the individual British and American teams working the scheme could never persuade their Russian counterparts to stray one inch from their instructions. Thus, productive capacity was often being destroyed in one corner of a factory while reconstruction and repair-work was being carried out in another corner.

Not that the dismantling ever progressed all that speedily —the German workers, and particularly the Krupp managers, saw to that. At Borbeck, for instance, barges would never arrive on time, railway wagons would take tortuously long routes and invariably land up at the wrong destinations, while people more often than not would simply not turn up for work. Occasionally the demolition-gangs would even down tools to stage so-called "spontaneous" demonstrations against what they described as the "needless destruction". There were endless arguments and countless petitions to stop the dismantling.

Luckless British administrators at times almost came to blows with Russian "liaison" officers in the Ruhr. Official complaints passed between Essen and Berlin, and between London and Moscow. Slanderous assertions were bandied about. Memos proliferated and reports piled up. Innumerable inspection teams checked and re-checked—and checked and re-checked each other. Reputations were lost in the Ruhr, and many a wartime friendship ended there. It was a sorry time for everyone—or almost everyone, for it suited certain people, such as the Krupp executives, who found, like the Communists, that the chaotic situation presented numerous opportunities for intrigue and delay, for casting doubts and encouraging divisions between the Allies.

To the Americans, it seemed as though valuable effort was being wasted that could have been better spent on putting Europe back on its feet again. To the Russians, every delay was interpreted as sabotage or else a going-back on agreed wartime policies. To the British, in whose zone most of this dismantling was perforce being carried out, the whole sorry business appeared both futile and embarrassing —for even in those first few years after the war, when the anger aroused by the Nazi atrocities was still intense, strong misgivings were being expressed in Britain, and indeed throughout the Western world, over the wisdom of continuing all this organised destruction.

At first the disquiet took the form of letters to the editors of liberal journals such as the *Manchester Guardian*—some even as early as the autumn of 1945. By 1946 and 1947 politicians as well as leader-writers had climbed on to the band-wagon. But then by this time too the whole Allied policy for the Ruhr was back again in the melting-pot, as post-war antagonisms had superseded wartime alliances. The American business magazine *Fortune* spoke up for an evidently growing and already sizeable body of opinion within the industrial community of the United States when, in a special cover-story on the area in December 1946, it called for the "Ruhr's revival", arguing that Germany could not be left for ever as "a physical, moral, and political slum".

The Ruhr lay of course in the British Zone, and was therefore a direct British responsibility, though obviously one in which she would take note of the feelings of her other Allies. Hence the way was open for pressures to be brought to bear upon Britain to alter some of her attitudes towards her defeated foe—and undoubtedly pressures, some subtle, some barefaced, *were* put on the British Government during those years to make them fall in line with American thinking on Germany as a whole, as well as on the Ruhr in particular.

The one thing that concerned British leaders most was the destruction of the political influence of Ruhr magnates like Krupp. As we have seen, socialists, such as Ernest Bevin, thought that this could best be brought about by public ownership and control of the Ruhr's major industries, coal and steel.

But the United States Administration would have nothing whatsoever to do with nationalisation—and as throughout 1946 and 1947 the British Government were having to go cap in hand on occasion to Washington to seek assistance in their financial difficulties, particularly their shortage of dollars, it became yet another instance of "he who pays the piper calls the tune". When in September 1947, the same month in fact in which Britain, plunged in yet another of her periodic economic crises, was asking the Americans for further aid, it was announced that henceforth Ruhr coal was to be administered jointly by Britain and the United States, it was assumed that possible public ownership of Ruhr industry was henceforth a complete dead duck.

Paradoxically though, the Americans were much more enthusiastic than their other Allies about carving up the big industrial concerns into smaller units. Whereas the British would have been well satisfied with dividing the market for each Ruhr product among, say, eight or ten medium-sized firms, the Americans were insisting on a much greater number of far smaller units. Compromises were inevitably struck in many cases—for instance, the notorious giant steel cartel, the Vereinigte Stahlwerke, which during the 'thirties had controlled something like three-fifths of the Ruhr's steel production and almost two-fifths of its coal output (and was therefore Europe's largest single industrial concern), was divided into twenty units.

Krupp's, however, presented a particularly difficult problem for even the astute American "decartelisers". It was of course relatively easy to rid Alfried's firm of its armament works—the U-boat pens at Kiel were simply blown up, and the gun-shops at Essen were razed to the ground. Inevitably too, Krupp's seemed to bear the brunt of the "reparations-in-kind" to the Russians and the other victims of Nazi aggression: it was estimated that some 40 per cent of the former "cannon-kingdom" was either destroyed or dismantled *after* the war was over, on top of the 30 per cent that had disappeared as a result of the bombing *during* the war. It was the problem of what to do with the remaining 30 per cent that was giving the Allied administrators all their headaches.

There seemed at least two alternatives, assuming public ownership was now definitely out of the question for all time. Either the Allies could try to find a politically "safe" member of the Krupp family to whom Alfried's residual properties could be given *en bloc*—his sister Waldtraut, who was married to a Bremen textile-magnate, thought to have been an opponent of Hitler, had in fact petitioned the Allies in June 1945 with this suggestion, namely that her husband be named as trustee of the firm pending a final decision concerning its future. Or else the Allies could separate out first the steel-holdings, so as to lump them together into a single company or a number of companies, and then do the same with the coal-mines and the engineering-yards, and so on.

But even this second alternative still shirked the thorny question of the eventual ownership of the Krupp assets, since both the British and the Americans were in principle against confiscation—unless of course Alfried could be convicted as a war criminal. This seemed to be the easiest way out, for some of the Allied delegations at Yalta had favoured confiscating property as an additional punishment to those convicted of major war crimes.

CHAPTER FOURTEEN

"Case Number Ten"

WHEN IN October 1945 the list appeared of the major war criminals to be tried at Nuremberg, Alfried's name was not, however, on it. But his father's was, just as it had been of course on the similar list drawn up in 1919 after the First World War. Such was the association, in the Allied mind, of the name of Krupp with the Nazi war machine and Nazi atrocities such as slave labour that Gustav had been singled out from all the other big industrialists and was to be tried alongside leading Nazis like Goering, Hess, Ribbentrop and Keitel. As Nazis went, Gustav was considered to be in the top twenty.

On the eve of his trial, however, his German defence counsel, Theodor Klefisch, applied to the International Military Tribunal for a postponement of the proceedings against him on the ground that the seventy-six-year-old Gustav was unfit to plead. A team of six doctors—one British, one French, one American, and three Russian—were immediately despatched to examine him where he lay dying, in the servants' annex of the Krupp summer castle at Blühnbach, high up in the Austrian Alps above Salzburg.

The castle had been originally built by that hapless Hapsburg, Archduke Franz Ferdinand of Sarajevo fame— or rather of Sarajevo misfortune. Gustav had bought the place during the 'twenties both as a summer haunt for his family and as a shooting-lodge for himself: the woods surrounding the eighty-roomed castle abounded in boar, chamois, and fallow deer. When the Allied bombing of Essen had got too hot for them in the autumn of 1944, Gustav had taken refuge in Blühnbach with his wife Bertha and their second oldest son Berthold.

Shortly after American troops captured Salzburg in the spring of 1945, General Mark Clark had sent one of his aides out scouring the mountainous area for a suitable week-end shooting-retreat for his senior officers. Lieutenant-Colonel Charles W. Thayer, who had been entrusted with this delicate mission, found himself in time hammering on the door of Gustav's castle. Ironically enough he was a distant relative of Gustav's, being in fact related by marriage to Charles E. (Chip) Bohlen, one-time United States Ambassador to Moscow and President Eisenhower's closest adviser on Russian affairs (and today's U.S. Ambassador to France). Bohlen shares the same great-great-grandfather as Alfried. Thayer looked the premises over but turned them down for General Clark's purposes. Instead, the castle was commandeered as a home for war refugees and Gustav and his family had to move into a near-by coaching inn that also served as the servants' annex to the castle—which was where the Allied team of doctors found them on 6 November 1945.

A stroke at the beginning of the year had left Gustav paralysed, unable to speak, hear, walk, or even eat, except with help. He had long suffered bouts of giddiness and faintness, and a succession of falls had virtually immobilised him even before the stroke. Although he was to linger in this limbo between life and death for another five years, to the doctors from Nuremberg it was obvious he was too senile to stand trial. What is less obvious is how no one had discovered his unfitness to plead a lot sooner. Apparently the first indication was when, early in October, James H. Rowe Jr., formerly one of President Roosevelt's legal aides, had travelled to Blühnbach to serve the Nuremberg indictment on Gustav. Unable to make himself understood to the old man, Rowe had merely left a copy of the indictment on the bed. Certainly no one among the British prosecutors had bothered to find out. Airey Neave, who in August 1945 had been put in charge of the team collecting evidence against Gustav, relates how he and his assistants were still at it even after the defence's application for a trial postponement had been heard. The doctors' report came as a complete surprise to them and their initial reaction was one of fury at having apparently been wasting their time. To be fair to the British, it is likely that the confusion arose because, as Essen was in the British Zone of occupation, the brunt of preparing the case against Gustav fell on them, whereas the responsibility for furnishing the body, as it were, rested with the Americans in whose zone Blühnbach Castle lay.

As though angry themselves too, the American prosecutors, backed by the Russians, now proposed that Gustav be tried *in absentia* or if that proved unfeasible that Alfried should be put in his place. Robert Jackson, the chief American counsel for the prosecution, thought that "public interests, which transcend all private considerations, require that Krupp von Bohlen shall not be dismissed unless some other representative of the Krupp armament and munitions interests be substituted . . . the United States respectfully submits that no greater disservice to the future peace of the world could be done than to excuse the entire Krupp family." In the bill of particulars accompanying the indictment against Gustav, Jackson had described the firm and family of Krupp as "the focus, the symbol, and the beneficiary of the most sinister forces engaged in menacing the peace of Europe".

The British and French, however, were reluctant to have anything to do with trying Gustav in his absence, saying that for one thing such a practice would not be permitted even under the American legal code, let alone under the British or French—and as for Alfried standing trial in his father's stead, Sir Hartley Shawcross, the leading British prosecutor at Nuremberg, was adamantly against this, arguing, in terms he thought the Americans might appreciate, that they were "in a court of justice not on a football field" and that "we couldn't play a substitute simply because one of the existing team of criminals had fallen ill". Lord Justice Lawrence, the eminent English jurist who presided over the Nuremberg Tribunal, was inclined to favour Shawcross's argument, as indeed was the French judge, Donnedieu de Vabres. Within a week of receiving the medical commission's report, the Tribunal announced their decision not to proceed with the case against Gustav, but to leave the indictment as it stood on the court's records against the possibility of a later trial should he ever recover.

Shawcross for his part had not excluded the possibility of

Alfried being eventually tried on his own account. In fact, while the trial of Goering and the other chief Nazis was still going on, he discussed with his fellow American, French and Russian prosecutors the question of their having another major trial of war criminals similarly organised by the four powers combined and in which a Krupp could figure. But the Americans were already beginning to feel the strain of co-operating with the Russians even in those early relatively halcyon days. Accordingly they expressed their reluctance to embark on another "Nuremberg". For a time the idea was entertained of a joint Anglo-American trial of one of the Krupps, but in the end the Americans opposed even this— and so, as the Americans from the start had really been more concerned than anyone else with the economic activities of the Nazis, the British handed over to them all the evidence they had been accumulating against Gustav in case they should ever want to try his son Alfried.

Indeed, once the International Military Tribunal had been disbanded after handing down its verdicts on the major Nazi leaders at Nuremberg in October 1946, the Americans in fact decided to go ahead on their own with prosecuting the German industrial bosses. Their interest by now had narrowed to the Big Three of German Big Business: Friedrich Flick, who had created the vast Vereinigte Stahlwerke and had financed Hitler in his early days, the directors of IG Farben, the giant chemical concern which had made most of the gases for the gas chambers, and of course Alfried.

Until the indictment was served on him in August 1947, Alfried was not allowed to consult lawyers of his own choosing. This had, however, not prevented other people, particularly members of his family, from preparing his defence. It was true that the Allied prosecutors had had a head start since they had begun the case against Gustav way back in August 1945, but there were some who had got in even before them, as Airey Neave for one vouches. When he searched the Essen headquarters of the House of Krupp that autumn immediately after the war, he found empty safes and empty filing cabinets, together with the burnt remains of letters and documents, suggesting that there had been some sort of systematic clean-out of perhaps the most incriminating papers. Even so, as the trial progressed, enough damning documentation came forward, particularly in the accounts of victims as well as eyewitnesses of the cruelty meted out to slave-workers in the Krupp factories—enough to make the guilt of Alfried and most of the other defendants clear beyond all doubt.

And so on 8 December 1947 "The case of the United States of America versus Alfried Felix Alwyn Krupp von Bohlen und Halbach, *et al.*"—the case known in the Nuremberg annals as simply "Case Number Ten"—opened in the same dirty-grey sandstone Palace of Justice building in which Gustav had been commanded to appear two years before. Alfried himself occupied the selfsame corner seat in the dock as Reichmarshal Herman Goering had during the 216 days of his trial. Alfried's appearance in the dock was to be almost as long—eight months in all. Indeed before the verdicts were delivered on 31 July 1948 some 227 witnesses were to be called, the prosecution was to introduce over 1,400 pieces of written evidence and the defence at least twice that number, the English transcript of the court's proceedings was to exceed 4,000,000 words. Krupp's for so long had liked to consider themselves a "special case" within German affairs. Now the Allies, in the persons of the Americans, were taking that Krupp boast to its logical conclusion and were treating the House of Krupp as a special case in international law, indeed as *Case Number Ten*.

Arraigned in the dock with Alfried were eleven other leading members of his firm. Among them Ewald Loeser in spite of the part he had played in the abortive anti-Hitler *putsch* of 20 July 1944; Erich Mueller the head of the artillery designing department, who had been closely involved with such projects as Fat Gustav; Heinrich Korschen, overseer of the various enterprises Krupp's had plundered in eastern and south-eastern Europe; and Friedrich von Bülow, chief of military and political counter-intelligence at Krupp's and their liaison man with both the Gestapo and the SS.

The judges who were to hear the trial were a curious bunch. Naturally they were all Americans. But since the United States Supreme Court had refused to spare American

federal judges, the war crimes people had had to make do
with men from the State Courts. Presiding over Case
Number Ten was a seventy-five-year-old judge from the
Tennessee Court of Appeals, Hugh C. Anderson. Unfortunately Anderson had a particular stomach complaint
which meant that he had frequently to leave the courtroom
and therefore the brunt of following the proceedings fell on
his two colleagues. They were fifty-five-year-old Judge
Edward James Daly of the Superior Court of the State of
Connecticut and fifty-year-old Judge William J. Wilkins of
the Superior Court in Seattle, Washington.

Defending Alfried was Otto Kranzbuehler who had been
Admiral Doenitz's choice of counsel during the trial of the
major war criminals. He had distinguished himself then
from the other defence lawyers by ostentatiously wearing his
German naval uniform throughout the whole of the Nuremberg proceedings. As Case Number Ten was to be conducted
according to American rather than German court procedure, Alfried had tried to hire an American lawyer—
Earl J. Carroll of California. But this the judges had declined
to allow. Petulantly, Alfried had threatened to withdraw
his counsel altogether, but the court had retaliated by
appointing Kranzbuehler an official defence aide, which
meant that he could not back out even if he wanted to.
Shortly after the proceedings began, one of the other defence
lawyers argued too vehemently with the prosecution for the
judges' taste, so much so that he was suspended—where-
upon the whole of the defence team, all thirty of them, filed
out of the courtroom and were only returned to their seats
under an armed guard. Six of them were in fact given three-
day prison sentences for contempt of court.

Leading for the prosecution was another Nuremberg "old
hand"—Colonel Telford Taylor, who had been Robert
Jackson's number two at the Nazi leaders' trial. Before
being drafted into the army, Taylor had served with Henry
Wallace on various New Deal agencies. He was just one year
older than Alfried but had worn better.

Alfried's thirty-two months of continuous custody was
beginning to make its mark on him. All too clearly he was
now no longer the dapper, well-groomed, scrupulously-

dressed man as seen with Hitler and the other Nazi leaders
in the photographs Airey Neave had found by the score in his
searches at the Villa Hügel during August 1945. Occasionally Alfried even turned up in the courtroom sporting a few
days' growth of beard on his chin and cheeks—a thing he
never would have done before. His face had become drawn and
haggard; he was beginning to look more and more like old
Alfred. His expression was serious—at times even almost
vacant. He appeared much older than his forty years.

The Krupp directors, including Alfried, were charged
under the same four main headings as the major war
criminals had been: that is, with having committed crimes
against peace, war crimes, and crimes against humanity, and
with having participated in a common plan or conspiracy to
commit crimes against peace and humanity. In the words
of the American indictment:

> These crimes included planning, preparing, initiating
> and waging wars of aggression and invasions of other
> countries, as a result of which incalculable destruction
> was wrought throughout the world, millions of people
> were killed, and many millions more suffered and are still
> suffering; deportation to slave labour of members of the
> civilian population of the invaded countries and the
> enslavement, mistreatment, torture, and murder of
> millions of persons, including German nationals as well
> as foreign nationals; plunder and spoliation of public
> and private property in the invaded countries pursuant
> to deliberate plans and policies intended not only to
> strengthen Germany in launching its invasions and wag-
> ing its aggressive wars and to secure the permanent
> domination by Germany of the continent of Europe,
> but also to expand the private empire of the defendants.

Case Number Ten is unique. If Gustav had stood trial
alongside Goering and the others the recitation of his misdeeds would have merely been an addition to an already
vast and mounting catalogue of corporate villainy. For
another thing, the delay of two years had enabled the
British and American investigators to delve more deeply.
But more especially, the singling out of Alfried and his eleven

Krupp confrères for a separate trial meant that for the first time the century-old machinations of that industrial colossus, the House of Krupp, could be publicly revealed and legally condemned. Because, as the prosecution's indictment made clear and the chief American counsel's opening speech made obvious, it was not the dozen defendants in the dock who were being tried in that dark-panelled courtroom, but the history and the heritage of the House of Krupp—that is what makes Case Number Ten perhaps the most historic, apart from the most histrionic, trial in the whole Nuremberg series.

Most German writers on the subject, particularly the official Krupp historians and biographers, have not realised —or have refused to realise—what the American prosecution team, backed by their British researchers and investigators, were trying to do beneath the solitary Stars and Stripes banner and amid all the microphones and the earpieces of the simultaneous translators during those winter, spring and early summer days of 1947 and 1948. It was a murderous machine and a mean method of making profits out of other people's miseries that was being judged, not a group of morally weak and cowardly concupiscent minor creatures. That Alfried should be free today and one of the richest men alive, that the House of Krupp should have once more attained a position of prominence and power not just in Germany but in the world, might seem to suggest that Colonel Taylor and his team failed at Nuremberg during those fateful eight months of bickering and bombast. But that is far from so. The stigma of "convicted war criminal" has been fastened for ever on a scion of the Krupp family, and those massive misdeeds in a century of blood and booty have once and for all been nailed to the name of Krupp. That is what Case Number Ten was all about.

Colonel Taylor's opening speech was so lengthy that at times he had to stand down while other members of his team read it for him. He lumped Krupp's with the other German militarists as "the indestructible common denominator of Germany's murderous and obstinately repeated lunges at the world's throat". Of all the names that had appeared in the Nuremberg indictments none, he argued, had been known for so long as that of Krupp. Nazism, he suggested, "was, after all, only the temporary political manifestation of certain ideas and attitudes which long antedated Nazism, and which will not perish nearly as easily". In the case that was before the court, he respectfully submitted, "we are at grips with something much older than Nazism; something which fused with Nazi ideas to produce the Third Reich, but which has its own independent and pernicious vitality". To Taylor, "the tradition of the Krupp firm and the 'social-political attitude' for which it stood was exactly suited to the moral climate of the Third Reich. There was no crime such a state could commit—whether it was war, plunder, or slavery—in which these men would not participate."

His speech was emotional and polemical. It was impressive and damning. But it was also unwieldy and perhaps the wrong tactic for the matter at hand—for immediately after the prosecution had concluded its main case, having taken some three months to do so, the defence surprised everyone by filing an application for the acquittal of all the defendants on the first and final counts, namely that of having waged aggressive war and of having conspired to wage aggressive war. What is more, the court upheld their plea. But this was in fact only half a feather in the cap of Otto Kranzbuehler and his team, for it meant that the court had now to focus its attentions on the two remaining counts, that of Krupp's having plundered and exploited the occupied countries and of having enslaved their citizens—and it was on these two counts that the prosecution was to produce its most damaging and devastating evidence of all, particularly damaging and devastating for the life-long pose of Krupp's as a "good" employer of labour.

Evidence was produced, for example, that Alfried had on 22 July 1942 attended a meeting with Albert Speer, Hitler's Minister for Armament and War Production, at which it was decided, in Colonel Taylor's words, "to impress 45,000 Russian civilian workers into the steel plant, 120,000 prisoners of war and 6,000 Russian civilians into the coal-mines and to place the medical standards for recruiting prisoners of war lower than those required of Germans employed in coal-mines".

Krupp executives used to make raids into the occupied

countries to choose at first hand the men to impress into Alfried's employ—rather like the naval "press gangs" of yore. Unbeknown to him they even forced one of his distant relatives, a Dutchman, to work and live in abominable conditions in Essen. Krupp women workers were specially trained by the SS to act as guards for the female slave-labourers—and witnesses galore testified to the cruelty of their behaviour.

Although the exact number of slave-workers used in the various Krupp armament establishments is not known, because the relevant documents were destroyed by Alfried's men during the closing days of the war, estimates put the figure as high as 75,000—and on top of this, it was alleged, some 21,000 French, Russian and Yugoslav prisoners of war were put to work for Krupp. Following that well-established economic principle of "locating units of production near to known pools of labour", Krupp's in 1943 actually built a factory for making shell-fuses inside Auschwitz itself—the extermination camp where perhaps the most villainous Nazi atrocities of all were perpetrated. In addition, about 5,000 concentration-camp inmates took part in constructing Krupp's new Berthawerke at Markstadt near Breslau in 1942—while further thousands were employed in the munitions plant once it was operating. All this was done with the approval of Alfried and the other directors, indeed Alfried acknowledged that he had watched the construction work four or five times and had also visited the nearby concentration camp from whence the workers all came.

But it was in the actual treatment of the slave-workers and the forced-labourers in their employ that Krupp's came in for the biggest condemnation by the court. Dr. Wilhelm Jaeger, the so-called "senior doctor" for these concentration-camp inmates at Krupp's, related in an affidavit how on taking over his job he had visited some hutments in Essen where over 600 Jewish girls and women who had been brought from Buchenwald to work for Krupp were living:

Upon my first visit I found these females suffering from open festering wounds and other diseases. I was the first doctor they had seen for at least a fortnight. . . . There were no medical supplies. . . . They had no shoes and went about in their bare feet. The sole clothing of each consisted of a sack with holes for their arms and head. Their hair was shorn. The camp was surrounded by barbed wire and closely guarded by SS guards. The amount of food in the camp was extremely meagre and of very poor quality. . . . I reported to my superiors that the guards lived and slept outside their barracks as one could not enter them without being attacked by ten, twenty, and up to fifty fleas. As a result of this attack by insects of the camp, I got large boils on my arms and the rest of my body.

Evidently Dr. Jaeger tried to interest some of the Krupp directors and even Alfried's personal physician in the plight of these unfortunate people, but all to no avail. Of another Krupp work-camp in Essen where French prisoners of war were living, Jaeger had this to say:

Its inhabitants were kept for nearly half a year in dog kennels, urinals and old bake houses. The dog kennels, were three feet high, nine feet long, six feet wide. Five men slept in each of them. The prisoners had to crawl into these kennels on all fours. . . . There was no water in the camp.

Workers from the East, however, fared worst of all:

The clothing of the eastern workers was likewise completely inadequate. They worked and slept in the same clothing in which they had arrived from the East. Virtually all of them had no overcoats and were compelled, therefore, to use their blankets as coats in cold and rainy weather. In view of the shortage of shoes many workers were forced to go to work in their bare feet, even in winter. . . . Sanitary conditions were exceedingly bad. At Kramerplatz only ten children's toilets were available for 1,200 inhabitants. . . . Excretion contaminated the entire floors of these lavatories. . . . The Tartars and Kirghis suffered most; they collapsed like flies from bad housing, the poor quality and insufficient quantity of food, overwork and insufficient rest. These workers were likewise afflicted with spotted fever. Lice, the carrier of the disease, together with countless fleas, bugs and other vermin tortured the inhabitants of these camps. . . . At times the water supply at the camps was shut off for periods of eight to fourteen days.

Inevitably the witnesses who appeared in person had the biggest impact of all on the court. Take for instance a twenty-five-year-old Czech girl called Elizabeth Roth who in 1944 had been shipped with her sister from Auschwitz to Essen after both their parents had been gassed:

When we arrived at Essen we lived in wooden barracks. It was August. On October 23rd there was an air-raid when all the barracks were burnt-down. Then we moved into one barrack, all the 500 of us, where the kitchen was before. We stayed there until January 12th 1945, when there was another air-raid. Then we moved into the cellar: we worked, no light, no heat, no baths, nothing at all. . . . We were beaten in the factory and beaten in the camp. We were kicked. We were beaten by the SS men, not by the soldiers, by the SS men in the factories.

And then there was the macabre exchange of letters on Krupp-headed notepaper which the court was shown:

To: Herr von Bülow,
We still need urgently ten leather truncheons or similar weapons for clubbing for our shock squads. As we have learned you still have such items in store we beg you to hand over the requested ten pieces to the messenger.
(signed) Herr Linder.

For discussion with Herr Wilshaus:
Do we still have any weapons of the black jack type?
(signed) von Bülow

To: Herr von Bülow,
I can supply the ten leather truncheons or steel birches.
(signed) Herr Wilshaus.

There were also enough stories to do with small children and young babies to make the heart weep for many a long year—stories of them being separated from their mothers and put in the charge of insensitive harridans without any experience of child care. The death rate among them was so high that even the usually thorough Krupp clerks did not bother to keep a close tally.

When he came to make his one and only statement at the end—this little procedure was of his own choosing, the court would have preferred him to have answered each and every point as it arose—to all these details of villainy, Alfried merely hid behind the defence that he did not know what his subordinates were up to and that they had not cared to tell him. To which of course the conscience of the world could only reply "Did you never bother to find out for yourself?"

He admitted to the presence of slave-workers and forced-labourers on his various plants, but argued, "These circumstances consisted, on the one hand, in a certain moral pressure exerted by the authorities in regard to an intensified production programme and to the employment of non-German workers, and, on the other hand, in the fact that the normally available manpower resources became more and more inadequate and finally gave out completely". And to the charge of having plundered the occupied countries, Alfried merely said, "This charge will remain incomprehensible to anyone who knows international economic relations" —and he went on, "Economics go beyond national borders in peace as well as in war."

To the three American judges, as indeed to the thinking world, his replies were not enough. When they came to deliver their verdicts on that last day of July 1948, Alfried was found guilty on both the counts of spoliation and slave-labour and was sentenced to twelve years. In addition, his property was ordered to be confiscated. Of the other eleven accused along with him, only one, Karl Pfirsch, head of the Krupp war materials sales department, was completely acquitted. The rest were all found guilty of the slave-labour charge, and five of them, as well as Alfried, guilty too of the plunder charge. Mueller and von Bülow both got twelve years like Alfried. Loeser got seven and Korschen six, while the shortest sentence was one of two years ten months meted out to Hans Kupke who had been in charge of some of the foreign workers' camps at Essen.

The additional sentence for Alfried of property confiscation came as a shock to many people. Although Stalin had proposed it at Yalta for all convicted war criminals, and the Soviet representative on the International Military Tribunal had brought it up again during the preparatory talks at Nuremberg before the major trials opened there in November 1945, the Americans in particular had always appeared adamantly opposed to the notion—indeed Robert Jackson, Colonel Taylor's predecessor as Chief Prosecuting Counsel for War Crimes, had described it as "somewhat obsolete as a punishment . . . like drawing and quartering".

On the other hand it would also seem that at least one of Alfried's judges might have wanted his punishments to have been even harsher, since in a dissenting minority judgement Judge Wilkins of Seattle declared:

I have no hesitancy in stating that in my opinion the vast amount of credible evidence justifies the conclusion that the growth and expansion of the Krupp firm at the expense of industrial plants in foreign countries were uppermost in the minds of these defendants throughout the war years. This huge octopus, the Krupp firm, with its body at Essen, swiftly unfolded one of its tentacles behind each new aggressive push of the Wehrmacht and sucked back into Germany much that could be of value to Germany's war effort and to the Krupp firm in particular. It is abundantly clear from the credible evidence that those directing the Krupp firm during the war years were motivated by one main desire: that upon the successful termination of the war for Germany the Krupp concern would be firmly established with permanent plants in the conquered territories and even beyond the seas. This was more than a dream. It was nearing completion with each successful thrust of the Wehrmacht. That this growth and expansion on the part of the Krupp firm was due in large measure to the favoured position it held with Hitler there can be little doubt. The close relationship between the Krupp firm on the one hand and the Reich Government, particularly the Army and Navy High Commands, on the other hand, amounted to a veritable alliance.

Alfried, it can certainly be said, behaved throughout the long court proceedings with great dignity and restraint. He had listened to the arguments of both the defence and the prosecution impassively and quietly. There had been no show of emotion at any time. Even when the sentences were were being read out his face displayed no feeling. "It was a mask", an eye-witness declared, "the mask of an exceedingly cold man."

So, with Alfried's property confiscated, a prison sentence of twelve years to be faced, 30 per cent of the works destroyed in the bombing and now another 40 per cent in the process of being dismantled and dismembered by the victorious Allies, the fall of the House of Krupp seemed pretty well complete. Yet even as the massive gates of Landsberg Jail were closing behind him—the same jail in which Hitler had been held in 1924 and where he had written *Mein Kampf*—world events were beginning to move in Alfried's favour. Already the pressures were starting to mount for an early release.

CHAPTER FIFTEEN

"Time will settle all"

WAR CRIMINAL Prison Number One, to which Alfried was taken from Nuremberg, was situated in the ancient fortress of Landsberg high above the river Lech in Bavaria. Landsberg had at one time been a mediaeval stronghold, but since Kaiser William's days had almost exclusively been used as a prison. Apart from his fellow Krupp directors and executives who had been sentenced along with him, Alfried shared Landsberg with some 200 other war criminals: Gestapo chiefs, heads of SS extermination squads, concentration-camp commandants, Wehrmacht generals, gauleiters, many of them as yet unsentenced, others convicted and awaiting execution.

Decked in a red-and-white striped prison uniform, Alfried was at first subjected to the same strict routine as the rest. Called at 6.30 every morning and expected to get up immediately, he had then to empty the "swill bucket" which served as both urinal and refuse-bin in his cell. Meals were eaten on command and Alfried had to take his turn like any other inmate at working in the kitchens or the laundry, in the gardens or the repair-shops. As the present-day Krupp public-relations men never tire of telling one, Alfried while at Landsberg shaped crucifixes and candlesticks in the prison smithy, some of which found their way into the prison chapel.

But Landsberg was of course no Belsen. Alfried's jailors where American G.I.s and it was not long before they were relaxing a few of the more rigorous rules and regulations. For instance, Alfried and some of his fellow prisoners were permitted to read newspapers, to write as many letters as they wished, to receive visitors as frequently as they liked.

They could smoke, and a blind eye was invariably turned on the copious food and other luxuries that were smuggled into them from friends outside. Although certain of his later biographers have tried to claim that during his stay at Landsberg he kept scrupulously out of politics and avoided having anything to do with his former factory-kingdom, the fact of the matter is that Alfried maintained a very close contact with Essen and with Krupp's. Lawyers with bulging briefcases would descend on him from time to time, and as free discussion was permitted among the prisoners it was perhaps inevitable that Alfried and his directors and executives should eventually hold in Landsberg what can only be described as unofficial board meetings.

All his life, Alfried had been used only to talk of production schedules and output charts, of delivery dates and budget targets, of profit margins and financial statements. His father knew few other topics of conversation—and friends of Alfried vouch that he had little "small talk" either. It was perhaps too much to expect of that sort of man that he should suddenly change his ways and think of starting his life anew. Instead, there is reason to believe that just as one Adolf Hitler used his time in Landsberg to plot out the course of his future career and to consider afresh his ambition and his goal, so Alfried Krupp pondered day in and day out during his two and a half years in that selfsame Bavarian fortress exactly how he was going to rebuild the House of Krupp and precisely what form the reborn factory-kingdom was to take.

His fellow prisoners did not share his optimism, nor did his former workers. But—and this is the most intriguing aspect of the rise of the House of Krupp—they had faith in him. Herr Alfried would bring them out of their difficulties. They had only to remain loyal and true to the House of Krupp and all would be well for them. Admittedly, they had a financial incentive to do so, since for most of them their "pension rights" in the firm were the only savings they had against old age—and some of course had recently passed the normal retiring time and were already due for a company pension. In addition there were the old employees who had not been paid their pensions since 1945 and who were suffering perhaps more than most from the terrible poverty of the post-war years. Significantly—and one must also say brilliantly and shrewdly—one of the first things Alfried did when he became boss again in 1953 was to pay his pensioners what they were owed, even though it cost him nearly £2 million and he had to sell off some of his land to do it. He knew then that he was going to have to rely on his workers' enthusiasm and devotion to rebuild Krupp's and he knew too that it was due to his employees' loyalty that there was anything left at all on which to base his firm's recovery.

But there is evidence that this loyalty sprang from other, as well as monetary, causes. There were for instance all those hundreds of letters that descended on the Nuremberg court-room both before as well as during Alfried's trial—letters purporting to come from ordinary Krupp workmen, Krupp foremen, Krupp pensioners, even from some who had been sacked by Krupp's. All expressed deep sympathy for the "head of the House" and all begged the tribunal to acquit him. At the time they did Alfried more harm than good with his judges—and journalists who heard about them were inclined to dismiss them as at best a clumsy sort of defence stunt or at worst yet a further indication of the absence of any feeling of guilt or desire for atonement on the part of the average German worker. But the letter-writers could have been sincere.

Then again, the Kruppians who were pressed into dis-mantling and into destroying Alfried's former munitions factories showed little enthusiasm or zeal for the job, as those unfortunate Englishmen whose task it was to supervise them can well vouch. Perhaps this was only natural and might well have been echoed by other long-serving work-men in similar situations elsewhere. But there were many servants and officials of the House of Krupp who were to boast afterwards how they had personally seen to it that the Allies' plans were thwarted and the British administrators were cheated, that the work of demolition was delayed and that essential equipment and key machinery were "saved for Herr Alfried". The British in particular were to under-estimate this *Kruppianer* spirit and it is from a feeling of having been somehow duped that much of the resentment and some of the antagonism towards Krupp's astonishing revival since 1953 springs.

But while Alfried and his colleagues, after their conviction, were planning their firm's recovery in the comparative comfort and absolute security of Landsberg jail, the Krupp workers—as indeed all the people of the Ruhr—were having a hard struggle to find food and shelter and warmth, were having a hard struggle in fact to keep alive. It was true that conditions had improved enormously from the nadir of 1947 when Herbert Hoover, the former American President, had reported to the United States Congress that in his estimation the Germans had sunk to a level of under-nourishment unknown in the Western world for at least a hundred years. Even so, in Essen for instance in late 1948 men, women, and children were still sleeping on the floors of railway stations, babies were being born in cellars, and families were being brought up in former air-raid shelters, nicknamed "bunker-hotels".

At first the official Allied attitude towards all this had been one by and large of letting the Germans "stew in their own juice", as a forthright American general put it, while every effort was concentrated on getting those countries that had suffered cruelly from Nazi aggression back on their feet again. But it was not long before food and clothing were pouring into Germany and not long either before many of the restrictions on a German recovery were being lifted.

It was not simply a humanitarian impulse that led the Allies—and particularly the Americans—to change their tune towards Germany. It was rather a calculated response to the differing circumstances of world politics after the war—a response which many neutral observers found hypocritical as they interpreted the well-publicised shipments of American grain to Hamburg or of British bacon to the Ruhr or of Russian clothing to Berlin as more of a battle for the hearts and minds of Germans by way of their stomachs and their backs than as a gesture of charity and mercy. Yet at the same time it was a response that was perhaps all too easy to dismiss as just so much cynicism and politicking.

Almost from the very moment the last German general had surrendered the last German soldier and the final inch of

Hitler's Reich had been won, the British and American administrators in Germany found their every action thwarted and their every move regarded with suspicion by their former Russian allies. For instance, on the very day the International Military Tribunal sentenced Goering and the other top Nazis, the *New York Times* carried the report of a Russian charge that the United States was already planning an atomic war against the Soviet peoples. Even in the spring of 1946, less than a year after the Allied victory, the Government-controlled press in Moscow described Winston Churchill as a "Hitler-like warmonger" and an "imperialist aggressor". In 1946 too were the first of what were to be a whole series of dramatic disclosures of widespread and successful Russian spy networks operating in North America.

1947 found the French desperately combating a Communist-led revolt in Indo-China and the British helping the Greeks to put down a Communist uprising in their country. In the Balkans and Poland the last façades of co-operation between the Communist and the non-Communist parties had crumbled. On the second anniversary of VE day the Soviet press had sought to belittle Britain's and America's contributions to the victory over Germany. In the very month that Alfried's trial had opened, a succession of particularly bitter attacks on America by Russian officials in Germany had prompted General Clay, the U.S. Military Governor there, to launch a massive counter-propaganda campaign extolling the virtues of democracy and capitalism as opposed to Communism. Already the Soviets had so tightened their grip on the Eastern Zone that it had become to all intents and purposes a complete Russian satellite. The Iron Curtain had become a reality.

In February 1948 came the Communist coup in Czechoslovakia—while a month later Marshal Sokolovsky proclaimed the end of the Four Powers Control Council for Berlin. On 24 June, just a little over a month before the three American judges were to convict Alfried and his Krupp colleagues of war crimes, the Russians began their blockade of Berlin. "Time will settle all", Alfried told one of his fellow prisoners shortly after they were taken to Landsberg—and as the months ticked by of the Berlin airlift it became increasingly clear that time was on Krupp's side.

It is perhaps the biggest irony of all in the German experience after 1945 that it was the Americans who were at first the most harsh in their attempts to prevent their soldiers from fraternising with individual Germans, were the most zealous in their hunting down of known Nazis, were the most strict in their interpretation of the Potsdam Agreement which called for the break-up of the big German industrial concerns (while the British favoured a unit no larger than 100,000 employees, the Americans would brook nothing bigger than 3,000 employees), and by and large were the most adamant in their opposition to a German recovery—whereas the British suggested an annual steel output for Germany of something like 9,000,000 tons, Washington wanted the figure as low as 3,000,000 and remonstrated with General Clay when he agreed on a compromise production rate of 5,800,000 tons. Yet in the end they were the most enthusiastic and the most earnest in their wish to restore the German economy, and were certainly the most generous of all the Allies in their bounty and their help towards such a restoration.

This volte-face in American policy towards Germany did not of course happen overnight. It was rather a slow development, though its stages can be clearly discerned. The first crack in the icy approach to their former foe was largely a genuinely humanitarian response to the poverty and wretchedness which individual Americans such as Herbert Hoover found in Germany. Hoover's report certainly struck a sympathetic chord in some quarters in Washington and prompted a somewhat reluctant State Department into easing the repressive restrictions on aid to individual Germans.

Then in March 1947 came the so-called Truman Doctrine which was the first and the most concrete indication that the United States meant to stop the spread of Communism, meant to contain Russian power within the limits it had then reached—"thus far and no farther" was to be the American catchword for the next five years at least. It was a shattering step for a President from the isolationist middle-west to take because it meant that the United States was firmly committed to holding the Iron Curtain as a "frontier of freedom" and to preventing any seepage of Soviet influence into Western Germany. In June 1947 the Marshall Plan was announced whereby America offered money and aid-in-kind to the countries of Europe to help them repair their economies. Its rejection by Russia and all the territories within the Soviet orbit spelt the division of Europe into two camps—particularly when in December 1947 the United States widened the Plan's scope so as to embrace West Germany.

Even so, while the American and to a lesser extent the British Governments were making their plans for putting Germany back on her feet the gutting of German factories and the dismembering of German industrial empires went apace—though at the beginning of 1948 the United States announced a 60 per cent reduction in the number of factories and plants scheduled for demolition in their zone of occupation. Britain was really in a cleft stick over the dismantlings. On the one hand she was finding the cost of supporting her zone of occupation a colossal burden—particularly at a time of rationing and intense austerity at home. Yet any hint of being "soft to the Germans" or of "feeding 'Nazi mouths' while freedom-loving British stomachs went unfilled" brought an immediate outcry against the Labour Government of the day, who were in any case having to balance the xenophobia of their extreme left wing with the mounting pressures from their economic experts to reduce the British commitment in Germany. But on the other hand as well as being reluctant to be a party to a resurgence of German political power, Britain also feared the re-emergence of German industry as a competitor in her export markets. As a result Britain was inclined to do nothing particularly positive either way, but rather to leave the running to the Americans.

By 1948, the year of Alfried's conviction for war crimes, the Americans had already made up their minds to aid Germany's recovery both as a means of reducing the burden of having to support her indefinitely but more so as a way of creating a stable non-Communist cushion between the

Soviet satellites and such countries as France and Italy in which there was a real danger of a Communist takeover. First, the United States organised and backed the reform of the West German currency in June 1948 from which, all economists are agreed, Germany's astonishing and dramatic post-war recovery really dates. Then, the merging of the three western Allies' zones of occupation into a single political and economic unit was largely carried out under American initiative and through American prodding. The tensions of the Berlin blockade brought victors and vanquished closer together, while the success of the Berlin airlift tightened the bond of respect and admiration of Germans towards their British, French and American occupiers. By the time Alfried's first year in Landsberg was over, a West German Parliament was in being, the Allied military governors had been replaced by civilian high commissioners, and the North Atlantic Treaty Organisation was in existence. An East German State had also been proclaimed.

Alfried's first indication of just how these changing attitudes of victors towards vanquished might affect him personally came in fact only eight months after his conviction at Nuremberg—and significantly two weeks before the signing of the NATO alliance—when, following a plea by him to General Lucius Clay for a remission of sentence, the American Military Governor promulgated instead a decree "confirming and revising" the sentence. The revision, however, was a particularly crucial one, for under the original Nuremberg judgement Krupp's properties had been taken over by the Inter-Allied Control Council, that is by all four Allies. But now, on the argument that the Russians had rendered that Council powerless and redundant, Clay was altering the relevant paragraph in the sentence to make the confiscation of Krupp properties the responsibility of the military governors in the zones of occupation where they were located. It meant for instance that the Russians could do what they liked with the huge Krupp machine-works at Magdeburg in their zone, just as the Polish Communists had already got their hands on Krupp's Berthawerke at Markstaedt in Silesia. The bulk, however, of the Krupp properties lay in the western zones, particularly in the British zone, so it meant that the Russians were now excluded from all further discussions as to the eventual destination of Alfried and most of his millions—for what the West took away the West could give back, and whom the Americans had imprisoned the Americans could release. Once more the course of history was running a Krupp's way—and paradoxically Alfried's best ally from now on was to be the Kremlin, for the louder the anti-American noises and the more menacing the anti-American moves the men in Moscow made the more would Germans and Americans be pushed closer together. For in their determination to stop the spread of Communism the Americans became ready to accept the friendship of almost anyone, particularly anyone who could help strengthen the West's economy. German helpers were to be especially welcome, since Germany, it had been decided in Washington, was to be Europe's "shield" against the East. And what better and more sure German helper to do this than a Krupp, than Alfried Krupp. One can safely assume that Alfried saw to it that the Americans were made aware of his willingness to help them.

Circumstances from the summer of 1949 onwards moved ever more rapidly to Alfried's advantage. The lifting of the Berlin blockade in May increased the confidence of the West. In June the American State Department declared that "German reconstruction is essential to the well-being of Europe"—and in September John J. McCloy became the new American High Commissioner. A lawyer turned banker, McCloy unlike Clay whom he was now replacing had no record of opposition to a full German recovery or of repugnance to the old German industrial régime. He came from American Big Business himself and was to prove a good friend to German Big Business.

Ironically, another good friend of Krupp was to be the British High Commissioner, Sir Ivone Kirkpatrick, who had been one of the few plaintive voices in the British Embassy in Berlin during the 'thirties, for ever warning his Foreign Office superiors in London of the dangers of a resurgence of German power. Towards the end of 1949, even before his appointment as High Commissioner, but while he was Permanent Under-Secretary of the so-called German Section at the British Foreign Office, Kirkpatrick was already arguing in favour of a stronger Germany and of a firmer backing by Britain and the West to the new Federal Government of Konrad Adenauer. He was later to say of this period in his memoirs, "The British and American Governments soon recognised that if Dr. Adenauer's administration was not to perish of inanition it must be given more power and something must be done to meet the Germans on the twin issues of dismantling and restrictions on German industry." In November 1949 Kirkpatrick prodded the British Foreign Secretary, Ernest Bevin, into persuading the French to agree to Germany being numbered among the "freedom-loving nations of the West" and to reducing some of the restrictions on German recovery, particularly to relaxing the dismantling programme which the Americans wanted to stop completely. Time by now was really on Krupp's side.

But the event that in the end tipped the scales fully Alfried's way was the Korean War which broke out in the summer of 1950. By Christmas of that year Western diplomats, especially American diplomats, were worrying lest Germany were to be the next "flash-point" on the Communists' list. All that summer and autumn, newspapers and magazines in Germany, regaining their confidence and preferring now to pander to their readers rather than as previously to flatter their occupiers, had been indulging in a veritable orgy of criticism of the conduct of many of the trials of war criminals, such as Alfried's. Petitions for clemency had been pouring into the offices of the Allied High Commissioners in Bonn from people such as the new West German President, Theodor Heuss, and the new West German Chancellor, Konrad Adenauer. The Americans were particularly sensitive at this stage to criticism from their newly found German friends—while on top of everything Kirkpatrick was continually pleading with his colleagues "to get Germany committed", an argument which went down well of course with McCloy. Just before 1950 finally gave way to 1951—and significantly a few days after the Chinese Communists had entered the Korean War—Alfried and his fellow Krupp prisoners in Landsberg heard that their sentences were being reviewed and that it was now extremely likely that they would be released early in the New Year.

Although the old year was now going out in great triumph for Alfried, it had in fact begun in sadness. On 16 January 1950, Gustav had finally died. For the last five years of his dismal struggle against death in the little coaching inn at Bluhnbach he had had Bertha almost constantly by his side. "Today all Germany stands in mourning at the coffin of one of her greatest sons", declared the Lutheran Minister at Gustav's cremation. But the turmoil of international politics that January, the world's pressmen paid scant attention to the passing of perhaps the most contemptible Krupp of all time—of the man who in adopting the name of Krupp brought as much infamy to the family as any pure-born Krupp before or since.

Shortly after her husband's death, Bertha had made a bid herself to win back the Krupp millions. She had sought to persuade the Allies to set aside the *Lex Krupp* on the ground that Hitler had imposed it on her and her family. She also had in mind to disinherit Alfried by claiming that in 1943 he had unlawfully taken unto himself the sole possession of the House of Krupp against her wishes as the true descendant of Alfred and Friedrich Krupp—and that, now Gustav was dead and Alfried was in prison, the ownership of the Krupp properties should revert to her and her other children. Needless to say the Allied authorities did not fall for Bertha's wiles—but she need hardly have bothered, for the New Year was going to see her family firmly back on the road to power and possession.

CHAPTER SIXTEEN

"There is no question of Krupp being allowed to assume either ownership or control of the former Krupp industrial empire"

THE OFFICIAL announcement that Alfried and his colleagues were to be released was made on 31 January 1951. It came shortly after American morale during the Korean War had reached its lowest ebb: Seoul, the South Korean capital, had just been captured for the second time by the Communists, while the United States Eighth Army had retreated 275 miles from the Yalu River, the longest retreat in American military history.

McCloy had in fact chosen to proclaim a more general amnesty—commuting the death sentences on nearly all the Nazi war criminals awaiting execution at that time and reducing the terms of imprisonment for the rest, in most cases to the time they had already served. He had also to many people's surprise decided to cancel the order confiscating Krupp's properties—it had not been expected that he would go quite that far. McCloy's justification for his generosity was that no other war criminal had been punished in this way:

> Confiscation of personal property does not belong to the practices of our legal system and in general is in contradiction of the American conception of justice. I am not able, on the basis of the evidence against the accused Krupp, to find any degree of personal guilt which would put him above all the others sentenced by the Nuremberg courts.

Later, when challenged by a number of eminent Americans to explain himself further, McCloy described his decision to release Krupp as the most "wearing" he had ever had to make. But to his eternal shame, in my opinion at least, he also endeavoured to play down the charges of slave-labour brought against Alfried at Nuremberg. The German press, however, were in no doubt as to the real reason for the release. They saw it simply as one of necessity for the Americans rather than of choice.

And so the incredible had happened. The Krupps were living up to their reputation for being indestructible. As with Gustav after the First World War, the pattern of arrest and early release was being repeated.

It took just three days to complete the formalities for Alfried's official return to freedom. Then on 3 February 1951 at precisely 9 a.m., while the cold, early morning mists were still shrouding the old Bavarian fortress, Krupp and his confrères walked out of the wicket-gate that served as Landsberg's side-entrance, clad in the warm overcoats their thoughtful American jailors had provided for them.

His younger brother Berthold was there to bunch him with a bouquet of tulips, his favourite flowers. In a puny attempt to escape the newspapermen and the photographers, Berthold had driven up to the prison in a battered old van specially chartered for the occasion and carrying the label "Snow White Laundry" emblazoned on its sides. But if Berthold had really thought the world's press were going to take this incident in the life of the House of Krupp so lightly then he was in for a rude awakening.

Ironically it was British newsmen who made the loudest and the most anguished noises of the lot—whereas of course it had been the British who had been the least enthusiastic of all the Allies at Nuremberg towards the notion of trying Alfried. The *Sunday Chronicle*, for one, sounded off against him personally, describing Alfried as "one of the most calculating brains in Germany" and suggesting that it would not be long before he would be producing guns again. This sentiment was echoed by the *Sunday Pictorial* who said that Bertha must be rubbing her hands "with glee" at the prospect once more of all those profits from armaments. Even the usually moderate *Observer* declared that "the American decision means that dangerous lunatics will again be at large".

Curiously enough, French newspapers despite their longer history of animosity towards the Krupps were several decibels lower than the British in their denunciation of McCloy's decision. *Le Monde* for instance merely referred to "the odium which after three wars has come to be associated with Krupp" and contented itself with the comment that no doubt Alfried would be prepared to "reap the benefit" of producing guns again no matter who asked him to—though *L'Aube* on the other hand advised Alfried to "Disappear! We have seen enough of you!" As perhaps was only to be expected, the bulk of the American press backed their High Commissioner's action up to the hilt. In any case they were much more concerned with the reports of a new Chinese Communist offensive in Korea.

But even while the ticker-tape machines of the news agencies were still typing out the reports and the reactions to his release, Alfried had been whisked off by Berthold to a champagne breakfast in his honour at a local hotel. There he held his first public press conference ever. Inevitably someone asked him whether he would ever produce guns again—and his reply was one that was to be discussed and argued over for years afterwards as to its true intent. "I hope that it will never again be necessary for a Krupp to produce arms", he said, "but what a factory makes depends after all not only on the decisions of its owner but also on the politics of its government." To many people it sounded as though the Krupps had still not learned their lesson and that so far as Alfried was concerned expediency would always outweigh morality.

This reply, on top of his release, brought forth a flurry of protest in the British House of Commons. Prime Minister Attlee tried hard to reassure his belligerent back-benchers by declaring, "There is no question of Krupp being allowed to assume either ownership or control of the former Krupp industrial empire." But many observers, as the *Manchester Guardian* at the time pointed out, thought that precisely the opposite would happen. Said that paper's Bonn correspondent ten days after Alfried's release, "There is very little chance that the Federal German Government will discriminate against a man who is as powerful and as popular as

Herr Krupp"—and he went on to add, "as a coalition of the Right Wing it has no wish to alienate private property rights in a single invidious case". In this matter at least, the *Manchester Guardian*, as we all now know, was to be more prophetic than the British Foreign Office.

Although Essen's Lord Mayor had planned a massive homecoming for him, Alfried preferred to slip away to Blühnbach to see his mother. His grand re-entry into the city of the cannon kings could wait—and in any case there were many more battles to be fought yet before the final victory would be his.

For one thing, British typists and British officials still occupied the Villa Hügel, and a British Controller was still running what remained of Alfried's empire. The dismantlings by now had dropped to an almost insignificant trickle—and within two months of Alfried's release they had stopped altogether. All in all, according to the official statistics, some 201,000 tons of machinery and equipment, valued at more than £8 million, had been taken out of the Krupp factories and sent as reparations-in-kind to Russia and the other sufferers from Nazi aggression.

In May 1950 the Allied Control Council had decreed in its now famous Allied Law 27 that "excessive concentrations of economic power" be eliminated from German industry. As a result, the House of Krupp in particular had been stripped of all its coal-mines, iron-ore deposits, and steel mills, and these had been put in the hands of Allied trustees. But what remained had already begun to boom again even while Alfried was still in Landsberg—and especially after the West German currency reform of June 1948.

The Widia tungsten-carbide plant had been one of the first to be given the go-ahead by its British managers to start up large-scale production again, since the hard-cutting tools it turned out were needed for such essential industries as coal-mining. The Krupp railway-workshops had been used throughout the occupation to patch up the goods-wagons and the steam-locomotives that right from Essen's first capture by the Americans had been in great demand for getting the coal and the iron-ore moving again. In time these selfsame workshops had begun manufacturing new locomotives, some even for export to places like Indonesia and South Africa. Rheinhausen had also been re-opened for heavy engineering products such as boilers and parts for bridges to replace the broken ones that were still littering the Rhine. The U-boat yards at Kiel had long since been razed to the ground, but in their place had sprung up factories producing machine-tools and electrical instruments. All told, Krupp's in the month Alfried left Landsberg were giving employment to some 12,700 workers. Even so, this represented less than one-twelfth of the number at the height of the war.

Although a free man after six years behind Allied bars, Alfried had still to tread warily. He may have straightaway gone out and bought himself a fast sports-car and he may also have moved with Berthold into a plush flat in the smartest suburb in Essen, but as yet he did not know whether the Allies really meant to return to him what remained of his properties. It was still possible that they might prefer to dispose of them in other ways and simply to pay him some form of compensation.

But he did not wait for them to make up their minds. Instead, he immediately began bombarding the Allies with proposals and counter-proposals—some people called them threats and counter-threats. He hired the best American lawyers Krupp money could buy and used every contact he and they could muster to prod and to cajole, to pressure and to impress. The major point at issue was how to reconcile the American High Commissioner's decision to give Krupp back his millions with the Allied Law 27 which called not only for the old industrial empires in Germany to be broken up but also for a bar to be put on "the return to positions of ownership and control of those persons who have been found, or may be found, to have furthered the aggressive designs of the National-Socialist Party"—it was hard to see how Alfried could escape this specific prohibition.

The Americans, however, were impatient for an agreement. They were anxious at this time for the west Germans to make what was euphemistically described as a "contribution to the defence of Europe". But to their intense annoyance the German people were far from eager to rearm. To help them perhaps change their minds, Washington

had ordered its officials on the spot to grant the We
Germans almost anything they wanted. Time was of the ver
essence in getting the Federal Republic firmly committe
to the anti-Communist cause: in the Far East the Korea
War was settling down into an uneasy stalemate, while o:
the European front too there was no let-up in the Cold War
Once again the men in the Kremlin were proving the bes
bunch of allies a Krupp could possibly wish for.

But the French and the British were less enthusiastic anc
less eager than the Americans for an agreement with Krupp
solely on his own terms. They wanted "concrete guarantees'
from him first that he would abide by Law 27 even after the
Allies had pulled out of Germany entirely and that he would
not try to buy back at the earliest opportunity the coal-
mines, the iron-ore deposits, and the steel mills that had been
unscrambled from his empire. Moreover, they were demanding from him an assurance that he would not attempt to
rebuild his coal and steel colossus on its former lines by
embarking on these "forbidden" activities elsewhere in
the future—and his reluctance to give them such an assurance only increased their suspicions.

In the midst of all this intense discussion, however, Alfried
for once found the time to think of something other than
business. In May 1952, just fifteen months after his release
from Landsberg, he married again. His bride on this
occasion was a thrice-wed, thrice-divorced daughter of a
German insurance official. Her first husband had been a
certain Baron von Langen. Then she had wed a film-maker
called Frank Wisbar, with whom she had emigrated to
Hollywood. But not making good there, she had found
herself forced to work: first as a shop-assistant in a Los
Angeles department-store and then as a receptionist to a
Dr. Knauer. After divorcing Wisbar in Las Vegas she had
married Knauer and through him had obtained American
citizenship. However, this marriage had not lasted long
either. Still in her thirties, she had returned to Hamburg
where she had met the forty-five-year-old head of the House
of Krupp during one of his frequent business trips to that
city.

Vera Hossenfeldt was her name—and after a lightning

courtship Alfried married her discreetly and almost surreptitiously in a registry office at Berchtesgaden, the Bavarian mountain resort which of course had been Hitler's holiday hide-out too. Such was their eagerness to keep their elopement out of the public gaze that they drove to the mayor's parlour in a baker's delivery van—shades of Berthold and the battered old laundry van at Landsberg! The only other two witnesses to the wedding were the proprietor and his wife of the hotel where they were staying. Alfried gave his bride a white Porsche sports-car and bunched her with the inevitable tulips.

But once back in Essen after a brief honeymoon, Alfried had begun the bargaining again in earnest. He had also straightaway started building another castle, this time fit for a re-crowned modern industrial king—a luxurious fifteen-roomed bungalow in the grounds of the Villa Hügel though not within sight of it (Alfried was at least trying to banish some of the more unhappy memories of his past).

Pretty, like his first wife Anneliese, but much more determined and much more worldly than her, Vera in the changed circumstances of the Ruhr in 1952 stood a reasonable chance of succeeding as the wife of Germany's richest and biggest industrialist. Evidently she played the part well of the perfect hostess at the big business parties Alfried started giving once he was back at Krupp's. She even accompanied him on many of his overseas trips. But there were no children of the marriage, and after just four years it ended in yet another divorce.

Meantime, despite the suspicions of the British and French officials, the American diplomats had had their way. Scarcely three months after Alfried's and Vera's nuptials, they presented them with the best wedding gift of all—a preliminary agreement whereby Krupp was to be paid something like £25 million in compensation for the coal, iron, and steel holdings the Allies had already taken away from him.

This prompted an even louder and more angry outcry in Britain than that of eighteen months before. Said the *News Chronicle*, "It is hard to stomach the vast compensation that is to be paid to Alfried Krupp to console him for the loss of control of his coal and steel interests." While the *Manchester Guardian* considered it "disquieting" and the *Financial Times* found it "baffling", the *Daily Telegraph* after first declaring it to be "monstrous" went on to point out that "The arch-profiteers of the régime are apparently to lose none of their gains". It was Anthony Eden's turn this time, as Churchill's Foreign Secretary, to try to reassure an indignant nation:

> It is the Government's purpose to ensure that Herr Krupp shall not be allowed to use the proceeds of the sale of his holdings to buy his way back into the coal and steel industries or otherwise to acquire a controlling interest. The means of achieving that end are under discussion in Germany between the High Commission and th: Federal Government.

But for many Britons this was not enough. The Liberal leader in the House of Commons, Clement Davies, spoke for a far wider section of the population than his party's meagre strength in Parliament indicated when he said, "The restoration of such a vast sum of money to the family whose activities were of such assistance to Hitler has deeply shocked people everywhere"—and he went on to ask, "Inasmuch as Krupp has been found guilty of using slave-labour and of taking other people's property, is it not possible to devote some of this wealth to the people who have suffered?" Alas, in the diplomatic turmoils of the Cold War, no one in authority at least was to pay much heed to such liberal sentiments. However, later that same year, on Armistice Day, a wreath inscribed "To the Dead from Alfried Krupp—Thanks a £40 million" was found placed against the Royal Artillery War Memorial at Hyde Park Corner in London. Two months after this particular incident, 4,000 French ex-servicemen demonstrated in Paris against the proposed Krupp compensation plan.

So far as the American public was concerned, the announcement came at the time of a Presidential Election— an election that was being fought on what degrees of toughness should be shown towards the Russians and on whether General Eisenhower's notion of "rolling back Communism" should be given the chance over the Democratic Administration's previous policy of merely "containing Communism". In all such discussions, issues to do with whether or not the Allies should continue to be "nasty to the Nazis" did not loom very large—and the Republicans were if anything keener to commit Germany to America's side than their Democratic opponents. After all, General Eisenhower as early as January 1951 had spoken of his former enemies as "honourable comrades". He had declared publicly that for him bygones were bygones and that it was his intention to secure for Germany equal status with the other countries of the Western alliance. What is more the Republican Party was the party of big businessmen, some of whom had had commercial relations with Krupp's before the war and had quickly re-established them shortly afterwards.

For Alfried an Eisenhower victory at the polls and a breakdown to the peace talks in Korea meant that he could afford to be even tougher in his bargaining with the Allies than hitherto. The American negotiators now made no bones about their sympathies lying entirely with him—and so he preferred to work through them, to get them to prod the British and the French. Alfried wanted a limit put on his pledge not to re-enter the coal, iron, and steel business— perhaps a limit for ten years only from the date of signing. But while the Americans were eager to agree to this, the British and French flatly refused. Another stumbling-block was whether he was to be permitted to make any alloy-steel at all, such as for instance in his Widia tungsten-carbide works. But on this point the Allies did give way, and in doing so they opened up a loophole in the Agreement through which Alfried was to drive a coach-and-four—for he interpreted the compromise clause banning him from making alloy-steel "except in small quantities incidental to the enterprises which will remain in the possession of Alfried Krupp" as allowing him to buy steel ingots elsewhere in unlimited amounts for re-shaping in his own foundries, and no one later was able to question this interpretation.

As the months of the bargaining dragged on, Alfried became more and more confident. Indeed, when the British coal control authorities moved out of the Villa Hügel he did not hesitate to petition Whitehall for the immediate return of some 300 to 400 "art treasures", the value of which he said approached £200,000 and which he claimed were missing. What is more, a group of British officials straightaway visited Essen and secured the return to him of several of the articles!

It took from August 1952 to March 1953 to turn a preliminary draft into a final agreement—and in the end another diplomatic *deus ex machina* came to Alfried's aid. In the early weeks of 1953 Western diplomats were concerned with clearing away the obstacles and creating the machinery for completing West Germany's sovereignty to enable her to rearm as a member of the European Defence Community and so enter NATO at some future date. A lot of loose ends left over from the Occupation remained to be tied up— one piece of such unfinished business was a settlement with Krupp. A fortnight only was allotted to obtaining Alfried's signature to a document binding him to the term of Allied Law 27. In such circumstances of acute haste Alfried was naturally in a strong bargaining position, and it would appear that he did not deign to help the diplomats over their shortage of days—at least that is how the officials responsible for the final agreement excuse its patent drawbacks.

Thus it came to pass that on 4 March 1953 signatures were put to the so-called Krupp Treaty. By it Alfried undertook to sell off his coal and steel companies within five years as a condition of the rest of his industrial empire being returned to him. At the same time he was made to provide for those members of his family who had been summarily disinherited by the 1943 *Lex Krupp*—for instance the shares in two small processing plants in Düsseldorf and Hamm were to be divided equally between his sister Irmgard and his nephew Arnold von Bohlen und Halbach, the son of his brother Claus, the Luftwaffe pilot who had been killed when his aeroplane crashed in 1940. Alfried was also bidden to give £1 million each to his other sister Waldtraut, to his two surviving brothers Berthold and Harald (although Harald at that time was still a prisoner in Russian hands and was not released until October 1955), and to his only son Arndt, to be held in trust for him until he came of age.

Significantly, Alfried did not sign the Agreement himself —he preferred to leave that to his American lawyers. On the day in question he had chosen to go off ski-ing in Switzerland. But the real reason was that by avoiding penning his own name to the document he could that more easily deny final moral responsibility for its contents should the occasion ever arise. So far the occasion has not in fact arisen—for as usual time has been on Alfried Krupp's side.

All in all the 1953 Agreement was unprecedented—for it was in effect a commercial Treaty between a private individual and three sovereign nations, Britain, France and the United States. It was yet one more indication of the now internationally accepted uniqueness of the House of Krupp.

It had its critics of course right from the start. British politicians were particularly angry. Many Conservative M.P.s harried their Government in the House of Commons with complaints that there was absolutely nothing in the Treaty to prevent Krupp, a convicted war criminal, from again becoming one of Germany's most powerful and influential men—nor were there even any specific provisions to stop him re-entering the armaments business. Some London newspapers were unusually virulent. The *Daily Telegraph* for instance argued that the Agreement's weaknesses were apparent to all and quoted an Allied official as saying that it "must be regarded largely as an academic solution". Even on the day before the signing, that selfsame newspaper had pointed out that German financial experts were convinced that because of the large sums of capital involved it would be difficult if not impossible to find a suitable purchaser for the companies Krupp was being ordered to sell. It also reminded its readers—and presumably they included the British Foreign Office—that the West German Government had already stated that it could not hold Alfried to his undertaking not to re-enter coal and steel because the Federal Constitution, largely written by the Allies, granted every West German citizen the right to enter *any* business.

But voices were raised in Krupp's defence at that time even within Britain. On the day after the signing, *The Times*, for instance, declared that "the settlement obliges Herr Krupp to take a very large sum, perhaps between £20 million and £25 million, out of the coal, iron and steel industries where it is needed and to put this money to other uses in which it will probably do less good"—and the editorial writer went on to argue, "The German shortage of capital for heavy industry is already a European problem, and there is no evidence for supposing that Europe as a whole can afford to have the shortage aggravated in an avoidable way." Special pleading like this on behalf of sectional interests was to be of enormous help and comfort to Alfried during the years to come.

Although, once the signing was over, his lawyers had promptly published a statement on his behalf denouncing the Agreement as not only recriminatory and reactionary but also harmful to the well-being of the workers' community of Krupp, Alfried himself did not protest too loudly. He knew that he had made a remarkably good bargain—so good in fact that he did not want to give others the chance of perhaps spoiling it. He had realised long since that the restrictions were unenforceable—and indeed that the whole Agreement was unworkable. All he had to do now was to be patient, for as usual "time would settle all".

Then, as though he had not had enough luck already, on the day following the signing, Stalin died. Straightaway Krupp disappeared off the front pages—and the attentions of Western diplomats and Western leader-writers were immediately switched to coping with that seemingly shattering event. So even if any of them had had second thoughts on the Krupp Treaty and might have wanted to do something about it before it was entirely too late, they now had the excuse that there was no longer the time.

If Alfried had been looking for a new motto for the armorial bearings of the House of Krupp he could hardly have chosen better than "Time is on my side", for that is really the theme and the explanation of his rehabilitation and his recovery in the Ruhr.

CHAPTER SEVENTEEN

"Looking back, we can note with satisfaction that on the whole our hopes have been fulfilled"

ON THE cold, blustery morning of 12 March 1953, to a hero's welcome not just from his workers but from many citizens of Essen too, some of whom even turned out to line the route from his home, Alfried Krupp von Bohlen und Halbach once more came into his inheritance. It was eight years almost to the day since that last fatal 1,000-bomber raid had laid low the city of his forebears and had brought production at Krupp's to a complete halt. Even now there were still reminders of that final holocaust: a ruined chimney or a charred pit-head. But most of the debris and the rubble had long since been cleared away—and in their place were vast, open brick-prairies, some so immense that they seemed to stretch as far as the eye could see.

As he re-entered the red-brick tower-block of the Krupp administrative building, tanned and refreshed from his ski-ing holiday, Alfried could not help noticing those gaping spaces. Nor could his gaze escape them as he made his way up to the fourth-floor office in which he had many a time entertained Hitler and the other Nazi leaders, and from which first his father and then he himself had master-minded Krupp's massive contribution to the Führer's war effort. The brick-prairies surrounded him, no matter from which window he looked out—for here at the historic heart of the House of Krupp, the site of the old Gussstahlfabrik, the "Cannon King's" cast steel works, the destruction had been at its most deliberate. Symbolically so, for what the bombers had not touched the victors later had torn out.

Whereas to an Englishman or to a Frenchman Krupp meant simply guns, to a German on the other hand Krupp

stood more for steel. Indeed originally Krupp's were solely a
steel-making concern. Old Alfred had only gone into the
armaments business in the first place because he thought the
new weapons Prussia was needing could more profitably be
made from his steel—and when in time the sporadic production of those first few cast steel cannons blossomed, if that is
the right word, into the regular and massive manufacture of
U-boats, battleships, tanks, and giant guns, it was principally because, to the Krupps, these were extremely lucrative
ways of using their steel.

The steel plants, with their auxiliary coal-mines and iron-
works, were the very core of the Krupp industrial empire—
and now to all intents and purposes that heart had been
plucked out, leaving Alfried merely a few of its bloodless
branches, such as the shipyards at Bremen, the bridge-
building and engineering works at Rheinhausen, and in
Essen the locomotive shops and the factories for making
heavy lorries. This of course had been the logic of the
Allies' original plan to dismember Krupp's: crush the
heart and you cripple the body. Keep Krupp's out of steel
and you would render them harmless and insignificant for all
time.

Yet it is perhaps the most supreme irony of all that by
placing these apparent strictures on his ever again producing
coal and steel, the Allies were in effect doing Alfried a great
service. Coal and steel, above all others, were the industrial
activities of the past. Now Alfried was being given every
encouragement to seek out and succeed in the industrial
activities of the future. No doubt if he had been left to
concentrate solely on his coal and steel he would have
still grown rich—though perhaps not as rich as he is today.
At the same time, however, Krupp's might have become
indistinguishable from other equally enormously profitable coal and steel concerns in the Ruhr such as Thyssen's
or Mannesmann. In that way too the spell of Krupp's
uniqueness might have been broken. But instead, Alfried
and his fellow directors have been pushed into pioneering
new ground—and their immense success at it has restored
some of the magic to the name of "Krupp" and enhanced
the myth of the firm's immortality. The Krupp saga is

indeed a path of paradox and irony, with Nemesis seemingly negated at every turn.

Once back as boss, Alfried in fact lost little time in beginning the long hard struggle to rebuild his House: his second wife has vouched for the intensity of his efforts on that score, to the detriment in her opinion of his health as well as of their marriage. Within two years he spent something like £12 million on new buildings and equipment. As chance would have it, he gained from what the Allies had done to him—for a lot of the machines and workshops destroyed by the bombers and the dismantlers had been obsolete. Now he replaced them with the very latest in design and efficiency.

To raise such capital he had to sell off some of those empty spaces and to rent out yet others. In all he disposed of something like 100 acres of Krupp land in the centre of industrial Essen—land that had been in the family for 200 years or so. But that still left him with more than 1,000 acres there. He peddled one of his coal-mines to the State for £2,500,000, which helped to swell the Krupp coffers. Like many another German tycoon he had managed to keep the larger part of his fortune out of Hitler's clutches: his financial director had testified at Nuremberg how from 1943 onwards Krupp's quietly sold their Nazi war bonds and accumulated the proceeds elsewhere. Now these nameless bank deposits in neutral countries such as Switzerland and Argentina were coming in handy. Significantly, four months after his release from Landsberg he made a secret trip to South America. The German banks too came to his rescue. Within no time at all, it seemed, his overdraft with them had grown to £5 million. Such is the magnetism of the name Krupp that unlike other German firms in similar straits Krupp's did not always have to provide security for their loans. Indeed Alfried's executives boast today that if the banks had demanded collateral in every instance then Krupp's would never have got restarted. The West German Government helped too by granting Alfried generous tax-abatements— and a part of the beneficent aid the Americans were pouring into Germany found its way to Essen and to Krupp's.

One of Alfried's fondest boasts himself is that when he

again took charge of Krupp's in March 1953 he found 16,000 pensioners as well as 16,000 workers on the firm's books. What is more these pensioners were for the most part owed substantial back-payments. But he paid them all that they were due, even though this cost him yet more of the firm's precious assets. Many of his executives and fellow directors opposed his action, arguing that there were more pressing things to spend the money on, but Alfried was shrewd enough to realise that he was going to have to rely heavily on his workers' enthusiasm and loyalty in rebuilding Krupp's—and as a piece of internal public relations it has paid off handsomely, for to date Alfried's firm has never been faced with a serious strike. Nor for that matter have the trade unions ever been able to get a firm grip on Krupp's. Both his great-grandfather and his father in their own different ways had seen to that: Alfred by fighting the growth of unionism tooth and nail, and Gustav by making the destruction of the unions his price for throwing in his lot with Hitler. But now Alfried was killing them with kindness and obtaining his workers' devotion through respect.

The recovery of Krupp's is startling enough, though in actual fact it is only one detail in Germany's astonishing recuperation in the 'fifties: the *Wirtschaftswunder* or Economic Miracle as it has come to be called. Business had begun to boom there even before Alfried had become boss again of Krupp's. The fighting in Korea had created an unprecedented demand from America and elsewhere for things German: from steel to sausages. Indeed, by the month of Alfried's return industrial production in the new West German Federal Republic had long since passed the level of that of pre-war—and by the end of the decade it was two and a half times the 1938 figure. By that time too West Germany had become an even bigger exporting country than Britain and was second in the world only to the United States.

Ironically enough it was Krupp's who led the vanguard in pushing Britain out of some of her oldest overseas markets such as Pakistan, India, South Africa and the Middle East. Denied in theory making steel, Alfried instead went in for making factories for making steel. Two of his first major orders were from India and Pakistan. The Pakistani project came up shortly after he returned to Krupp's. For some time the Pakistanis had been seeking to establish a steel industry of their own. British and American experts had been called in for advice, but they had argued that Pakistani's deposits of coal and iron-ore were of too low a quality to make the enterprise worth while financially. Then the men at Krupp heard about it and devised a process for using the inferior ores economically. As a result they won the contract to build a steel works with a capacity of 300,000 tons a year, and on top of that were granted a 10 per cent stake in the new steel industry out there.

In December 1953, despite stiff competition from the Russians who at that time were out to woo India away from its neutrality and into the Soviet camp, Krupp's along with DEMAG, another Ruhr firm making machinery, entered into a ten-year partnership agreement with the Indian Government to establish a £52,500,000 complex of steel industries at Rourkela, some 250 miles to the west of Calcutta. The project also included the building from scratch of a new city with a population of 100,000 designed to be "Asia's Essen". The whole contract was one that the British had been hoping to land themselves. As Alfried was quick to discover, in dealing with many of these newly emerging countries Germany had the advantage over Britain in not ever having been a major colonial power. This was to stand Krupp's in good stead, particularly in Africa and the Middle East.

It was early successes like the Pakistani and Indian projects that prompted Alfried to set up his now famous and immensely profitable "consulting engineering department". Since again in theory he could not sell Krupp steel, or mine Krupp coal or forge Krupp iron, he decided that he would sell Krupp "know-how" in making and marketing steel and in mining coal and forging iron. Working teams of geologists, engineers, foundrymen, and mining experts, complete with their own aircraft, caravans, mobile offices and mobile laboratories, were despatched from Essen to the four corners of the globe to explore at a price for coal and iron-ore on behalf of governments as well as private individuals. What is more they were prepared to furnish their potential customers with detailed blueprints for completely integrated coal, iron and steel industries. Nor were they content to confine themselves merely to steel, but soon became adept at offering "package-deals" to establish almost any industry anywhere.

Within twelve months of returning to the firm, Alfried had won orders to build a cement works near Bombay with an initial capacity of 300 tons daily and to erect for the Greeks two huge £7 million plants for processing nickel and brown coal. A year later he signed contracts to exploit tungsten and tin in Bolivia, to construct factories for producing vegetable-oil in Pakistan, Persia and the Sudan, and to instal new harbour-equipment in Iraq, Thailand and Chile. In October 1953, just seven months after Alfried had resumed command, the *Manchester Guardian* was already warning its readers, "Krupp is emerging as Britain's most dangerous competitor as an exporter of constructional machinery to the under-developed areas of the world".

On top of all this, his shipyards at Bremen were turning out oil-tankers for the Turks and the Americans, his crane factories at Wilhelmshaven were supplying Egypt, Norway and Mozambique, while the products of his locomotive shops and heavy lorry assembly-lines at Essen were being sold as fast as they could be produced to customers in India, South Africa, South America, Indonesia and the Middle East. Not only had Krupp's bettered American as well as British exporters in some of their most traditional preserves, they had also ousted Soviet salesmen from countries where their campaigning had a political rather than a purely commercial edge to it.

"Looking back", Alfried boasted to a group of his workers one spring afternoon at the Villa Hügel in 1955 as he presented them with long-service medals and other labour trophies, "we can note with satisfaction that on the whole our hopes have been fulfilled." Krupp's had done £83 million worth of business in the first complete year of his resumption of power, while their labour-force had leapt from 16,000 to 80,000. In the eyes of more than one British newspaper it was all evidence of "a remarkable post-war metamorphosis"— and to others of "an almost unbelievable progress", Krupp's having become again in their leader-writers' opinion a "mighty force" and a "major factor" on the world industrial scene.

In most cases Krupp's could outbid their rivals not just on price and delivery-dates, but more especially on the length of time they gave their customers in which to pay. British exporters in particular sounded off about this, jealous of the apparent ease with which Alfried could obtain almost unlimited credit from his Government. In 1957 for instance it leaked out that the Frankfurt Export Credit Bank for one had loaned him the better part of £27 million for such purposes.

But it was not simply a matter of lower costs and longer credit-terms with Alfried. He had the edge over his international competitors in other ways too. The thoroughness with which Krupp's during the war had stretched out their tentacles in the wake of the Wehrmacht to grasp the choicest morsels of plundered industry that were going was now being put to studying in detail the world's export markets: not just the richer sophisticated areas in the West, but more particularly the needs of nations newly emerging or yet to be developed. Similarly, the meticulous regard for precision and the relentless drive to surmount apparently insurmountable problems that had hitherto been expended on weapons of war like Big Bertha, Long Max and Fat Gustav now went into designing gear-boxes easy enough for even the most primitive peasant from off the pampas to operate or even the most illiterate Arab from out of the desert to service. The men too who had devised the armour-plating for the terrible Tiger tanks that had decimated the doughboys in the Battle of the Bulge in 1944 were now engaged in beating the Yanks in a different sort of struggle—this time the fight to be the first to develop diesel engines for locomotives capable of withstanding the harsh gradients and extreme temperatures of Brazil and the Argentine.

Krupp's overseas business was not always plain sailing in those early days of recovery. For instance, they very often had to take payment in local products. But the Polish bacon, Egyptian cotton, Russian caviare, Siamese rice, Turkish raisins, Brazilian coffee, and Bulgarian tobacco that they received in this way they turned to profit by moving into the retailing and wholesaling business in a big way. Today, Alfried has a chain of 120 supermarkets and stores throughout the Ruhr selling anything from Krupp wine and Krupp shirts to Krupp toys and Krupp orchids.

Alfried even had the audacity in March 1955 to ape President Truman by launching his own Point Four programme for helping the under-developed countries. The main difference about his scheme was that he did not propose giving the aid away free. He wanted others, chiefly the Americans, to put up the money, while he profited by exchanging that money for machinery from his factories. But Washington soon saw through his "philanthropy"— and in the end even his own executives were derisively calling the scheme "Alfried's Point 4½ Programme". As such it never got off the ground, though more than half of Krupp's business overseas was, and still is, with countries under-developed.

The year before making his "Point 4½" announcement, and almost exactly twelve months to the day after wresting control of what remained of his industrial empire from its British overseers, Alfried was brazen enough to visit London —his first trip there since 1937. With Vera at his side he dined at the Savoy Grill in March 1954 but few Englishmen recognised him and there was no outcry. The couple then went on to the Bahamas, a British colony, to spend a few days with Axel Wenner-Gren, the Swedish millionaire industrialist and business-associate of Alfried's—Wenner-Gren, as we shall see, was to prove a valuable and willing ally of Krupp's in their circumvention of the 1953 Agreement. The final port of call on this particular trip for Alfried and Vera was Mexico to visit a German Industrial Fair at which Krupp's inevitably were exhibiting.

The couple were back again in Britain the next year, this time for a quick look at the Farnborough Air Show: Alfried was already about to launch himself again into aeroplane manufacture in a big way. They also had a stop-over lunch at London Airport with Henry Luce, the *Time-Life* tycoon. Luce too was to be a good friend of Krupp's, for in August 1957, on the occasion of Alfried's fiftieth birthday, a largely complementary cover-story entitled *The House That Krupp Built* appeared in *Time* magazine. *Time*'s proprietor was also believed to be instrumental in Alfried's getting a visa to attend a conference for international businessmen and statesmen which his magazine was sponsoring in San Francisco that same autumn, at which Alfried had been invited to speak on "The Partnership Approach". Strictly speaking Alfried should have been denied a visa, since he was after all a convicted war criminal and such people were beyond the pale so far as the United States immigration laws were concerned. To the *New York Herald Tribune*, the whole ploy was "one of the slickest advertising promotional schemes yet devised". Nor did it escape the attention of certain senators, many of whom began to get angry. Alfried in the end preferred not to go—and his visa application has never been renewed.

But his never having visited America has been no bar on his doing business there. Not only has he sold oil-tankers to American shipping firms and built the world's largest shiploading installation of its type at Toledo, Ohio, but he has exchanged technical information with at least one American company, Blaw-Knox, since October 1956, and it is thought that he has similar, though less publicised, agreements with several more. He has been making plant to produce synthetic fibre under licence from the American firm, von Kohorn's, since before 1957, and the United Aircraft Corporation of Connecticut is a major shareholder in his airframe-assembly company. There is also a reported tie-up in heavy-lorry production between Krupp's and the White Motor Coporation—the latter lies second in the United States to International Harvesters in heavy-vehicle production. A group of American banks and insurance companies helped him set up a new shipping subsidiary in January 1959 to transport iron-ore.

As the magic has returned to the name and the myth been restored, so a new crop of Krupp stories and legends has sprung up since 1953. One of these, most probably apocryphal, concerns how four companies from four different countries were invited to tender to build a steel smelter in one of the newly emerging African nations. The French, so the story goes, never replied, the British asked for more details, the American company sent a junior salesman, but Krupp's despatched Alfried to the scene—they also got the contract. The thousands of miles covered every year by Krupp executives have become legendary in West Germany —and Alfried has certainly done his share of the leg-work.

In February 1956 he made an extensive tour of the Far and Middle East, dropping in to talk to business-heads in such capitals as Cairo, Bangkok, Delhi and Karachi. He was in fact the first major German industrialist to set foot in the area since the war. At the outset the trip was described as "a serious attempt" to counter the Soviets' economic offensive in the underdeveloped countries of Africa and Asia, but on his return, discovering that the Russians were now interested in buying from him, he changed his tune and hastened to deny that he was waging "a private crusade against Communism"—to the chagrin of many American diplomats whose blue-eyed boy he had recently become. He even announced that he was tendering for Egypt's mammoth multi-million-pound Aswan Dam project, just at the time when John Foster Dulles, the scourge of the uncommitted nations, was himself blowing cold on the scheme as Colonel Nasser seemed to be courting the Communists. Later that same year while the world's statesmen toiled over the Suez Crisis, Alfried took in Chile, Peru, Brazil and Mexico— picking up here and there the odd lucrative contract for constructing a complete copper refinery or a whole shipyard.

In 1957 it was the turn of the Turks. They greeted him ecstatically, and with equal enthusiasm on his part he discussed building blast furnaces and railways, mining coal, wolfram and chrome, and even bridging the Bosphorus for them—though the latter project so far has not come to anything.* Within a few months he was off again to Canada —though unlike the Turks, Canadians were not so ecstatic at having a convicted war criminal in their midst and showed their discontent by staging demonstrations everywhere he went in their country. Alfried's reason for going there was his participation along with Cyrus Eaton, Kruschev's famous capitalist friend from Cleveland, Ohio, in a joint £77 million German, Canadian, and American scheme for developing a vast new iron-ore field in northern Quebec. But before he could visit the site of the bonanza, news

* But see p. 314.

reached him of Bertha Krupp's death in Essen at the age of seventy-one. He hastened home for his mother's funeral, and in the event, at least so far as Alfried was concerned, the Quebec partnership never came to anything.

After Gustav's death, Bertha had returned from Blühnbach to live in Essen. She even on occasion appeared in public at some of the massive receptions at the Villa Hügel Alfried gave for visiting heads of state: such as those in November 1954 for Emperor Hailie Selassie of Ethiopia and a few months later for the Shah of Persia. Always austerely dressed, her very presence, eyewitnesses recall, made guests ever mindful of the cold and steely Krupp past which Alfried and his public relations men were trying so hard to dispel. Having been fondled as a babe by old Alfred the "Cannon King", fêted by both the Kaisers in turn, had her hand kissed—however reluctantly—by Adolf Hitler, and her name immortalised through an infamous giant gun, Bertha so long as she lived exuded Krupp's past from every pore. Her going, sad personally of course for Alfried, must nevertheless have made it that little bit easier for him to throw off his history.

But it was still not all that easy, as he found out when in February 1958, a few months after his mother's death, he visited Australia and New Zealand. Irate ex-servicemen picketed his arrival in Melbourne, while Opposition politicians reminded their listeners of the thousands of Australian lads who had lost their lives to Krupp guns and Krupp tanks during Rommel's various desert campaigns. Some demonstrations were particularly noisy. Banners inscribed "Achtung Belsen" and "Keep Out War Criminal Krupp" were thrust at him—and perhaps for the first time in his life Alfried was called "butcher" and "Jew-killer" to his face. But apparently it all left him unperturbed, for at the airport before departing he remarked to newsmen that he had been "a little sorry" to see that some Australians were still angry with him.

A year later he was back again in the Far East, showing his face in Japan, Hongkong and the Philippines. He also for the first time took along with him his son and heir Arndt, now aged twenty-one, though not in the same plane—for a dynastically conscious family like the Krupps that would have been tempting fate too much! When journalists tried to press the point, a spokesman for the firm simply explained that travelling in separate aeroplanes was quite usual among important families, including the British royal family!

And all this journeying brought him enormous dividends: by 1959 Krupp's foreign sales alone netted some £58 million and the total business for the firm grossed £372 million, a rise of nearly 500 per cent in just five years! Meantime too, Alfried's labour force had grown to some 107,000 strong, a bigger number than the population of whole towns like Blackburn or Gateshead, or cities such as Oxford or Cambridge. Krupp products were certainly reaching out into every continent and almost every country. The contracts were mounting and growing ever larger: a £19 million order from Angola to exploit iron-ore deposits there and to lay down a railway and to reshape a harbour, a £12 million one from Turkey to extend the steelworks at Karabuk, a £9 million one from Greece to fit out a new oil-refinery, an £8 million one from Portuguese West Africa to supply railway equipment, a £6½ million one from Liberia to build a paper and cardboard factory, and so on, and so on. The list seemed to go on for ever as nations as different as Japan or the Yemen, and peoples as varied as the Nepalese, the Tunisians or the Australians scrambled to buy Krupp in that first decade of Alfried's return.

Some projects naturally were more spectacular than others and hence more likely to catch the public's imagination—such for instance as the bathyscaphe *Trieste* Krupp's built for Professor Piccard, in which he made his record-breaking seven-mile descent in 1960 to the bottom of the Marianas Trench off Guam Island in the Pacific. It was to hit the headlines again when it was used to try to locate the lost U.S. submarine *Thresher*. Another Krupp exploit was the raising for Egypt's President, Colonel Nasser, of the 3,000-year-old thirty-foot-high statue of Pharaoh Rameses II by means of hydraulic jacks, transporting it over treacherous terrain, and finally resiting it outside Cairo's new main railway-station. In absolute terms such schemes were perhaps only pifflingly profitable, but in publicity for the firm they reaped rich rewards, bringing not only extra

business in Egypt in the shape for instance of a couple of
bridges over the Suez Canal and one over the Nile at Cairo,
together with a shipyard and a paper-mill at Alexandria,
but also more importantly in adding a lustre of daring and
romance not hitherto associated with the name of Krupp.

No fortress of prejudice seemed too impregnable and no
walls of bitter memories appeared too high for Alfried's
salesmen to scale. Some of the countries in which Krupp's
did their best business in the years immediately after 1953
were those they had been plundering ruthlessly only a
decade or so before: for example, Holland and France in the
West, and Greece, Poland, Yugoslavia and even Russia in
the East.

Krupp's of course had had a long history of lucrative
commercial relations with the country of the Czars, dating
back to old Alfred's days—and as we have seen they had
also thought it quite fitting to clinch a deal or two with the
commissars between the two world wars. Their campaigning
for sales behind the Iron Curtain incurred the wrath of their
American mentors who considered it a wretched way of
showing thanks for recent kindnesses: Dulles for one had
expected Krupp's faithfully to toe the anti-Communist line.
But it soon emerged that their wooing of the Soviets had the
blessing of at least some members of the West German
Government, though apparently not Chancellor Adenauer
who displayed his disapproval by immediately snubbing
certain Krupp senior executives at a Bonn diplomatic reception. However, he did not keep up this arraignment for very
long.

Alfried's first major Russian order came in 1957, after he
had exhibited at the Leipzig East German Trade Fair
the previous March—an action which at the time had
shocked many West Germans. The contract was worth
just over £4 million and was for a chemical works and three
synthetic fibre plants which ironically he was making
under licence from an American firm. This quickly led to
closer and warmer relations between Moscow and Essen.
Indeed when Mikoyan, the Russian Trade Minister,
visited West Germany in 1958 he went out of his way to
talk to Alfried's general manager, assuring him that "the

products of Krupp have an excellent reputation among our people". A few weeks after this remark of Mikoyan, Kruschev, then Russia's Prime Minister, declared in a speech to the Central Committee of the Soviet Communist Party in Moscow that "the Soviet Union has in the past entertained good trade relations with the Essen firm of Krupp".

Later that same year, a group of Krupp senior officials headed by their general manager were fêted in Moscow; Mikoyan called them "the first swallows of commerce from the western world". The Russians were evidently very eager to do business with Alfried's men, but negotiations broke down on credit terms—though rumour had it that the real reason was that Alfried had been nobbled at the last moment by the Americans.

Kruschev himself took a hand in the next stage of the wooing when, at the Leipzig Trade Fair in the following March, that is March 1959, he made the East German press drop their usual denunciations of Krupp's as warmongers, and of Alfried in particular as a convicted war criminal. Moreover, he visited the Krupp stand at the Fair and drank a toast to the firm out of a Krupp stainless steel tumbler filled with French Cognac, expressing regret that the head of the House was not there in person, but sending Alfried his good wishes all the same. Today, Alfried's name no longer appears on the Soviet's list of war criminals and until quite recently the House of Krupp maintained a permanent office in Moscow: perhaps the two most remarkable, and at the same time the two most paradoxical, facts in the whole post-war rise of the firm and family.

But although Alfried's overseas exploits have hogged the headlines, exports in fact have never amounted to more than 20 per cent of his total business in any one year since 1953. It was his sales inside Germany itself that supplied the solid core of his success. Already by 1961, for instance, he held 40 per cent of the West German market in power-shovels, 35 per cent in electric locomotives, 33 per cent in aeroplane manufacture, 12 per cent in building cranes, and 10 per cent in chemical plants. And some of his domestic projects have been equally as noteworthy as his coups overseas: particularly his joining with a group of other German firms to build the Federal Republic's first nuclear reactor. Begun in March 1958 it is already past the experimental stage. Its graphite core is made from Ruhr coke, but its uranium has been supplied by the United States Atomic Energy Commission. In addition, as early as the spring of 1955, and long before Britain or any other country outside North America had done so, Krupp's began making titanium, the new "wonder" material that is as strong as steel but some 80 per cent lighter and much more resistant to rust. Its chief use then was in engine parts for jet aircraft and supersonic rockets, though Krupp's have since helped to widen its application throughout industry. Alfried has also been one of the pioneer manufacturers of monorails in Europe.

To the West German Government he has long been considered a sort of unofficial "industrial ambassador", to be entrusted on occasion with important messages of policy for foreign leaders on his travels abroad—and when heads of state come visiting the Federal Republic a meeting with Alfried is usually included in their programme. Out come the Krupp candelabra and once again the Villa Hügel resounds to talk of matters of State. Where kaisers and führers once pontificated, presidents, shahs, kings, emperors, and even communist cabinet ministers now mingle and chatter. *Mirabile Dictu*. The House of Krupp has risen, fallen, and risen again.

CHAPTER EIGHTEEN

"The American"

KRUPP PUBLIC relations men are apt to make a great play of Alfried's oft-repeated wish to break completely with his past and his declared determination to project an entirely new image for his firm. It is a point they tend to bring up at the outset of any initial encounter with visiting journalists and politicians, particularly those from Britain, America or France—presumably they do not have to do it quite so heartily or so readily with fellow Germans or with, say, Persians, Africans, Brazilians and Japanese, even if they actually bother at all.

The way in which it is done is in the manner born of smooth P.R. men the world over—and Krupp's P.R. men must number among the smoothest of that particularly smooth calling. Counts abound at Krupp's for one thing—not only do they sport a real live Prussian count at the head of their P.R. outfit in Essen, but they have a dashing Danish one holding the fort for them in London from an Eaton Square address. "The only offensive weapons we produce these days, old boy, are orchids, designed to demolish the defences of even the most chaste *Fräulein*" is one clumsy version of the gospel, while another is "Why we even draw the line at selling toy guns in our supermarkets".

Even so, despite the efforts of his P.R. department, Alfried's attempt to brush the past under the carpet received something of a setback in November 1954 when the Christian Democrat newspaper the *Rheinische Post* came out with a story that Krupp's had working for them in the Argentine the infamous Nazi, SS Colonel Otto Skorzeny, the man responsible for Mussolini's daring rescue from his captors on Monte Sasso in September 1943, and the man whom

Himmler from time to time had entrusted with less savoury tasks. Evidently a picture had come to light allegedly showing a group of Krupp officials being entertained by President Peron of the Argentine. A member of the authoritative Swiss newspaper, *Neue Zürcher Zeitung* had recognised Skorzeny among the bunch. Promptly a spokesman for Alfried retaliated by arguing that Skorzeny was really acting on behalf of the Argentinian Government in the talks that were taking place there on whether or not Krupp's should participate in the so-called "South American Ruhr" the Argentinians were building for themselves north of their capital, Buenos Aires. But true or false, such was the outcry that Skorzeny was never heard of again in connection with this particular deal. The whole incident went down very badly with the Americans especially and Alfried's image in the United States suffered accordingly—though not, as it turned out for long.

The year before "The Skorzeny Affair" Alfried made perhaps his most important single act on the score of changing the old Krupp tune, when he appointed Berthold Beitz as his general manager. It was certainly his most symbolic and, at the same time, also his shrewdest move—for although Alfried has been extremely energetic and resourceful on his own account in endeavouring to dispel the old image of the firm there is little doubt that no one has done more to improve the way in which the world now regards Krupp's than Berthold Beitz. Indeed it is joked around Essen that if Alfried had not found Beitz then he would have had to invent him!

Only six years Alfried's junior, Berthold Beitz, as he loves to boast, knew absolutely nothing about coal, iron or steel when he joined Krupp's in November 1953. He also quips that he thought the Bochumer Verein, a long-standing Ruhr steel concern and one which Krupp's now own, was merely the name of a local football team. But Beitz brought to Alfried the priceless asset of having an excellent anti-Nazi record. Not only had he never been a Hitler-follower or behaved badly to the Jews or exploited slave-labourers or plundered other countries, instead, as many resistance-fighters were only too willing to testify, he had helped countless

numbers of Poles to escape the gas-chambers and had
prevented leaders of the Polish underground from falling
into the Gestapo's clutches—and all this while filling the
critically important post of administrator of the captured
Polish oil-fields at Borislav to which the Nazis had appointed
him in February 1940. As a result today he is very much
persona grata, not simply in Poland but throughout the whole
of the Eastern bloc—perhaps the only leading German to be
in this happy position, and certainly an enviable one for a
leading German businessman. It is this fact which helps
explain the remarkable success of Krupp's in trading
behind the Iron Curtain: Berthold Beitz, the humane
German and the sympathetic friend of the Polish resistance-
movement neatly cancels out Alfried Krupp the plunderer of
Yugoslav and Russian industry and the exploiter of Hungar-
ian and Czech slave-labour.

The British occupation authorities too had been unable to
find a blemish on Beitz's character—and so while many
business executives formerly employed by the Nazis swept
the streets, cleared away the rubble, or did other similarly
menial chores considered fitting for suspected Hitler-
sympathisers, he was singled out, given a car, and put in
charge of insurance for the British in Hamburg.

How Beitz eventually swam into Alfried's ken reads
rather like a travesty of an early "poor-boy-makes-good"
Hollywood film-script. In fact they met quite by chance in
the flat of Jean Sprenger, a sculptor friend of Alfried's
younger brother Berthold. Beitz had commissioned Sprenger
to do a nude statue for the outside of the new headquarters
building in Hamburg of the Iduna-Germania Life insurance
company he was then managing.

One spring evening in 1952 Beitz went to Sprenger's flat
in Essen to discuss some of the designs for the statue. While he
was there they were joined for a drink by Alfried and his
younger brother who were living in the same apartment-
block as Sprenger at the time. Afterwards they all went out
for a meal to the Krupp-owned Essener Hof Hotel in the
centre of town which Alfried's grandfather Fritz had built
some sixty or so years before and which had become the
venue for hearty, unphilanthropic Krupp junketing ever

since. Beitz and Alfried evidently hit it off together right from the start, although they are in many ways entirely opposites, Beitz being extrovert, for ever joking, and extremely forthcoming, while Alfried is introvert, shy, retiring, almost donnish.

Even so, several months went by before they met again—and when they did it was at Alfried's own arranging. Krupp in the meantime had of course got married. One autumn evening later that same year he invited Beitz and his wife to join Vera and him in a foursome for dinner at Hamburg's Vierjahreszeiten Hotel. The get-together was apparently a success. Afterwards, while the ladies chatted in the lounge, Alfried took Beitz on a short walk around Hamburg's Binnenalster lake. There in the autumnal darkness he popped the Krupp question to Berthold: "How would you like to come and manage the firm for me?" Beitz was bowled over by the suggestion, since he had thought the whole point of the dinner and the late-night stroll was simply that Alfried wanted to touch his insurance company for a loan. Nor did he jump at the job immediately—preferring to say merely that he would think about it. In any case Alfried at that time was not strictly in a position to offer Beitz anything, for as yet the Krupp empire had not been restored to him. That he had made such a definite approach was a measure of his confidence in the final outcome of his negotiations with the Allies. Inevitably, he had discussed the matter with his mother, for despite her years, Bertha still wielded a substantial influence over her son. She had insisted, typically, that Alfried look a little more closely into Beitz's background.

Berthold Beitz in fact hailed from Pomerania: from the tiny village of Zemmin in the county of Demmin to the north-east of Berlin, now of course behind the Iron Curtain. His forebears had been factors for some of the local Junkers. But his father, tiring of the land-agency business, had first enlisted as a sergeant-major in the Pomeranian Lancers at the beginning of the First World War, and then after 1918 had become a bank clerk in one of the neighbouring small towns.

Born on 26 September 1913, Berthold went to grammar-school at Greifswald. When he was twenty he joined his

father in the local bank, moving later to Stralsund and then
to Stettin, the chief city of Pomerania. Bored with banking,
and fired with a much wider ambition than his parents,
Berthold applied for and eventually in 1939 secured a job
with the German Shell Company in Hamburg just before
hostilities started. After Germany had overrun Poland,
Shell, as we have seen, sent Beitz to help administer the
captured Polish oil-fields at Borislav, although he was even
then barely twenty-seven years of age. What is more the
job was deemed crucial enough to Hitler's war effort for him
to be excused military service.

When the Russian Army liberated Poland in 1945, Beitz
was taken prisoner. But he soon escaped, met up again with
his wife, Else, and their two children, Barbara and Bettina,
and together made their way back to Hamburg in the
autumn of 1945. For a while they all lived with his aged
parents in a tiny wooden bungalow some distance outside
of that city. The times were hard for the Beitzes, as indeed
they were for all Hamburg's citizens. But an accidental
encounter one day in 1946 with a secretary of his from
before the war at Shell brought him in touch with the
British occupation authorities who were on the look-out
for "reliable" Germans to help them administer their zone.
Berthold seemed to fill their bill and after a careful screening
was given the job of Vice-President of the Zonal Office of
the Reich Insurance Supervisory Board. The pay was small
but the bait was a brand new car.

But Beitz's knowledge of the insurance business was
minimal—as was his spoken command of the English
language. However, there were many ex-Nazi insurance
officials wandering the streets who for a few cigarettes
or a little food were prepared to "advise" Beitz without
his British bosses knowing anything about it. Within no
time at all he was an expert. As Germany began to recover,
and the old private insurance companies started up in
business again, Beitz's services were eagerly sought after.
In 1949 he plumped for being general manager of the
tottering Iduna Insurance. By pushing his salesmen hard
and using every selling gimmick in the book, he managed so
to increase the business that they could absorb one ailing

company after another and rise within four years from sixteenth to third position in the German insurance league table. This drive and energy had given him a reputation for being something of a "whizz-kid" long before Alfried met up with him.

When Alfried was told by his lawyers in the first week of March 1953 that everything had been settled with the Allies, he immediately telephoned Beitz to make him a firm offer. It so happened that Beitz was holidaying at the time with his family/at St. Moritz. Promptly he motored down to Zürich to meet Alfried, and there over brandies at the Hotel Baur-au-lac Beitz made his fateful decision. Nor was it one that he was ever to regret financially—today he is the highest paid man in Western Germany and probably in all Europe, earning something like £150,000 a year and with a cast-iron contract that he has virtually written himself. Esseners quip that it would be easier for Beitz to sell Krupp's than for Alfried to sack him!

In fact Beitz did not join the firm until November 1953. His departure from the Germania-Iduna Life had been delayed because of eleventh-hour difficulties with his former directors who had tried desperately to dissuade him from leaving them.

But if Beitz had thought his last few days in insurance were somewhat stormy, his first few days with Krupp's were certainly far from rosy. When the news of his appointment leaked out, reactions within Essen and the Ruhr as a whole ranged from utter bewilderment to extreme anger. His reception from the other Krupp managers and directors was coldly hostile, to say the least. Naturally many of the more experienced senior executives felt rather bitter at the prospect of a complete "outsider" to their business being hoisted above their heads.

When some of Beitz's early decisions came unstuck, it seemed to suggest that he was in fact "a fish out of water" as they claimed—and there were many of course to take delight at his discomfiture. But Beitz persisted, for above all he had Alfried's firm backing. Within a relatively short time the hostile elements among the upper echelons of Krupp officials had been weeded out and some of the older directors even persuaded to retire early.

There are many stories, some probably apocryphal, about those early days of Beitz: how one senior manager who had disputed a decision of Beitz's was given fifteen minutes in which to leave the premises; how another found his desk and even the door to his office had disappeared when he returned from holiday; how a venerable and aristocratic director was shocked by Beitz quipping at a board meeting that at one stage in their lives they had both been fondled by the same woman, for it turned out that Berthold's mother had been the Prussian count's nurse! This ruthlessness and this brashness in the face of Krupp tradition and Krupp accepted ways of doing things quickly earned for Beitz the nickname of "The American"—and the fact that he speaks English with a Brooklyn accent and peppers even his German conversation with American slang has served to perpetuate that soubriquet among his workmen and his officials ever since. On top of this, he prefers Count Basie to Johann Sebastian Bach, dresses more in the mode of Madison Avenue than with the cut of Essen's Kettwigerstrasse, drinks Manhattans and whisky-sours rather than schnapps and beer, hangs Impressionists on his walls rather than family portraits, and talks incessantly of efficiency and motivations much more so than any other Krupp executive before or since.

It was typical too of Beitz that almost his first action on taking charge was to speed up the lifts in all Krupp offices—and as well as arguing in favour of getting out of coal-production altogether he could also show how untraditional he was by suggesting that Krupp's should give up making locomotives too. Alfried overruled him on both points, however—the only time he ever has on major issues. But Berthold has been proved right, for since that time Krupp's locomotive business has dipped further and further into the red, and one coal-mine after another has had to close down in the Ruhr.

Just eighteen months after Beitz had arrived at Krupp's *The Times* was already describing him as "one of the most up-and-coming industrialists in Western Germany" and was declaring that his career to date had been "meteoric". In a profile of him a few years later, that same London newspaper referred to him as "a man of drive and powerful ideas".

Beitz is typical of the breezy breed of new managers that have grown up in the Ruhr since the Allies left: men supremely confident in their ability to handle people and situations of all kinds, men more often than not without a financial holding in the firm they are managing and directing, yet acting with all the power and authority of the old-time entrepreneur and self-proprietor. Beitz like the rest of them has a great flair for organisation and in "picking the right man for the right job". He boasts that he has what he describes as a "sixth sense for business". In point of fact he has very little technical knowledge of Krupp processes even today, preferring to leave the details of any contract to others once he has made the decision in principle. He dislikes his desk being cluttered with documents and relies on the spoken rather than the written word. Every year he flies thousands of miles in his Krupp-owned British-built private jet, but likes nothing better of an evening than to cook cosy little meals for his family or for certain visiting ambassadors and other dignitaries. He exudes charm all the time and, unlike Alfried, enjoys appearing in public, even on American or German television, though not so far on British television. Again in contrast to Alfried, Beitz readily accepts invitations to Bonn diplomatic receptions. He makes a particular point of keeping in very close touch with the various ministries, especially the department of foreign affairs: it so happens that his holiday retreat on the island of Sylt in the North Sea is next door to that of the Foreign Minister, Gerhard Schroeder. The Krupp office in Bonn is virtually an embassy in itself, being one of the most imposing and best-situated buildings in the West German capital. It is right next to the new Königshof Hotel where journalists and visiting delegations usually stay—and the Krupp man in Bonn is often jocularly referred to as "the Ambassador from Essen". Beitz is also on excellent terms with Willy Brandt, the Mayor of Berlin, and with Otto Brenner, the leader of the big metal-workers' trade union and described by some as the Frank Cousins of West Germany. But his biggest asset at Krupp's is the complete trust Alfried undoubtedly has in him.

Beitz in effect is Prime Minister in Alfried's constitutional monarchy—or perhaps the better analogy is Chancellor in Krupp's Reich, for there is no *primum inter pares*, no "first among equals", nonsense about Berthold's relationship with his board of directors. They are strictly advisers and do not participate collectively in every decision of principle that he makes. A board decision at Krupp's means a Beitz decision, perhaps belatedly agreed to by Alfried. Indeed Berthold has boasted to at least one visitor that he sees his boss on the average no more than twice a day, although their offices adjoin each other: first thing in the morning when arriving and sometimes last thing at night over a cocktail before leaving. Their talk is invariably of business, because they have little else in common.

Perhaps the key to the success of their partnership is that they are such opposites, for by and large they complement each other. Alfried is shy and hesitant, while Beitz is forceful and direct. Alfried is correct and formal, while Beitz is brash and prefers to call a man by his first name rather than to follow the German custom of addressing him as "Herr Doktor" or "Herr Direktor". Alfried is dignified and paternalistic, while Beitz positively enjoys being aggressive with his staff as well as with his competitors. In short, Alfried is still steeped in the Krupp traditions of before the war, while Beitz has been schooled in the harsh realities of post-occupation Germany. As it might well have been put by that same Madison Avenue which continues to colour much of Beitz's thinking and to affect much of his behaviour, theirs has been a marriage of an Old Heritage and a New Look.

Berthold has led the way in not wanting Krupp's to re-assume the mantle of the Nation's Armourer—not out of strong principle but by the simple yardstick of economic fact. To his mind there are many more profitable ways of employing their capital than going in for making guns and shells again—apart of course from the obvious fact, as he himself has pointed out, that armaments today no longer mean the weapons in which Krupp's were once proficient, but rather ballistic missiles and H-bombs, in neither of which the Essen firm has any production advantage over its competitors. That no pacifist streak runs through Krupp's thinking despite the 1945 débâcle can be judged from the evidence that Alfried and Beitz have undertaken contracts for NATO, albeit such relatively harmless things as mobile water-purifiers or such clearly defensive things as radar reflector-aerials for Europe's early-warning system. At the same time, some of their heavy trucks, for instance, have found their way into military use—as indeed have the helicopters and aircraft they have been assembling at Bremen under licence from American companies. On the other hand, their great, private artillery-range at Meppen is today the site of a Government oil-refinery.

It was for the same reasons of reduced profitability that Beitz tried at first to dissuade Alfried from becoming associated again with coal and steel. Coal, as he unfailingly points out, is a declining industry—and as for steel, he argues that it will not be long before German and other West European basic producers are undercut drastically by the new steel industries in the developing countries, many of which have of course been built or equipped by Krupp's themselves. "Our competitors can be grateful to us we didn't sell our coal and steel," he is on record as saying, "if we had done, we would have put all the money into becoming the suppliers for the fastest-growing industries: petro-chemicals, plastics, and atomic-energy, for example." As it is, even now Krupp's have to import their iron-ore from Sweden, Liberia and Brazil—and the profit margins on their most modern steel plants at Rheinhausen have dwindled year by year.

Beitz's most remarkable achievement to date has been his pioneering of West Germany's "trade opening to the East", a sort of latter-day commercial *Drang Nach Osten*. "Why go all the way to Indonesia or Bolivia when East Europe is on our doorstep?" is one of Berthold Beitz's most quoted utterances. Said *The Times* of him in February 1965:

He has personally engineered West Germany's otherwise rather clumsy efforts at a reconciliation with Poland. The West German Government, hampered by the Hallstein doctrine (which does not permit the Federal Republic to have any dealings with those countries

which recognise East Germany) and the dispute over
the Oder-Neisse territories, has virtually handed over
its relations with Poland to this very diplomatic
businessman.

As early as 1957 Berthold was broaching the idea with
Adenauer of setting up trade missions in Poland and the
other Iron Curtain countries. In 1958 the Poles invited him
officially to Warsaw and when he arrived received him as an
honoured guest. A little later, Dr. Adenauer, although
somewhat sceptical about his chances of success, entrusted
him with a letter to the Polish Prime Minister which Beitz
delivered in person. Thereafter he began an unofficial
mission to try to improve relations between the two countries,
and over the years has become a familiar figure in Warsaw,
highly regarded in fact by the Polish leaders. He has already
been described as "the only German with credentials
acceptable in Eastern Europe"—and by another as West
Germany's unofficial ambassador to the Soviets. Not only
was he able to coax a reluctant Chancellor Adenauer into
co-existence with the Poles in particular, but he also secured
the blessing of the Americans who had at first been alarmed
by his hobnobbing with the Communist world. After
being rebuffed by Republican Washington in 1956, the year
of the Suez Crisis, over Alfried's "Point $4\frac{1}{2}$" programme,
Berthold persisted with them and was rewarded in 1965,
the year of the Vietnam Crisis, by the Democratic Administration's approval of his plan to establish factories in
Poland jointly owned by Krupp's and the Warsaw Government.

In essence, the idea is that Krupp's would furnish the
machinery, the technical knowledge, and the managerial
skills, while Poland would supply the land and the labour.
Beitz's boys would handle the marketing of the products in
the West, leaving the Poles themselves to look after the sales
outlets within the Eastern bloc—and the profits of course
would be shared. Its attraction to Warsaw is that it would
help ease their unemployment problem and provide much-
needed foreign currency, as well as giving them a chance to
benefit from Western technical and managerial "know-

how". Krupp's interest in it is that it offers them a firm commercial footing behind the Iron Curtain and is a way too of getting round the acute labour shortage in the Ruhr. The first plants would probably be for making something like gear-boxes or transmission units for cars and heavy lorries. At the time of writing (July 1966), nothing had been definitely signed or agreed in detail—as Beitz has said "the devil is in the details"—though it was clear that since February 1965 there has been some sort of agreement in principle between Warsaw and Krupp's.

If Beitz accomplished nothing more in his life than to have come up with this imaginative idea then history would still have remembered him. Should his plan ever take practical shape then it will be an event of momentous significance, for it will have broken through the harsh mantle of the Cold War and pierced the icy shroud of political co-existence. Declared *The Times*, "It will represent a bridge not only between West Germany and Poland but also between East and West Europe and between the capitalist and Communist economic systems." Said the *New York Times* when the scheme was first mooted, "The proposed deal is clever of Krupp, bold of Poland, and challenging for ideologies . . . if the once largest 'sword' in Germany can persuade one of Hitler's first victims that it now beats only ploughshares, a significant East–West barrier would seem surmounted."

The leader-writer could also have added of course that Beitz's project if sufficiently successful might dispel once and for all Krupp's ugly past reputation for destruction and might give them the name, perhaps even in Britain itself, for constructive and peaceful endeavour—should Beitz ever achieve that, then apart from all his other notable contributions to Krupp's recovery since 1953, he will have more than proved his worth to Alfried.

CHAPTER NINETEEN

"The Americans of Europe"

IF BERTHOLD BEITZ's appointment as Alfried's general
manager is Krupp's best symbol of their break with their
past, it is also indicative of the change in the rest of the Ruhr
today. The Ruhr has broken with its past too. No longer is
the emphasis simply on coal, iron and steel: on the so-called
"heavy" industries with which the word *Ruhr* has become
synonymous. The Ruhr now is a centre for glass-making,
tailoring, oil-refining, petro-chemicals, electronics, medicine
—even for manufacturing motor-cars, television sets and
kitchen food-mixers. You can buy a shirt or a pair of socks
made in the Ruhr; you can also buy a packet of Ruhr
margarine.

Like Krupp's, the Ruhr has diversified—has broadened the
range of what it produces. In doing so, however, it has lost
its uniqueness (and at the same time its notoriety) as the
home solely of the big coal and steel empires. Although many
of these industrial colossi still of course remain, their influence
has been blunted and their supremacy has been supplanted
by the rise of the Ruhr's newer baronies, such as supermarket
chains, banking houses, construction concerns, and even
mail-order businesses. Today, the white-collar worker and
the shorthand typist are becoming more typical of the Ruhr
than the soot-faced coal-miner or the brawny foundry-
man. Indeed, twice as many Ruhr citizens now find their
livelihoods in commerce and finance than in coal and
steel.

The pace by and large has been set by coal's decline. In
1950 it accounted for 92 per cent of the Federal Republic's
energy needs. By 1955 the proportion was down to 70 per
cent, and by 1965 to 41 per cent. Sixty-eight collieries have

been closed in the Ruhr since 1958, when the crisis really began—and the numbers employed there in actual coal-production have shrunk from nearly half a million in 1957 to under 300,000 by the end of 1965. As the use of oil increases, and as the new natural-gas field just 100 miles away in Holland is more and more opened up, so coal's share of the fuel market can expect to diminish yet further. Though still relatively abundant, most of the Ruhr's coal lies deep down in narrow veins not easily adaptable to automatic mining techniques.

By contrast to coal, steel is still in great demand—1964 was in fact a record year for output in the Ruhr. But times are becoming tougher and tougher for steel producers, such as for instance Krupp's Rheinhausen subsidiary. Competition from the other Common Market countries, as well as from Japan, has intensified in recent years: between 1961 and 1965, for example, the share of imported steel in West Germany's total steel consumption rose from 14 to 22 per cent. To shave costs, most manufacturers are automating heavily—which means of course fewer jobs. They also argue that they could reduce prices still further by using the cheaper American coal instead of the more expensive local product; that in this way the removal of the Federal Government's high duty on coal imports could save them something like £30 million a year. But as the steel companies are practically the only major customers still faithful to Ruhr coal this would aggravate that industry's difficulties as fast as it solved their own. In addition, many steel producers, including Krupp's Rheinhausen subsidiary, have their own coal-fields—all of which makes the problem of what to do about the Old Ruhr a particularly complicated one.

Even so, the 5,000,000 people who live and work in that oval-shaped, fifty-miles-long by twenty-miles-wide industrial belt, stretching from Dortmund in the east to Duisburg in the west, enjoy today one of the highest standards of living anywhere in Europe: higher certainly than South Wales, Clydeside, or the north-east coast of England, and at least as high as London or the Midlands. Shop-windows fairly bulge in the Ruhr—while the atmosphere in most town centres is on the whole more cosmopolitan, and the choice of goods for sale more sophisticated, than in the average northern English town. The *Hausfrau* of Essen, Dortmund or Bochum does not feel the same pull towards the neighbouring "big city" of Düsseldorf or Cologne as the housewives of, say, Bacup or Batley do in regard to Leeds or Manchester. Furthermore, there is no shortage of jobs in the Ruhr, and unlike his confrère in the coal-fields of for instance Durham or West Virginia the displaced Ruhr coal-miner can usually find an opening fairly easily in another industry right on his doorstep.

Perhaps the most vivid example of the Old Ruhr giving way to the New is to be found at Bochum. Headquarters of the German Miners' Union, and almost at the geographical heart of the Ruhr, Bochum was the typical tough, grimy, ugly, smoke-stack town of the Ruhr's "Coal-Pot". Most of Krupp's coal-mines, for instance, were located there —and Bochum is the home too of the Bochumer Verein steelworks, once old Alfred's fiercest competitor for specialised steels, but now owned by his great-grandson Alfried. During the last eight years or so the number of coal-miners in Bochum has dropped by well over half to just under 20,000 at present. Nine collieries have been closed there so far, leaving four still open, though their day of execution cannot be far off either.

In 1959, when pit closures were already under way, and when morale was particularly low among its citizens, the Town Council of Bochum boldly began courting General Motors who at that time were looking round for a site on which to set up a second factory for their German subsidiary, Opel, which had outgrown its Frankfurt home. Months of anxious bargaining followed before America's biggest automobile concern succumbed to Bochum's blandishments. Then in 1962, to the plaudits of politicians and P.R. men alike, what was described as the world's most modern car factory was opened there for making Opel Kadetts, Germany's fastest selling small-car. Built above a veritable honeycomb of worked-out coal-mines, the project when finally completed will have cost General Motors about £100 million and will give employment to some 20,000 people—almost exactly the number of Bochum coal-miners so far displaced. What is more, should the old pits ever subside, and the factory fall in, then the company would be fully compensated by the Bochum Town Council, who to date have lavished another £50 million on laying down roads, drains, and water-supplies to the site.

Not far away from Opel's new factory, on a 1,200-acre site above another group of disused collieries, is arising the mammoth, American-style University of the Ruhr: the first major seat of higher learning in the whole industrial belt. When finished in 1975, some £200 million will have been spent on providing places for 15,000 students and on erecting a satellite-village to house the 25,000 teaching staff and administrative personnel, together with their families. Yet another modern acquisition at Bochum is a television-components factory supplying jobs for 4,000 citizens of the town, mostly women—just one of the 200 or so new enterprises Bochum boasts have opened within its boundaries since 1952. A still further proud possession there is a brand new theatre—one of Germany's finest provincial theatres in fact.

Some parts of the Ruhr have inevitably been less successful than others in attracting the newer industries. Their relative failure tends to be marked by the greater persistence of the older sub-standard housing of the past, instead of the tall, modern blocks of workers' apartments that are going up almost everywhere else in the Ruhr. Essen, for instance, hitherto the front-runner in the Ruhr's growth, largely because of Krupp's, has in fact dropped way behind many of its neighbouring cities. Although never more prosperous than it is today, and laying claim to having some of West Germany's most up-to-date shopping facilities, Essen's income per head of population increased just 15 per cent between 1957 and 1961—whereas a place like Gelsenkirchen, once known solely for coal and steel, but now a centre for petro-chemicals and electronics, rose by more than 30 per cent, while Leverkusen, the home of Bayer's, the successors to IG Farben's medicine division, grew 23 per cent. At the other end of the scale is an old "Coal Pot" town like Castrop-Rauxel with an expansion of barely 4 per cent to its name in that same time-period.

Similarly, the Ruhr itself, although still termed the "power-house of Western Germany" in most literature on the subject, has lagged behind the rest of the country's industrial growth. In the five years between 1957 and 1962 for instance, production in the world's most famous industrial belt increased by only 30·1 per cent, compared with 45 per cent for the entire province of North Rhine-Westphalia, of which the Ruhr is simply a part, and compared with 54·4 per cent for the Federal Republic as a whole. As south-east England is to the traditionally industrial north, so newer "growth areas" within Western Germany like Bavaria and Baden-Wurttemberg, with their absence of slums, industrial greyness, and factory smog, have been attracting away vital labour from the Ruhr, particularly the younger workers.

But faced with losing its historic pre-eminence in the nation's economy, the Ruhr has fought back. As well as wooing newer industries, it has set about improving the area as a place in which to live. Already under way is a Government-backed project to landscape the whole industrial belt: factory eyesores are being screened by trees and shrubs, and the more populous parts are being laced with so-called "green wedges" of woods, farms and lakes. By the beginning of 1968, for instance, regulations will be in force requiring automatic cleaners on all smokestacks within the Ruhr—though it is expected long before then, as a result of what has been described as "Europe's biggest campaign against industrial smog and chemical waste in the atmosphere", that the skies above cities like Essen, Duisburg and Dortmund will be a lot bluer than they are today, and a lot bluer perhaps than the skies above (say) Sheffield or Rotherham or Stoke-on-Trent. To date, individual industrialists have spent something like £90 million on installing air-purification plants inside their works—while the police in the Ruhr now have powers to shut down offending industries or even to halt private road traffic when smog reaches a certain density. Thyssen's, for example, have lavished £4 million on controlling the smoke from their stacks at Duisburg.

Attempts too have been made to beautify some of the old

company towns of yesteryear and to turn them into handsome modern cities; Krupp's for instance have steam-cleaned many of their buildings in Essen. Ruhr local authorities, controlled for the most part by the Social Democrats (Herr Willy Brandt's party) have led the way in improving the standard of housing within the area and in raising the level of the cultural amenities and the public services they have to offer—not simply as a means of perhaps stemming the migratory flow of workers to the south, but rather as a way of attracting back ambitious executives and their families.

Besides the new university going up at Bochum and the new Shakespeare Theatre already built there, the Ruhr town of Wuppertal now boasts Germany's most modern swimming pool—and even Essen, at long last, has a cultural centre, helped financially by Alfried, who has also given over a part of the old Villa Hügel as an art gallery for visiting collections.

There is also in existence a comprehensive plan for the Ruhr, drawn up by the provincial government of North Rhine-Westphalia, whereby the population of the region will be "decanted" from the centre to a series of new towns to be built ten miles away to the north and south, each with light industries of their own. This redistribution of the population will give the opportunity, it is hoped, for the existing "infra-structure" of the industrial belt, such as roads, railways, power-lines, water-supplies, sewage, schools, hospitals and so on, to be brought up to date. Inevitably, too, there are schemes for an elaborate network of monorails, to be built perhaps by Krupp's, who already market a mobile steel flyover for roads—and a Dortmund city official has even proposed an intricate tunnel system some sixty to eighty feet below the surface, consisting of massive concrete tubes in which fast underground trains would run, connecting all the towns of the area, and in which vast subterranean shopping-centres could also be located.

Ideas are certainly not in short supply in the Ruhr—and as ever it has the reputation of being one of the liveliest focal points for industrial research and technical development in Western Europe.

But gone are the days when it was a breeding-ground for autarchy and for nationalism—when Ruhr scientists slavishly strove to make Germany industrially independent of the rest of the world, and when Ruhr tycoons like Krupp or Thyssen led the rest of the Reich in their fervour for first the Kaiser's call for a greater *Lebensraum* and then the Nazis' notions of racial supremacy. Today, the talk in Essen and Bochum beer-halls is of inter-dependence—and Krupp officials and Krupp workers, for instance, are among the most enthusiastic anywhere on the Continent for such supranational bodies as the European Common Market or the United Nations.

The Ruhr today is indeed international. British firms, Canadian firms, Japanese firms, but above all American firms, abound there, attracted by the Common Market and preferring stable, friendly, prosperous Germany to, say, de Gaulle's volatile and occasionally petulant France. Such has been the influx of United States investment into the Ruhr since the early 1950's that more than one German headline-writer has seen fit to term it "the second American invasion of Germany". Some thirty American companies are in fact located there, mostly subsidiaries of larger home-based corporations such as U.S. Rubber, Minnesota Mining and Manufacturing, American Metal Climax, and General Motors' Opel. In 1965 for instance Du Pont's announced they were building a massive multi-million-dollar factory for making synthetic fibres at Uentrop near Hamm, to be completed within three years.

All in all, nearly 150 foreign firms have settled in the Ruhr since the establishment of the European Common Market. Curiously enough, over half of them are Japanese—a fact which does not seem to displease the Americanophobe headline-writers quite so much. At the moment the tradesmen from Tokyo and Nagasaki are relatively small fry, but if sheer numbers count for anything in business—the Japanese sales staffs alone are said to total 800 in the Ruhr—then somebody someday could be in for a rude awakening. One German industrialist I questioned on the subject during the autumn of 1964 merely replied, "But of course we had quite good contacts with most of these Japanese firms during the War."

Such well-known British companies as Courtaulds, I.C.I., Bowater's, and Reed's, all have subsidiaries in the Ruhr, including of course B.P. and Shell who boast two of the biggest oil-refineries there. As for the rest, there is even a battery manufacturer from Israel.

But apart from foreign businessmen, the Ruhr's immense wealth has always attracted different nationalities to go and work there, ever since Irishmen sank the first coal-shafts at Gelsenkirchen two centuries ago. Nowadays Greeks, Turks, Moroccans, Spaniards, Italians, Africans, Poles, Yugoslavs, and even a few South Koreans, have flocked to the Ruhr, drawn by some of the highest wages paid anywhere. In 1965, for instance, 30,000 foreign miners were working down Ruhr pits, while the total number of foreign workers in the Ruhr was approaching 100,000.

Coal may symbolise the Old Ruhr, and Opel's car factory at Bochum may symbolise the New Ruhr, but for the moment at any rate the visible Ruhr is still steel, despite the intense competition encountered by its manufacturers. The concentration of steel plants along both sides of the Rhine at Duisburg makes Pittsburgh and Sheffield look positively underdeveloped. Over one-third of the Federal Republic's steel is produced here—and Duisburg is Europe's biggest inland port mainly on account of the trans-shipment of steel and iron-ore. Not for nothing is this stretch of Germany's mightiest river known as "the Road of the Dragons". Nor is it so surprising that the Ruhr as a whole is called "the Land of a Thousand Fires". Driving east from Duisburg to Dortmund by way of Essen, along the new super-highway that cuts through the middle of the Ruhr, you are rarely ever out of sight of a smokestack or a belching furnace. Dotted in between are the rickety-looking gantries of the old coal-mines, with here and there a mountain or two of slag— but not much slag, for most of it has been sold over the years to the Dutch to help build their dykes to keep out the sea. What *is* new, however, on the Ruhr skyline today are the skyscrapers—the locals call them *hoch-haus* (high-house) or, less reverently, "status-symbols". Usually they vary between twenty and twenty-five floors in height, but the style is invariably identical: the up-ended slab. Most of them are steel-framed (even though concrete would probably be cheaper) and the majority are in fact the headquarters of steel companies.

But besides boasting the tallest office-blocks of the whole industrial belt, the old steel companies are again much in evidence in other ways. Their former immense political influence has certainly gone (for good one hopes), but their economic power remains. Old habits die hard—and head-line-writers still link the word *Ruhr* with steel.

Despite the efforts to break up the coal and steel empires into smaller units, most of them have in fact come together again. The one victory the Allied "decartelisers" can point to is that the Vereinigte Stahlwerke, the notorious giant steel cartel that dominated the Ruhr before the war, has not been re-formed. But even that is only a hollow victory, for the Thyssen Group, welded in 1963 out of just two segments of it, is today far bigger than the old VS ever was. Similarly with IG Farben, the mammoth chemical concern, which was split into three by the Allied "trust-busters"—now each of the three offshoots is larger than its former parent!

But today's £400 million Thyssen colossus is not merely bigger than the Vereinigte Stahlwerke was before the Allies dismembered it, it also happens to be Europe's largest steel producer—and the third by size in the world, coming after the top two American steel producers, U.S. Steel and Bethlehem Steel. Its annual production amounts to more than half the total British output and is about three times as big as that of its nearest British rival. Yet such has been the growth in the Ruhr's steel capacity since the end of the Occupation that even Thyssen's represents only one-quarter of the area's steel production, compared with the much more dominant two-thirds that the Vereinigte Stahlwerke possessed during the 'thirties.

Thyssen's, however, are not the only Ruhr steel giant today. They are followed closely in size by the product of another recent (1965) merger: that between the Dutch-controlled Dortmund-Horder (a segment of the broken-up VS) and the hitherto independent Hoesch concern also located at Dortmund. The yearly output of this new titan is not much behind Thyssen's in fact, and in any case puts it easily in the top ten of world steel producers. Not to be outdone, Krupp's steel subsidiary, Rheinhausen, has taken over the Bochumer Verein (still one more offshoot of the former Vereinigte Stahlwerke) to give Alfried a 15 per cent share in the Ruhr's total output. But even so he has dropped to third in the German—and hence European—steel stakes. Before the war of course Krupp's were second to the VS and had a slightly larger proportion of the market then than they have today. Another of the "Big Six" steel producers in the Ruhr before 1945, Mannesmann, although divided into three, too, by the Allies has come together again—and yet a further reversal of the Allied "deconcentration" policy has been the linking-up of the steel plants with their former coal-mines despite the efforts of the British and Americans to sever such connections for all time.

During the 'thirties, six massive steel groups controlled 97 per cent of the Ruhr's steel output. The victorious Allies determined to break up these concentrations of economic power, considering them not only unhealthily large economically, but also that their sheer size had encouraged their bosses to be politically irresponsible. In fact they increased that number to eight, effectively sharing 99 per cent of the Ruhr market, but much closer in size to each other than before. As a result of recent mergers, however, we are back to six firms dominating the Ruhr, of which four account for well over three-quarters of the area's production of steel—indeed two of them share just under half of the market. All in all, of the fifty biggest steel companies in the world ten are German.

To add an extra touch of piquancy to the irony of all this, these mergers that have unashamedly undone the work of the Allied "trust-busters", have in fact been carried out under the auspices (some would claim the active encouragement) of another Allied creation, the European Coal and Steel Community. Set up in 1952, it was meant really to be a final solution to the "Ruhr Problem" since all the powers previously held by the allied occupiers in the Ruhr were vested in this new supranational organisation.

Both Britain and the United States at first welcomed this idea of a common market for Europe's coal and steel

industries—but Britain eventually backed out of the negotiations, though in the end she did nothing to prevent the other
six (France, West Germany, Italy, Belgium, Holland and
Luxembourg) from going ahead with pooling their "heavy"
industries. A sort of cabinet of the Community, the so-called
High Authority, was established, whose decisions affecting
the whole of the industry were binding on the Governments
of all member-nations.

France had been enthusiastic for the idea from the start—
indeed it was the then French Foreign Minister, Robert
Schuman, who had initially proposed it in May 1950.
France had never really taken her eyes off the Ruhr since
1945—and if she was to be denied "internationalising" it
then at least she would "supranationalise" it. To her mind,
once a German Government had lost total sovereignty
over the Ruhr then France would never again have to
fear an attack from her Teutonic neighbour across the
Rhine.

But in June 1950 Winston Churchill warned the French
people that "without Britain, the coal and steel pool in
Western Europe must naturally tend to be dominated by
Germany, who will be the most powerful member"—and
this of course is how it in fact has turned out, for of the
eleven major steel producers in the Community today seven
are German, including the two biggest.

The High Authority's basic concern is with the efficiency
of the coal and steel industries within its jurisdiction—that
is with the economics rather than the politics of coal and
steel. It is on this criterion alone that applications for
mergers and take-overs are judged. If Thyssen's or Dortmund-Horder or Krupp's had had to seek approval for their
actions from the Federal Government in Bonn then it is just
possible that they would not have been able to contravene
the clear intentions of the Allied "decartelisers" quite so
blatantly. It is likely that Chancellor Adenauer or Chancellor Erhard might have found it just too embarrassing
politically to have set their seal on such mergers. But since
the High Authority has only to consider *economic* arguments,
it has been an admirable instrument in the hands of the take-
over tycoons of the Ruhr—just how admirably so far as

Alfried Krupp is concerned is the subject of the next chapter.

Yet although the pre-war pattern of a few vast groups dominating coal and steel output in the Ruhr would seem to be re-emerging (even down to the reappearance of the same pre-war names), there is, however, one key difference. The Ruhr today is no longer the private province of the rich steel families of yesteryear: of the Thyssens or the Haniels or the Stinnes or the Flicks, or even of the Krupps. No more do these "smoke-stack" dynasties rule the roost in the Ruhr, wielding immense power and political influence. For the most part they have either died out or sold out or moved out.

In the case of the Thyssen family, for instance, the major shareholding in the Group is still held by two lady-members: the eighty-eight-year-old Frau Amelie, Fritz Thyssen's widow, and his fifty-four-year-old daughter, Countess Anita de Zichy, although like Alfried they were both required by the Allies to sell. But the two ladies, said to be worth about £80 million between them, very rarely visit Germany, least of all the Ruhr, preferring to live in their fastnesses, at Lugano in the case of Amelie and Buenos Aires in the case of the Countess—though they have also set up a £16 million philanthropic foundation in Germany. The active member of the family, young Baron Heinrich Thyssen-Bornemisza (better known to English readers through his previous marriage to the Scottish model, Fiona Campbell-Walter) has his money invested not in steel, nor concentrated in the Ruhr, but instead widely spread throughout Western Germany in such things as shipyards, utilities, and engineering.

Friedrich Flick is another case in point. Although a convicted war criminal, he is again one of Germany's wealthiest men. But today his £300 million fortune is not solely in steel, but also in paper, chemicals and particularly motor-cars: he owns the prestigious Daimler-Benz (Mercedes) corporation.

The notable exception in all this is of course Alfried Krupp who has sat tight in Essen. In this way he is unique in the Ruhr today—far more so than either his father Gustav or his grandfather Fritz were in their day.

But in one important particular Alfried has followed the prevailing trend. Today's Ruhr bosses by and large are salary-earning and business-school trained, with little or no direct financial stake in the firm they are managing. Berthold Beitz conforms almost exactly to this pattern. In this sense these managers are like the German mercenary generals of old. Their allegiance can be bought, albeit at a high price, but can also just as easily, and just as expensively, be un-bought. In most cases they have not grown up with the firm. Very often they are outsiders even to the Ruhr, having been poached not just from other industries but also from other areas—again like Berthold Beitz. Accordingly they are inclined to be far less sentimental towards age-old accepted ways of doing things and tend to be tougher with tradition: not paternalistic but judging every activity of the firm they are running by the simple yardstick of its profitability— again like Berthold Beitz. In a word they are *professional* managers, rather than scions of proprietorial industrial families. There is less of the "Herr Direktor" of yesteryear about them. They do not retreat into their capacious oak-panelled family-portrait-filled offices, merely sallying forth once a year to present the long-service awards to loyal, forelock tugging employees. Today's Ruhr tycoons, like Egon Overbeck of Mannesmann or Guenther Henle of Klockner's or Hans Guenther Sohl of Thyssen's—and of course like Berthold Beitz of Krupp's—are far more ap-proachable to their staffs and far more familiar figures to their workers, even to popping up from time to time on German television, than the big magnates of yesteryear. In this sense too they are nearer to their American than to their British counterparts—just one more reason in fact why the Germans are becoming known as "the Americans of Europe".

In his appointment of Berthold Beitz, as with his wide-ning of the firm's activities, Alfried Krupp has shown himself to be brilliantly in accord with the trends of his time. But he has also been partly pacemaker as well as trend-follower.

Beitz stands for the New Ruhr—Alfried for the Old. Between them the House of Krupp spans both Old and

New. In this way it is unique in the Ruhr today. But over the future of the House of Krupp there still hangs the question whether or not Alfried should be made to carry out his promise to sell off his coal and steel interests—and it is to this that we now turn.

CHAPTER TWENTY

"The British Government has no reason to believe that the undertaking will not be fulfilled"

VISITING BONN UNIVERSITY in the autumn of 1964, I asked many of the students there whether or not they thought Alfried Krupp should be made to abide by his 1953 undertaking to dispose of his coal and steel holdings. Not one of those young German men and women but were convinced in his or her maturing mind that Alfried should not for one moment contemplate selling a single penny-piece of his interests in the Ruhr. Indeed I got the distinct impression that his refusal so far to sell was to them both an. act of courage and a moral standpoint.

Without exception, those youngsters had been brought up entirely since the end of the war. For the most part they would not have been born, or else have been still only babes, when Nazi Germany went down to defeat. Their only recollection of hearing Hitler speak was in old newsreels recently re-shown or in television programmes dealing with some aspect of their country's history during the last thirty years. On other issues their views were quite liberal, more often than not democratic, and certainly far from nationalistic, almost passionately so. It seemed true, as I had been warned, and as much of my reading hitherto had led me to believe was so, that Germans no matter how young or how old had this "blockage" in their thinking when it came to considering the past, present, and future of the House of Krupp; that Krupp's were indeed almost a "sacred cow" in German life and in German politics; that to criticise the firm or the family was wellnigh tantamount to blasphemy.

Putting the same question to a group of certainly more varied British people, the responses predictably were totally different. Older ex-servicemen were bewildered and baffled, some bitterly so, as to how Krupp's "had got away with it". There was a definite feeling among many of them that they had "somehow been let down". "I thought that that was what the war had been all about—stopping people like him from getting started again." Others had assumed that Alfried had been "made to sell up ages ago" and were surprised, and some even alarmed, to hear that he had not but was back in business.

To younger men who had fought in the Second World War, the fact that Alfried had not "of his own free will" done what he had promised to do, seemed "typical". "That's all you would expect of a man like him", said many. The exasperation appeared to come from Krupp not having been *compelled* by the Allies to sell—from, too, the Allies not having confiscated his properties when they were legally entitled to, that is while he was in Landsberg. The blame, if any, they wanted to lay at the Allies' doorsteps, curiously enough not at the German Government's, nor even at Alfried's own.

While many a brawny ex-serviceman brandished his fists at me, or else rolled up his sleeves and looked belligerent, when I put it to him to tell me exactly how he thought the Allies at this late stage should go about trying to compel Alfried to sell—most of the others were inclined to agree that it was now too late really to do anything about it. A common phrase that kept cropping up time and time again in their answers was "the pass has already been sold on this one long ago".

A Conservative M.P. with a distinguished war record argued thus:

Of course I recognise that a big firm like Krupp's is important for the economy of Germany. What I object to is that a man who's a convicted war criminal, and who has been found guilty of crimes against humanity of the most terrible kind, should remain as proprietor of this great firm with its enormous capital assets. I believe that to be morally wrong for this reason: at Nuremberg we attempted to set up a code of conduct

in war-time. We tried people on the basis of international law as it then stood—and I think it makes a
mockery of those trials if Alfried Krupp is allowed to
remain in his present position.

While another British politician, this time a man of the left
and for long an inveterate opponent of Alfried felt that the
British were just about "the only people left in the world who
really feel still deeply that Krupp's should be made to carry
out their promise to break up their organisation". "But,"
he added, "I don't think that that will probably ever happen
now."

The plain fact of the matter is that Alfried has not waited
to see. Although saying publicly, soon after the signing,
"we have a moral obligation, and I will not look for escapes",
the truth is that he has done very little himself to carry out
the spirit, let alone the letter, of the 1953 Agreement.
Equally, there is little doubt too that in circumventing the
Allies on this one he has had the active encouragement and
moral support of the rest of German industry—and if not
the active encouragement, then at least the clear connivance
of the West German Government as well.

Apart perhaps from the Communists, who in any case do
not exist as a party there, no organised body of opinion in
West Germany has ever called on Alfried to abide by his
1953 undertaking to sell. No German trade unionist, no
German left-wing politician, no German writer or journalist,
actor or painter, housewife, labourer or businessman that I
have talked to has ever argued that he should. Perhaps,
Alfried's best argument then—though surely not a justification—for "taking the Allies for a ride on this one" (the
phrase is that of a distinguished British diplomat) is that
it has met with the clear and obvious agreement of the mass
of West Germans.

One of the key links in this chain of cheating and chican-
ery, of humbug, hoodwinking and hypocrisy, is of course
Berthold Beitz. The fact that Beitz joined the firm only some
eight months after the 1953 Agreement had been signed,
and is still there, suggests, so some Krupp men would have us
believe, that the Agreement, if not exactly invalidated

thereby, has at least been made irrelevant or outdated. Beitz for his part has not publicly shown any inclination to pursue this particular trail of sophistry—though he has nevertheless privately made plain his position as not being compromised in any way by what was undertaken, no matter by whom or for whom, on that certain day in March 1953.

What had been the actual sequence of events? The 1953 Agreement, though billed at the time as the means whereby the Krupp empire was being broken up for ever, was in actual fact simply the instrument by which Alfried's properties were being legally returned to him. As the price of this little bit of tomfoolery, he undertook within five years of the date of signing (though there were built-in arrangements for at least two more years' extension on top of this) to dispose for a reasonable sum his holdings in certain companies. These companies were the Hüttenwerk Rheinhausen, a steel-producing plant; the iron-ore mining concern of Sieg-Lahn Bergbau; the collieries of Bergwerke Essen, Hannover-Hannibal, Constantin der Grosse, Gewerkschaft Emscher-Lippe, together with the coal-fields of Rossenray, Rheinberg, and Alfred. Except for two of the coal-mines, situated in the Bochum area and expected to be sold separately, the rest of the coal, iron and steel interests were lodged with a holding company specially created for the purpose, the Hütten- und Bergwerke Rheinhausen. The shares of this holding company were to be retained by so-called Disposition Trustees: three distinguished German gentlemen* who were given the responsibility of negotiating the sale and who if it ever went through were to receive for their pains a commission of half of one per cent on the going price. Even at the early valuation of £90 million on those shares, this commission could have easily amounted to £150,000 per trustee! No restrictions were placed on who could buy the stock, save for Alfried's "immediate family or . . . persons acting on their behalf".

It fell to the luckless Selwyn Lloyd to have to announce in the British House of Commons on the day following the

* The three were the former German Chancellor, Hans Luther, together with two bankers, Herbert Lubowski and Carl Goetz.

actual signing ceremony just what Alfried had apparently undertaken to do. Significantly, the British Government's statement began with the phrase, "The Krupp Organisation has been broken up in the following manner". Alfried had in fact made two other promises in addition to his undertaking to sell. They were that he would not "through the use of the proceeds of the aforementioned sale of securities, acquire or own any securities of or any interest in any enterprise engaged directly or indirectly in the steel or iron producing industries in Germany or in the coal-mining industry in Germany"; and, that he would not "directly or indirectly, acquire or own a controlling interest in, or occupy a controlling position in any enterprise engaged directly or indirectly in the steel or iron producing industries in Germany or in the coal-mining industry in Germany". In view of what follows it is as well to bear in mind the wording of those promises, particularly that of the second one.

At the same time, too, the British Conservative Government saw fit to rub their socialist predecessors' noses in the Essen mud a bit by detailing what to them appeared to have been the difficulties under which the British delegation had been operating during their most recent negotiations with Alfried. In the first place, it seemed that the Allied Governments had decided among themselves long ago (in August 1946 in fact) to limit any "deconcentration" of Krupp properties to his holdings in coal, iron and steel—so that had ruled out any later tampering with his other interests. Secondly, no steps had been taken to confiscate his properties by either the Attlee Administration or Alfried's American captors during the two-and-a-half years he had been in Landsberg, although of course his sentence ordered such confiscation—a remarkable oversight on somebody's part for sure, and an extraordinarily lucky break for even that extraordinarily lucky man, Alfried Krupp. And thirdly, the Allied Law 27 which was the basis of the recent negotiations (and which of course the British Conservative Government had also inherited from the Attlee Administration) contained no specific powers for confiscation, but rather, quite the reverse, proposed compensation.

What the official statement scrupulously avoided men-

tioning, however, was just exactly how the British Conservative Government intended upholding the Agreement
once Allied Law 27—the Krupp Treaty's legal validity—
had lapsed in two years' time when West Germany became a
sovereign state. Although pressed on the point by the
Opposition, Selwyn Lloyd would only repeat, "The British
Government has no reason to believe that the undertaking
will not be fulfilled".

Krupp PR men have of course never concealed their hope
that the 1953 Agreement if not actually ever buried by the
Allies would at least die a death through attrition. Their
arguments for Alfried not selling are no doubt *economically*
sound—for instance, they say that the reputation of the
House of Krupp has always been founded on the high quality
of the steel that goes into their finished products. If the firm
were not to have direct control over the manufacture of this
steel in the first place how, they claim, could the mainten-
ance of their standards of workmanship be guaranteed.
Krupp's renown in the past, they go on to argue, has come
from the closeness with which Krupp salesmen and Krupp
engineers have worked together at every stage of manufacture; to separate these functions for all time would be to
remove this safeguard to quality. Invariably, they go on to
quote Beitz's epigram, "Krupp's without steel is like a
woman without any lower part to her body". Once when
Aristotle Onassis, the Greek shipping millionaire, complained bitterly of a fault discovered in a turbine-engine
supplied to him by Krupp's, spokesmen for the firm immediately took the opportunity not of concealing the complaint
but of blaming it on the quality of the steel, saying that it
would never have happened if the engine-makers and the
steel-manufacturers had been under the same control: an
argument which had a lot of people, including Onassis
himself, nodding assent to.

An additional argument the Krupp PR men proffer is that
coal and steel are no longer the dominating—and hence in
terms of Germany the notorious—industries they once were.
So why do the Allies persist, why not quietly forget the
whole thing? Beitz has preferred to put it a bit differently,
pointing out rather that the war criminals after the next

holocaust will not be the gun-makers or the steel-tycoons but the ballistic-missile merchants and the electronics experts.

Krupp executives also like to tell one that whereas within the strict wording of the 1953 Agreement Alfried would have been perfectly entitled to have built new steel furnaces for himself on foreign soil, he has so far resisted this temptation, despite the blandishments of many overseas Governments. Nor, again they argue, has he tried to acquire existing steel capacity in countries like Holland and Belgium right on Essen's doorstep, although to have done so would once more have been entirely within his rights by the terms of the 1953 Agreement.

Such moderation, these Krupp spokesmen would have us believe, indicates Alfried's "moral integrity"—but others, not quite so naïve or perhaps not quite so committed, interpret these "denials" differently, as rather an expression of his determination to hold on to what he already possesses and of his absolute confidence that in the end he would never be called on to sell.

No heads have rolled; no noses have been bloodied; no sons have gone to prematurely early graves. Yet the battle for Krupp's coal and steel has been fought, on one side at least, with all the ruthlessness of an eighteenth-century dispute between dynasties and all the blandness of a twentieth-century sales-struggle among competing car-manufacturers or detergent peddlers.

"Safe" journalists have been primed with the Krupp version of the story and have duly puffed their way into print at regular intervals. A whitewashing official biography of the Krupp family crept into Anglo-Saxon bookshops in 1954 and got reasonably well reviewed even in Britain and particularly so in America. Discreet shooting parties were arranged for the British and American Ambassadors. A Danish count with "top" connections was expensively installed in the heart of London's Belgravia, there to court the "Commonwealth Set" and only sallying forth by special jet to lay on at the behest of his masters in Essen discreet meetings with the Henry Fords and the Harry Oppenheimers, the Onassises and the Niarchoses, the Rockefellers and the Rothschilds of this world. University students have been taken on conducted tours of the Krupp establishments and entertained lavishly in the Villa Hügel; many of the Bonn undergraduates I talked to in the autumn of 1964 had been on such jaunts.

November 1955, for instance, saw Krupp's chartering a special train to bring 150 young foreign diplomats and 250 other notables from Bonn to a sumptuous reception in Essen. Blue-uniformed "Krupp hostesses" from his guest establishment served champagne cocktails, canapes, and cigars on the pullman cars. First of all the guests were taken in luxury motor-coaches to see the modern Rheinhausen steel plant and were lectured on the "impracticability" of Alfried ever selling it. They were shown too the peaceful products of the present-day labours of the House of Krupp: the false teeth, the diesel-locomotives, the bridges, the oil-tankers, even the sausages and the shoe-polish. All the while of course the thought was being gently ushered into their minds of why a firm of such clear benefit to mankind as this one should be threatened with premature death. Afterwards a champagne dinner was laid on for each visitor followed by a splendiferous ball at the Villa Hügel where the dancers had a choice of not only three different bands but also twenty of Germany's choicest wines, many of them from Krupp's own vineyards. Gossip columnists had a field-day. As well as remarking on the presence of Max Schmeling (Germany's most famous boxing champion), they also wrote of the stir Vera Krupp's diamond ear-rings had caused: it was said they contained single-stone diamonds the size of starlings' eggs. Before being whisked home in one of the Krupp fleet of black Mercedes limousines or else back on the first-class train, each guest was given a bottle of brandy together with a silver-plated cigarette lighter and ash-tray, both adorned of course with the Krupp trade-symbol of the three interlocking rings.

The *Christian Science Monitor* described this as the opening salvo in Krupp's campaign to win back their coal and steel (not that they had ever really lost them of course) and quoted Alfried as saying, "I won't sell a single brick more". One can only surmise how many of the 400 or more guests present were busily nodding approval to Alfried's remark by the end of the proceedings—particularly as it was discreetly but persistently repeated to them by the myriads of Krupp PR men present.

All that Alfried had in fact sold so far were two coal-mines: one to the State-controlled Hibernia Company, and another to the Bochumer Verein, makers of high quality and specialised steels. His choice of the Bochumer Verein as a purchaser passed uncommented on at the time and it was only much, much later that its significance became evident. It so happened that shortly after Alfried and Vera had sojourned with him in the Bahamas in 1954 that Axel Wenner-Gren, the millionaire Swedish businessman had bought quietly and completely unnoticed through a "cover company" in Cologne a 40 per cent share in the Bochumer Verein—and within two years he had increased the share to over 76 per cent. Hitherto, Wenner-Gren had shown no interest whatsoever in steel manufacture, nor did he acquire one now—for after only a brief while he sold out to a group of German banks and insurance companies, though with the clear understanding to them that they would give Alfried long-term, first-refusal rights to buy both the Bochumer Verein and its Krupp coal-mine, the Constantin der Grosse. The Bochumer Verein was of great interest to Krupp's since it almost precisely modelled the Borbeck specialised-steel plant they had lost to the Russians through the Allied dismantling programme after the war.

The Krupp campaign to hold on to their coal and steel now began to gather momentum. Two months after the Villa Hügel binge, Fritz Berg, the chairman of the powerful Federation of West German Industry, declared in public that the 1954 Krupp Agreement had in his opinion been "signed under duress" and that "disposal abroad would meet with the most energetic opposition among industrialists and workers alike as well as among the mass of the German people".

In March 1956 the *Manchester Guardian* was quoting Alfried as saying of his having hung on to his coal and steel holdings, "the only way they could have stopped us would have been to have killed us all". Spokesmen for the firm were also arguing at this time that the 1953 Agreement had created an unfortunate precedent in singling out Krupp's for special treatment.

The day after the *Manchester Guardian* report, it was announced in Bonn that the West German Government intended bringing up the subject of the "Krupp Treaty" with the three Allied powers at the earliest opportunity. Yet Chancellor Adenauer was almost as firmly committed as Herr Alfried himself on this issue, since in autumn 1954 as part of the price of securing the Federal Republic's full sovereignty he had undertaken to complete the programme of "deconcentration" begun during the Occupation and had promised to have the West German Government eventually draw up its own anti-cartel laws. This suggested to most commentators that the spirit, if not the actual letter, of Allied Law 27 was to become part and parcel of the Federal Constitution—and that this included the sale of the Krupp concern. Indeed, in a letter dated 23 October 1954 to James B. Conant, then the United States High Commissioner at Bonn, Adenauer promised that "the Federal Government will also oppose all efforts to repeal or modify Allied legislation which now prohibits restraints of competition and monopolies before the coming into force of a German law containing general provisions against restraints of competition".

That there was no doubt in the British Government's mind of the West German Government's commitment on this score was made clear in May 1957 when, Adenauer having persisted in yet another request to the British Ambassador in Bonn to permit the Krupp Agreement to lapse, London retaliated by promptly demanding from the Federal Republic to know how far it had gone in discharging its obligation to persuade Alfried to sell. This move of the British Government's produced a spate of vehement articles and editorials in the German press denouncing Britain as the most anti-German of all the three Allies. No reply was in fact received to the British note until 29 April 1958, almost a year later—and even then the reply was prompted only by a leader in *The Times* of that very morning drawing the British Government's attention to the lack of a German response. As it turned out, Bonn had merely answered somewhat superciliously that coal and steel was no longer the province of the Federal Government but was now that of the High Authority of the European Coal and Steel Community in Luxemburg.

At the time of the despatch of the original note, Selwyn Lloyd, replying to a question in the House of Commons, had repeated that it was still the British Government's policy to see that both Adenauer and Krupp were kept to their pledges on deconcentration. The *Manchester Guardian* in another leader about this same time had pointed out that the West German Government's frequent argument that the German capital market was not big enough to absorb the sale of the Krupp properties "would be more convincing if the German Economics Minister [Herr Erhard] had not recently been 'very happy' to announce to his party's congress that the Volkswagen works are to be handed over to 'a widely scattered private ownership' ".

Just five days after this leader appeared, it was announced in Essen that Alfried intended to take up his option to buy the Bochumer Verein. Four months later he renewed control of his coal and steel assets (not that he had ever *practically* given up control—indeed to the annoyance of the three Disposition Trustees Beitz had persistently turned up as a so-called observer to every board meeting of the "deconcentrated" companies) by appointing Berthold Beitz as chairman of the supervisory board of the Hütten- und Bergwerke Rheinhausen, the holding company of all the assets he was supposed to be selling. The timing of this particular move was impeccable—just three days before the West German elections—and hence it was comparatively neglected by both the German and other European newspapers. But the "three wise men", as the Krupp Disposition Trustees had been nicknamed, protested to the Bonn Government. However, Chancellor Adenauer merely retorted that he did not feel that Alfried had overstepped the mark in any way and that it appeared a "natural" appointment. Two months after this stratagem, on 1 November 1957 to be precise, Alfried pushed his private U.D.I. a stage further by disclosing that he was seeking approval from the High Authority of the European Coal and Steel Community for permission to merge the Rheinhausen and Bochumer Verein steel companies.

On 17 February 1958 Alfried appointed one of his directors, Karl Hundhausen, to be general manager of the Bochumer Verein, thus indicating his firm intention of knitting the two companies closer together. Later that spring, on the occasion of his annual presentation of long-service awards to his workers, Alfried spoke out for the first time in public against the 1953 Agreement and indeed challenged the Allies' right to force him to sell against his wishes. He denounced the Agreement as "insupportable in an age of European co-operation" and declared that he believed it "contrary to the basic rights of West German citizens".

On 16 June 1958 Beitz moved the headquarters of the Rheinhausen company to Essen, the home of Krupp's, and at the same time Alfried appointed the general manager of Rheinhausen to be a director of Krupp's.

The High Authority of the E.C.S.C. emerged as a strong ally of Alfried in his campaign, when in that same month of June 1958 it issued a judgement that Krupp's would not constitute a prohibited cartel within the constitution of the Community if it were allowed to ignore the Allied order to sell its coal and steel. Seven months later, in January 1959, the High Authority took the "Krupp Rebellion" a stage further by approving the merger between Rheinhausen and the Bochumer Verein. This take-over when it finally went through in November 1965 gave Krupp's 16 per cent of Ruhr steel output and made them then the second biggest German steel producer after Thyssen's. It also meant that they had a larger steel capacity than at any time in their history.

Meantime, back in Britain, although there had been a fairly regular and constant flow of questions in Parliament on the Krupp issue, official attitudes had begun to soften —perhaps showing that Alfried's PR blandishments were succeeding. Already by December 1957, for instance, Lord Gosford, the Government's Foreign Office spokesman in the House of Lords, was refusing to give Viscount Elibank (perhaps Alfried's most resolute opponent among the British peers) a definite answer to his request for an assurance that Krupp's were not going to be released from their under-takings. In January 1959 *The Times*, too, was declaring,

"There is nothing to be gained by pressing too literally the terms of a settlement which cannot be executed without hard feelings on both sides." And even the *Manchester Guardian* was now arguing, "Herr Krupp has relied on the healing effect of time and he seems to have been proved right."

The day after both these editorials appeared, it was announced that Alfried had been given a year's extension of the time period in which he was supposed to be still selling his coal and steel interests. As though to assuage his critics it was revealed too that a "mixed-nationality" commission was to be appointed to examine the whole future of the 1953 Agreement. But since this seven-man committee, consisting of three Germans, one Briton,* one American, one Frenchman and the inevitable neutral Swiss chairman, took more than six months just to meet for the first time, it soon became clear that this was yet another delaying device heavily weighted in Alfried's favour—particularly when in January 1960 it was to announce the first of what has become a fatuous annual repetition of twelve-month respites for Krupp.

Alfried's confidence now began to know no bounds. In an interview to a *New York Herald Tribune* reporter in February 1959 he declared that for the West German Government to force him to sell against his wishes would require an amendment to the Basic Law. Such a constitutional change, he pointed out, would need a two-thirds majority which he thought would be "virtually impossible to obtain".

When the time came round again that year for him to present the annual long-service awards to loyal workers, Alfried used the opportunity to sound off on what was rapidly becoming his pet obsession. "We have so far showed patience, but now we must have clarity"—and by clarity he meant an early release from his pledges to sell. As a further indication that he meant business, in September 1959, on the eve of a British General Election that was being fought on the simple issue whether or not British voters had "never had it so good", Alfried announced that he was merging

---

* The British member was a seventy-two-year-old former judge, Sir Edward Jackson. When Sir Edward died in 1962 he was succeeded by Sir Sidney Littlewood, a past president of the Law Society. Sir Sidney was sixty-six years old at the time of his appointment.

into a single company all the coal-mines belonging to both
Rheinhausen and the Bochumer Verein—thus undoing the
Allies' own organisation of his holdings as laid down in the
1953 Agreement. He completed this "reorganisation" in
April 1960 by turning the Hütten- und Bergwerke Rheinhausen holding company (specially created by the Allies in
1954) into an operating company of which Alfried was the
sole shareholder. Beitz was still its chairman, but with Otto
Brenner, the Metal Workers' Union leader, as deputy-
chairman, and with Josef Hermann Dufues,* the Minister
of the Interior for the province of North Rhine-Westphalia,
as another member of the board—perhaps one of the most
subtle pieces of political "window-dressing" ever known in
West Germany.

Inevitably, though now belatedly, Viscount Elibank sallied
forth with a question to the British ministers in the House of
Lords. Once again the British Government's answer showed
a further softening in their resistance to Alfried's obstinacy:
this time the Marquess of Lansdowne, the Under-Secretary
of State at the Foreign Office, merely replied that "there is
no provision in the 1953 Agreement which prohibits the
reorganisation".

As though this set the final seal on his reinstatement as a
coal and steel producer, Alfried promptly sought and
obtained permission from the E.C.S.C. to put £25 million
into expanding the Rheinhausen steelworks.

Then what seemed like the first serious possible purchaser
of Rheinhausen appeared on the scene. He was a Dutch
scrap dealer by the name of Louis Worms, who in November
1959 offered £125 million for Alfried's coal and steel interests. This offer, made to the West German Government in
Bonn on behalf of what Worms described as an international
consortium, prompted an immediate visit to Chancellor
Adenauer's office by both Alfried and Beitz. Shortly after
this meeting, Worms was rebuffed by Erhard, the West
German Economics Minister, who told him that his offer
was not the concern of the Bonn authorities but should be
directed to Alfried himself. Worms retorted that he refused

* A prominent member of the Christian Democrats, Adenauer's and
Erhard's party, he later became that party's general manager.

on principle to do business with a convicted war criminal and that either the West German Government must take up his offer or else it would lapse. But Erhard did not budge, despite Bonn's firm commitment under the Paris Convention of 1954, and Krupp's did not approach Worms either with a view to doing a deal. In any case, the London *Daily Telegraph* had just then put a new valuation on the Rheinhausen interests at nearer £212 million than the £125 million Worms was offering.

When Worms persisted with his offer in September 1960, this time directed to Alfried, Essen again tried to fob him off by asking him to furnish "particulars" of the capital available to his consortium and refusing to name a negotiable price until he did so. Eventually the seven-man Krupp Commission came to Alfried's rescue by turning Worms' offer down out of hand.

The only other offers that have been forthcoming over the years have been from a small American company whose price was also brushed aside as being too low and from another "international consortium" that turned out to be organised by an American student—though from time to time there are rumours of Japanese approaches to Alfried to sell Rheinhausen to them. But in any case, under the original Agreement no bids from abroad need be considered —and it has clearly now become a point of principle among German steel companies not to bargain among themselves for Krupp's. Indeed, at the one hundred and fiftieth anniversary of the firm in November 1961, Fritz Berg, chairman of the German Federation of Industry, not only declared that no German industrialist would ever make an offer for Alfried's coal and steel but called on all industrialists everywhere to take the same attitude.

These Krupp anniversary celebrations were held in a *Traglufthalle*, one of the firm's latest products and a kind of giant tent 100 feet high which was supported only by air under pressure. Inside was the reconstructed early home of old Alfred, the "Cannon King", around which the 6,000 guests present gathered to hear the speeches and to eat a sumptuous buffet complete with separate bottle of champagne for every person. Since the tone of all the orations was, without exception, laudatory, the quips remarked that it was this "hot air" of the speakers that was really holding up the tent's roof!

Erhard in his speech declared that the Allies' demand for Krupp's to sell was "unjustified and an anachronism". Theodor Heuss, the former President of the Federal Republic, in a somewhat gushing account, even for that sugary occasion, of Krupp's achievements over the years proclaimed that it was high time the Allies renounced the 1953 Agreement. Alfried for his part, in reply to all these righteous remarks, simply argued that what he had done, or rather not done, had been inspired by what he considered to be his duty to preserve the unity of his various enterprises. But the reporter from the London *Times* found all this talk particularly sick-making and pointed out that no one had mentioned, not even quietly, the contribution of the wartime forced-labourers to all these "Krupp achievements".

Having so far got away so easily with his circumvention of the 1953 Agreement, Alfried in recent years has gone even further in re-creating his former factory-kingdom. In December 1962 he secured approval from the E.C.S.C. for the Bochumer Verein to buy back for £2,200,000 Capito und Klein, one of the two companies the Allies had made him give to his sister, Waldtraut, and his nephew, Arnold von Bohlen, nine years earlier. He also arranged for Rheinhausen to re-purchase from them in October 1964 the other company, the Westfaelische Drahtindustrie Hamm, which his father had first bought in 1914 and which had supplied much of Germany's barbed-wire in two world wars.

These two purchases meant that apart from a single coalmine, the Gewerkschaft Emscher-Lippe, sold to the State in 1954, Alfried's empire in terms of companies at least was back to its pre-1945 dimensions. In terms of sales turnover and absolute size it was of course far greater. A remarkable metamorphosis for the firm—and a remarkable instance of one man hoodwinking three of the greatest sovereign nations in the world, Britain, France and the United States.

Exactly what sort of man *is* Alfried Krupp?

CHAPTER TWENTY-ONE

"My life has never depended on me, but on the course of history"

WHEN SENTENCED at Nuremberg in July 1948, Alfried became a mere penniless convict. Now, less than twenty years later, he is a multi-millionaire, richer certainly than any member of his family has ever been, and one of the richest men alive in the world today. A recent valuation of his properties put them as being worth around £1,500 million give or take the odd hundred million. His spendable income every year runs into at least seven digits.

Yet he is a man of few expensive tastes. He sails a magnificent yacht, the sixty-six-feet-long Olympics-designed *Germania V*, has one or two private jets to his name, drives a whole fleet of custom-built sports-cars, each with the number plate "ERZ", meaning "ore", specially reserved for him by Essen Council, but his only hobby is taking endless amateurish home-movies of his travels with which he then proceeds to burden his closest business associates. He chain-smokes American cigarettes and prefers Scotch to schnapps. He attends no church, although the Vatican has seen fit to bestow on him from time to time various medals "in recognition of his services to Christianity". He rarely reads a book, has hardly any friends, and lives alone in a modest, modern, fifteen-room ranch-style house in the grounds of the Villa Hügel—though with a sentry at the gate and a barbed-wire entanglement for a garden-fence.

Today, although approaching his sixtieth birthday and despite having spent six of those years in Allied jails, he is remarkably well-preserved: handsome still, stiffly erect, tall, fine-boned, but gaunt nevertheless. There is in fact an almost incredible likeness between Alfried and his great-grandfather Alfred. "Shave off the old cannon-king's beard, and you have Alfried", you hear time and time again from Krupp senior executives as well as from Essen parlour-room gossips. But it is a likeness that does not stop at facial features. Both men have performed "miracles" with their firms, yet both have been singularly inept in their human relationships. Both have been very hard, very impersonal men, sticking strictly to business throughout their lives, extraordinarily indifferent to anything except the expansion of the Krupp empire. Indeed, the whole story of Krupp's is an exercise in power not personality.

At first sight and at first meeting, Alfried does not give the immediate impression of a cunning, calculating, ruthless, amoral man. He is almost English-looking and could easily be mistaken for an Oxford don. Quiet, unassuming, modest, scrupulously polite, rather retiring, extremely dignified, immensely self-controlled, he is neither prodigal nor over-generous. Yet behind all this is a certain arrogance, an undoubted coldness and disdain, an evident insensitivity.

Despite all the efforts of his PR men, there is very little personal regard for "Herr Alfried" even among his employees—perhaps he is too much of a recluse to warrant warmth. Yet there is respect: one hears very little criticism or even gossip about him in Essen itself. But the deference and the esteem comes more from the name he bears than on account of the man himself—particularly from the remarkable ability of the Krupp family to survive all vicissitudes.

One of the least comprehensible, and certainly least forgivable things about him is that he has never really publicly expressed any regret for the hundreds of luckless souls, many of them women and children, who died or suffered miserably in his works during the war years—labouring for him, not out of choice, but by dint of a Gestapo boot or an SS whip that had been provided more often than not from his own firm's funds. His main excuse at Nuremberg for these terrible crimes carried out on his premises and occasionally by his men was that he did not know anything about them. Whether or not he actually did know seems immaterial now, but the fact that he would let himself appear as not caring, or as never having bothered to find out, what was happening to the unfortunate thousands who were being forced to work for him against their will but not against his, must put the lie once and for all to the pose that Krupp's were "good" employers of labour.

Nor has he ever seen fit to renounce Nazism. Even when, just before Christmas 1959, he was persuaded by his public relations advisers that it would help his "image" among influential American Jews if he were to make available a sum of money by way of compensation to those Jewish slave-labourers still alive who had been forced to work in his factories during the war, he was at pains for his spokesmen to make absolutely clear that he was in no way accepting responsibility for their miseries, but that the gesture was simply one of helping "to heal the wounds suffered during the Second World War".

The figure in fact that he was offering was 6,000,000 Deutsch Marks, or roughly £510,000: that is about £425 per slave-worker still alive. Not a very princely sum—though he did say at the same time that if more forced-labourers came forward he was prepared to raise the amount to around £830,000. This offer was the result of two years of negotiations between Krupp's and Jacob Blaustein of the Conference on Jewish Material Claims Against Germany. Blaustein had already made a similar deal with IG Farben's directors in February 1957. But IG Farben had put up more than four times the amount of money that Alfried was now offering: £2,300,000 as against £510,000.

It was significant too that Alfried was not offering to compensate any non-Jews among his former slave-labourers —although Jews amounted only to between one-quarter and one-third of the 80,000 or so forced-labourers who passed through Krupp factories during the four years of the Nazi "extermination through work" programme. Presumably this was because the non-Jews did not have any strong organised pressure-groups to look after their interests—certainly not one wielding considerable influence with prominent American businessmen and political leaders.

One or two European refugee organisations did, however, approach Krupp's during the early part of 1960, only to be pretty promptly brushed off. On 17 March 1960, a spokesman for the firm announced that Alfried was "unable to make further voluntary payments". What the statement did not make clear was exactly who or what was stopping Alfried if he had really felt so inclined. Certainly the West German Government was not putting obstacles in his path on this or anything else at this stage—and it could not have been that he was short of money either at this time. Indeed when his second wife had divorced him just four years before she had alleged that he had more than £90 million stashed away in cash in Swiss, Swedish and South American banks.

His second divorce had been much messier and much more bitter than his first. After barely three years of marriage Vera had left him and returned to America. Long before that, however, she had been seen less and less often in public with Alfried. Her complaints in private to her friends and acquaintances were that her husband spared too little time from his work for her and also that his mother, Bertha, tried to run her son's household, as well as her own, with a rod of iron.

When Vera's petition for divorce was made known from Las Vegas in October 1956, its harsh legal language recorded her complaint that "the defendant did, wilfully and without cause, withdraw from the marriage bed and has persistently refused to have matrimonial intercourse with the plaintiff". In addition, she also claimed that Alfried had refused her a home life and had demanded she give up her American citizenship. By way of financial settlement, Vera asked for an annual allowance from Alfried of £90,000, together with an immediate capital payment of £1,800,000.

Although, according to West German law, divorce trials should be held in public, it comes as no surprise to learn that an exception was made in the case of Alfried. Indeed, the first intimation most West German people had that Alfried's marriage had broken up was when the divorce was pronounced final in January 1957. What is more, since the actual proceedings were held *in camera* we do not know how far Alfried's lawyers met Vera's money demands. As it happened, she was herself almost straightaway cited in another divorce case, this time as a co-respondent in an action brought by a certain Mrs. Annabel Manchon against her husband Louis. Louis Manchon, it turned out, was president of a construction company belonging to Vera Krupp who, Mrs. Manchon alleged, had "openly and notoriously carried on a romance" with her husband.

Vera was also, later that same year, subpoenaed to appear at an enquiry concerning a luxury hotel and gambling casino in which she had invested about £70,000 just before it went bankrupt through owing the inevitable large back-payments of tax. For a time American gossip-columnists had a field-day following her around and endeavouring to link "the divorced wife of the German armaments tycoon" with almost every prominent unshy public beau from George Sanders downwards. Then Vera retired to a 400,000-acre ranch not far from Las Vegas, there at long last to escape the weary eye of the Dorothy Kilgallens of this world.

Perhaps the real key to Alfried is to be found in the two words that follow his firm's name in all official Krupp literature: *Fried. Krupp Essen, sole proprietor—Alfried Krupp von Bohlen und Halbach*. Sole proprietor. There is only one share in Krupp's main company—the keystone and at least one of the pillars of Alfried's very personal imperial arch—and that share is held by Alfried himself. It is Alfried's *rationale*, since without the power that comes from possessing that particular wealth he would be nothing, he would be a nobody. No one would notice him—and no one would especially want to notice him. He has no distinctive abilities or talents that would otherwise set him apart from his fellow men, that would otherwise set him head and shoulders above the common herd.

Without wealth—and without the singular power that comes from possessing his sort of immense wealth—shallow, purblind, impassive, insensitive Alfried would be no more or no less interesting than, say, Hans Schmidt who keeps a corner grocery-store in Cologne today or Fritz Schultz who led an SS Commando troop in Breslau during the last war. What else would have caused Konrad Adenauer, then West Germany's Chancellor, to take time off from the cares of his important public office to issue a press statement on 13 August 1957 drawing everyone's attention to the fact that he had just sent off a telegram congratulating Alfried on the occasion of his fiftieth birthday?—he certainly would not have done that for even the ninetieth birthday of either his Economics Minister or his Foreign Minister, nor for any other industrialist. Similarly, how otherwise can you explain that when Alfried visits Tunisia, for instance, he does so only at the personal invitation of the Tunisian President, Habib Bourguiba, who puts him up for the duration of his stay at the "First of July" palace usually reserved for visiting heads of state?

If anyone should be seeking an epitaph for Alfried Felix Alwyn Krupp von Bohlen und Halbach then I would humbly suggest that they look no further than those self-same words *Sole Proprietor*—for they more than any other two or one hundred and two or one thousand and two words seem to signify his true being, his whole existence, in fact his only *raison d'être*.

In February 1959 the *New York Herald Tribune* quoted Alfried as telling one of their reporters that he intended keeping Fried. Krupp Essen as a family concern without shares for all time, even though Rheinhausen and many of his other subsidiary companies are now joint-stock enterprises. In this way, he argued, "it is possible to take major business decisions with maximum speed ... it is not necessary to pay attention to the wishes of stockholders as regards dividends —we can leave as much money as we want in the company for development purposes". It means too of course that no one other than Herr Alfried need know how he disposes of the immense profits and revenues of his massive combine—for as a family enterprise he avoids having to disclose most essential facts about his firm. He could be using the vast income that accrues from his enormous interests for the most wicked, morally degrading, and potentially treacherous purposes for all the Federal authorities in Bonn might know.

More than eighty years after his great-grandfather had compiled the original one, Alfried on 1 January 1958 signed and published a new constitution for the firm. Significantly, in one basic fact the new *Plan and Principles of Organisation for the Firm of Fried. Krupp* did not differ from the old— its first paragraph ran thus, "The owner, or his general plenipotentiary, shall lead the whole firm". One day the West German Government will have to consider whether it is politically, economically, or socially healthy for so much power to be held by one man who is responsible in no sense to anyone—and whether in fact huge private empires like Krupp's have any place in the modern world.

Unlike a Rockefeller or a Ford, a Nuffield or a Nobel, Alfried Krupp has not seen fit—so far at any rate—to use his great wealth to further some personal ideal or some national, or even international, benefit. His donations, when he makes them, are puny and parochial. They are usually far from philanthropic, and more often than not have a business purpose that is only thinly disguised. For instance, each year Alfried rewards his ten best apprentices with a sailing holiday at his expense. Able sons of Krupp workers bent on a scientific or technical education can hope to get financial aid from the firm towards their studies— and there are similar bursaries for suitable foreign students wishing to obtain experience in some of the Krupp establishments. Alfried has also dipped into his deep pocket on occasion to help make Essen a city of culture and artistic light—and so perhaps prove a more attractive place for ambitious Krupp executives to live in—by subsidising visiting musicians and acting groups, and also by providing a gallery at his former home, the Villa Hügel, for itinerant art collections.

In contrast to Berthold Beitz, Alfried shuns politicians, even party leaders. He avoids political debate of any kind, no matter how privately conducted—and whatever political lobbying there is to do he tries to leave to his General Plenipotentiary. Of course in eschewing politics Alfried is being true to his family's tradition—that of being *unpolitisch*, outside politics, without politics. Though naturally the man at the head of such a mammoth concern as Krupp's cannot ignore politics or politicians altogether—nor has his family ever done so in the past.

What the Krupps appear never to have possessed—and this is certainly true of Alfried—is any firm political convictions. They have no burning ideal or exciting image of the world which they would want to wish on to their fellow men. When it comes to politics they are not pacemakers but rather train-bearers. Old Alfred started with virtually nothing, yet created great wealth for himself. He supported the political *status quo* so long as it helped him build up his fortune—and he resisted all reformers who would have undermined his mint of money. It was the same story with his son Fritz. On the other hand Gustav, Alfried's father, feeble-minded, the puniest Krupp of them all and hence the most dangerous, sought out whichever was the strongest political band-wagon at any moment of time and saw to it that he got on just before it started rolling. Alfried too is a trimmer: a follower, not a shaper of events.

As Germany goes, Krupp goes. In that way of course there is likely to be less commercial risk and probably more profit. The family's mystique, and hence its immortality, has come from matching the mood of the moment. As such they have long considered themselves historical phenomena rather than just ordinary mortals. Indeed Alfried is quoted as having once said, "My life has never depended on me, but on the course of history."

What makes a Krupp tick is not an easy question to answer—the ground is slippery and surely fairer game for a psychiatrist or a psychoanalyst. But all the same it is a question that no one attempting to relate the Krupp saga can possibly avoid. What makes Alfried in particular tick would seem to be a mixture of plain ordinary acquisitiveness and lust for power on his own account, yet also a sense that Krupps have always done this, even though at times they may have hidden it beneath thin veneers of social welfare and so-called workers' paternalism. Alfried is very aware of the traditions of the House he heads—and his desire to keep the Krupp dynasty strong and the Krupp empire intact is obviously a very powerful one with him. It is a desire he has really inherited from his great-grandfather and from his mother—and it helps in part to explain his intransigence and his single-mindedness of purpose, his ruthlessness and his persistence, his doggedness and his dullness. It helps explain too the almost unnatural restraint and aloofness, the lack of any trace of deep feeling, that he has shown at every stage of his self-appointed task of rebuilding the House of Krupp from the shambles of 1945: from those very first interrogations by American intelligence officers on the night of his capture, right through his behaviour at the trial, his conduct in Landsberg, and his attitude towards the 1953 Agreement since then. The arrogance of it all is irritating and horrifying. Its success is a reflection of the abject muddle that the world, particularly the Western world, has been plunged into since the end of the war.

To be a Krupp is to be lonely. Alfried, perhaps the loneliest Krupp of them all, has also been the most successful. There is a seeming riddle in this second rise to riches of the House of Krupp that would satisfy the most captious sophist. But there is no logic in it at all, just as there has been no justice.

Not many years ago, while ski-ing in the Bavarian Alps, Alfried met again one of the Americans who had borne the brunt of much of the interpreting during the Krupp trial at Nuremberg in 1947 and 1948. By way of conversation—for small talk never comes easily to Alfried—he asked the exlinguist how Brigadier-General Telford Taylor, the American chief prosecutor at Nuremberg, was faring these days. Back came the reply across the ski slopes, "He's doing fine, just fine —though not as well as you, Herr Alfried!" In that remark you have perhaps the sharpest irony of all in the recent Krupp story.

CHAPTER TWENTY-TWO

"Krupp: Symbol of Leadership in Industrial Progress"

MIDWAY THROUGH 1965 a series of eye-catching though otherwise discreet half-page advertisements began appearing in American glossy news-magazines. Each one was headed "Krupp: Symbol of Leadership in Industrial Progress". Each one boasted of some special achievement of the firm —and each one contained a photograph of a particularly complicated piece of machinery or equipment made by Krupp's. Just as they had come on the scene quietly un-announced in the first place, so they disappeared equally silently. Yet they represented a considerable landmark in the "public face" of the House of Krupp.

Only the year before, a public opinion poll carried out within the Federal Republic showed that the majority of West Germans placed Krupp at the top of their list of all West German industrial concerns for the quality of its products and for the welfare it bestowed on its workers. So having re-won the respect of his own countrymen Alfried was now setting out to conquer the hearts of the world, particularly of the Anglo-Saxon world. On that count alone, it surely cannot be long distant before his face —or more probably that of his general manager, Herr Beitz—will be beaming at us from the advertising pages of even the *Daily Express*.

1965 was clearly a year to remember for the House of Krupp. For one thing it had never been bigger: by the year's end its annual rate of business was topping the £600 million mark, a figure larger than the whole output of a country like Ghana or Iraq or Ceylon or Morocco or Malaysia, and more than twice that of Kenya or Southern Rhodesia or Jamaica. What is more it is still growing—its turnover having increased by 4 per cent during that twelve-month period (though this was less than the 16 per cent achieved in the previous year). Much more importantly, in November 1964 Alfried had bought what *The Economist* described as "the jewel" of the tottering Hugo Stinnes Jr. chain of industrial companies. This was the great Atlas-Werke of Bremen, manufacturer of ships and diesel-engines, of electronic equipment and engineering goods, quite a sizeable proportion of it on defence contracts to the West German Government. Nor did it appear as though this particular take-over was the limit of Alfried's ambitions on that score. Indeed, when giving his usual yearly address to the senior employees of the firm, Alfried in April 1965 had gone out of his way to reiterate his strong belief in the need for big corporations: "the right kind of concentration is of vital importance to the German economy . . . only soundly based large companies can be of help to the many specialised medium-sized and small undertakings in a highly developed economy in the long run". At the same ceremony the year before he had said, "The technical achievements and progress of the twentieth century cannot be imagined without large industrial organisations."

But 1965 would seem destined more likely to go down in the annals of Krupp history as the year when they finally tore up the 1953 Agreement, as the year when once and for all they thumbed their noses at the Allies' long-drawn-out attempt to make them sell their coal and steel interests— for if the merger completed in December 1965 between the Rheinhausen and the Bochumer Verein coal and steel complexes does not do precisely that, then it is difficult to know what will, short of course of the Allies actually repudiating the so-called "Krupp Treaty" themselves. Indeed *The Times* declared that the merger amounted to a "tacit acknowledgement of the fact that the Order will no longer be enforced—something which the Allies, unofficially at least, have recognised for some time".

As a further display of his complete disregard for the 1953 Agreement, Alfried even changed the name of the parent company for his coal and steel holdings from the Hütten- und Bergwerke Rheinhausen that the Allies had originally chosen to that of Friedrich Krupp Hüttenwerke. However, the disdain was tempered with a little bit of window-dressing a month later when he put on public sale just under one-fifth of the new company's shares—the first time in fact that Krupp shares had been quoted, let alone sold, on the stock exchange. But the shares were non-voting ones—to have risked dealings in voting shares would, for a Krupp, have been tempting fate too much! *Time* magazine quoted one observer as describing the transaction as rather "like Wotan selling shares in Valhalla".

Today, Alfried's personal industrial empire is spread over more than 100 different companies producing everything from giant 500-ton steel cranes to sets of false teeth, from whole processing units to book-binding and bottle-filling machines, from 150,000-ton ocean-going oil-tankers to the tiniest of watch springs, from jet aircraft to cantilever bridges, from diesel-locomotives to heavy lorries, from orchids and sausages to lemonade and vintage wine. In fact the latest Krupp catalogue lists upwards of 3,000 different items beginning at *abattoir by-products plants* and ending with *zirconium*. To the layman there seems little that Krupp's cannot and do not produce. At the end of 1965 Alfried had 112,000 people working for him—more people than in a town the size of Berkeley, California, or Trenton, New Jersey, or Northampton, England, or Amiens, France, or Ravenna, Italy. As a steel manufacturer he is now ranked third in West Germany, eighth in the European Coal and Steel Community as a whole, and twentieth in the world. Although his is still the biggest privately-owned factory-kingdom in the world in terms of sales, it is also the fourth largest industrial undertaking in the Federal Republic, the fourteenth outside America, and the sixty-second biggest anywhere. The firm has once and for all burst out of its Essen cradle—indeed no steel has been produced there since 1964. The Krupp factories and offices have spread throughout Germany and the world.

More than one-fifth of Alfried's present business is done abroad—and at the last count he had some 355 agents in 116 different countries seeing that the flow of such business was kept up. Pride of place in his overseas interests probably goes to his wholly-owned factory at Campo Limpo in

Brazil producing chassis and other parts for heavy lorries. Otherwise, Krupp's tend to steer clear of direct, permanent investment outside Germany, preferring merely to have market-sharing, information-exchanging, or process-leasing agreements with their foreign competitors. In addition to Campo Limpo they have only a small crane factory in Canada, a half-share in an insignificant coal-carrying company in Britain (the Anglo-Hanseatic), and various degrees of ownership and control over a couple of shipping companies in Panama, two manufacturing concerns in Switzerland, a trading house in Holland, and a French sintered-carbide plant, none of which amounts to very much. Their speciality of course is still the large-scale lucrative civil engineering contract such as that for supplying an eight-mile stretch of monorail in time for the 1964 Olympic Games at Tokyo. At the moment they are participating in a £32 million iron-mining project in Liberia, often described in the West German press as the Federal Republic's biggest single private overseas investment, and an £18 million iron-ore development in Angola, though hardly a month goes by without some new multi-million pound order being announced—such as, at the moment of writing, to build a £50 million bridge over the Bosphorus for the Turks and to help erect a mammoth-sized steelworks for the Spaniards at Veriña, near Gijón.

Since 1959 Krupp's have signed deals worth over £30 million with the countries of the Soviet bloc to supply everything from fishing-boat equipment for Bulgaria to a cement factory for the Yugoslavs. Currently, over one-tenth of Krupp exports find their way every year behind the Iron Curtain—and this is a steadily growing proportion. Until recently Alfried kept a permanent office in the Soviet Union, but although they withdrew their man from Moscow in January 1966 Krupp's still maintain representatives in Warsaw, Prague, Sofia, Budapest and Belgrade. Beitz's own frequent trips "East" have earned him the title of West Germany's "unofficial ambassador to the Soviets". Indeed seldom a year goes by without him bringing off some big commercial coup there. In 1965, for instance, to the chagrin of a group of British industrialists who firmly thought they had clinched the deal, Krupp's wrested a £9 million contract to build a synthetic-fibre plant in Bulgaria.

Nor does there seem to be any limit to the range of possible Krupp activities. Again in 1965, during a visit to Tunisia at the personal invitation of the Tunisian President, Alfried announced that in addition to building a shipyard and an industrial complex at Bizerta on the site of a former French military base, he was also thinking of entering the tourist business. As a start he was proposing to develop as a holiday resort the Mediterranean island of Djerba, some 370 miles south of Tunis. It so happens that most of the travel-writers in British newspapers this year are tipping Djerba as the place to go for a "with-it" holiday—I doubt, however, if any of those writers know who is the money-bags behind Djerba's sudden development.

In January 1966 British newspapers were full of the joint Anglo-Dutch and German project to build a medium-sized civil jet airliner. Vereinigte Flugtechnische Werke of Bremen was the name of the West German company involved, but what no Anglo-Saxon journalist had tumbled to was the fact that it is 40 per cent Krupp-owned—the rest of the shares belong to the United Aircraft Corporation of America (better known as the makers of Pratt and Whitney engines and the only aero-engine manufacturer that ranks with Rolls-Royce), Focke Wulf, who produced the famous German wartime fighter-plane, and Ernst Heinkel, the company started up by the designer of the equally famous Luftwaffe bomber that blitzed Britain and other European countries during the early 1940's. Krupp engineers are also active in the European space programme.

Not of course that everything has always been plain sailing for Alfried in recent years. Towards the end of 1963, for instance, there were constant rumours that Krupp's were in some form of financial difficulty. It appeared that they had accumulated between £10 million and £20 million worth of short-term debts which many of their creditors were anxious to be repaid. This came shortly after the collapse and failure of a number of well-known West German industrial firms, such as Borgward's the car-manufacturers, Schlieker's the ship-builders, and of course Stinnes the heavy industry

and banking group. As a matter of fact most Ruhr steel
producers were having a rough time just then on account of
tough competition from Japan and other Asian suppliers.
Rheinhausen had been running at a loss: some people
estimated this at about three-quarters of a million pounds a
year. On top of this, the locomotive- and lorry-building side
of Alfried's business was in the doldrums too, and the
establishment of some of the newer activities such as plane-
making was proving a heavy drain on the firm's resources.
Allegedly Alfried was also losing money with his shipyards at
Bremen and Bremerhaven.

Naturally the British, French and even American press
had a field-day over the story—and just as naturally the
German press leapt to Alfried's aid. For once, Krupp's
bankers actually came into the open and issued statements on
his behalf trying to reassure a worried West German public.
Even the Federal Government felt obliged to speak up too,
though the official spokesman also attempted to turn the issue
against the British newspapers who had had the "audacity"
to report the rumours. Said Herr von Hase, State Secretary
at the Federal Press Office, on 11 November [sic] 1963, "One
has the impression that what has up till now been reported
about this on the other side of the Channel is a mixture of
the British Krupp trauma and certain material interests."

But in the event the crisis did not last long. How near
Germany's most famous industrial concern was to the
brink of financial disaster during those fateful months is still
hard to discover even at this later stage. However, it would
appear extremely likely that Alfried was under some form of
pressure from many of his creditors at the time—though
not nearly as badly as a few of the reports would have had us
believe. Indeed, more than one commentator has concluded
that this was probably the reason why within two years
Alfried was prepared to float £10 million worth of public
shares in the coal and steel side of his business. Although
inevitably that sale was hailed, particularly in the West
German newspapers, as a great moment of history for West
German industry, it is significant that as yet Alfried shows
no eagerness to let the general investor participate in his
more profitable ventures!

CHAPTER TWENTY-THREE

"The British Krupp Trauma"

WHITHER KRUPP?

Alfried Krupp is now fifty-nine years old, while Berthold Beitz is fifty-three. Although Alfried has never mentioned, publicly at least, at what age he might wish to step down from the proprietorship of the House of Krupp, Beitz is certainly on record as stating that *he* intends to retire when he reaches sixty, that is in 1973. The House of Krupp is therefore rapidly taking on a middle-aged look at the top and the problem of succession is beginning to loom large.

Alfried of course has a son Arndt, from his first marriage, now aged twenty-eight—though he is not obliged to turn over the massive inheritance to him. By the strict terms of the *Lex Krupp*, Alfried can name as his successor whom he likes, so long as he does not divide the inheritance and so long as the inheritor takes the name of Krupp (at the moment Arndt is called Arndt von Bohlen und Halbach—he will only become Arndt Krupp if Alfried in fact names him as his successor). It remains to be seen of course whether or not Alfried will abide by what is after all a Hitler-signed law. Equally it remains to be seen whether or not the West German Government will choose to recognise this relic of the Third Reich.

Being traditionalists, and since the *Lex Krupp* was not imposed on them by the Nazis but is rather a law of inheritance originating within the family itself and certainly following on the will of old Alfred, the Krupps would be expected to want to keep to the 1943 ruling, particularly as there do not seem to be any other successors to Alfried within the family, apart from Arndt.

Arndt was born in a suburb of Berlin on 24 January 1938,

the year of Munich and the Nazi *Anschluss* with Austria. He was barely four years old when his father divorced his mother—it was the year that Fat Gustav thundered out against the walls of Sevastopol. His mother took him to live with her in Bavaria: to her house near the little town of Tegernsee, a famed local beauty spot on a lake, just south of Munich and not far from the Austrian border. It also happens to be on the route by road from Essen to Berchtesgaden, Hitler's hideout, so it can be presumed that during his frequent trips to visit his Führer in the celebrated mountain-retreat, Alfried stopped off to see his son and perhaps even his ex-wife, since the divorce was not of his own choosing but had been imposed on him by his parents.

When Arndt was little more than seven years old, Alfried was already in an Allied jail and from the mood of the time did not look like ever again emerging with his life. Like the dowager she undoubtedly aspired to be, and conscious as ever of her responsibilities to the dynasty of which she was the true descendant, Alfried's mother, Bertha, had taken Arndt with her and Gustav to Blühnbach Castle, the Krupps' own mountain retreat, long before the war had ended. When Gustav finally died there in January 1950, Arndt represented his father at the funeral—for although the American Governor of Landsberg jail had been prepared to let him attend, under strict security guard of course, Alfried had preferred not to go.

Arndt was thirteen before he saw his father again. Meantime his mother had sent him to a fashionable, cosmopolitan Swiss boarding-school. A year after Alfried's release, he was confirmed into the Protestant religion, the venue being a small church near the Villa Hügel. The confirmation was the suggestion of his mother, Anneliese, who despite Bertha's efforts, had remained the biggest influence on Arndt in his early years. Alfried did, however, come to the confirmation, although he is, as we have pointed out, a completely irreligious man and accepts no church. What is more, Alfried brought along Arndt's new step-mother, but there does not seem to have been any *rapport* between the new Frau Krupp and Alfried's first-born, and, as it has turned out, only-born.

Arndt's first major appearance in public was at his grandmother's funeral. Aged nineteen, he walked with his father behind Bertha's bier. Two years later, on the occasion of his twenty-first birthday, Arndt received from his father the inevitable fast sports-car and even accompanied him on a business trip to the Far East.

Undoubtedly Alfried has been at pains to introduce—and to be seen to be introducing—his son into the ways of the House of Krupp. When West German notabilities by the score came to Essen in November 1961 to help the firm celebrate its one hundred and fiftieth anniversary, Arndt stood in line next to Alfried and Beitz to receive the guests —and Krupp PR men sought every opportunity to have the three of them pictured together.

Remembering perhaps his own early frustrations, Alfried has not forced an Essen apprenticeship on his son. After studying economics at Freiburg University, Arndt's only contact with the business has been in Brazil, at the Campo Limpo outpost of the Krupp empire. Tall, slim and as elegant and as handsome as his father, Arndt nevertheless does not give the impression of being a Krupp—and it is perhaps this immediate, albeit superficial first feeling that is the basis for all the rumour of rift between father and son (and between Alfried and Beitz over the question of the son's possible succession), and for all the insinuation about Arndt's unsuitability for such a massive inheritance as the House of Krupp. Essen gossips allege that he refers to Alfried and Beitz as "V1" and "V2", that is Vater-One and Vater-Two (*Vater* being the German word for father). They also recall how he seems to spend more time in fleshpots like Tangier and Rio than getting to know people in the Ruhr.

Every time some malicious story appears about Arndt, this sets off again all the talk of a possible Krupp Foundation, of Alfried following the precedent of other industrial dynasties by placing the family fortune in the hands of a bunch of worthy trustees rather than a single, uncertain heir. This of course would also be one way of "depersonalising" the world's most personal industrial dynasty and so perhaps ending what Herr von Hase has chosen to call "the British Krupp trauma". Another way would be for the firm to "go public", that is for it to float all its shares on the

markets and so become another General Motors or I.C.I.:
one among many similarly large impersonal industrial
undertakings in the world today.

Rumour has it too that Alfried has been looking into the
question of other heirs within the family. Chief favourite
here might be his nephew Arnold, son of his brother Claus,
the Luftwaffe pilot killed in 1940. A year or so back, newspapers across the world made great play of a flight this
young Oxford-educated German took one summer with a
fellow undergraduate of his own age. The two safaried in a
Piper Comanche around Africa and the Middle East,
dropping in for a meal or two with people such as Emperor
Haile Selassie of Ethiopia and King Hussein of Jordan.
Nothing remarkable in that perhaps, except that Arnold
von Bohlen's flying companion was by name Winston
Churchill, grandson of *the* Winston Churchill! As can be
imagined, headline-writers and gossip-columnists everywhere
had a field-day pinpointing the apparent paradox of "these
illustrious scions of two immortal foes" touring together and
purpling their stories with sentences such as "with a Krupp
and a Churchill in the same cockpit the day of European
disunity must be over". What pleased the Krupp P.R. men
about the incident, however, was that young Arnold got a
"good press" wherever he went, particularly in the Anglo-
Saxon world. Other observers noted that after Oxford
Arnold was going to study business administration at the
new European school for technocrats at Fontainebleau.

Arnold was not of course the first member of his family to
go to Oxford. Apart from his father Claus, who was up at
Balliol before the war, another of Arnold's uncles, Berthold,
Alfried's younger brother, is an Oxford man too. Alone of
the family, Berthold has chosen science, but even this did
not keep him out of the Wehrmacht when Hitler's war came.
Like two of his brothers, Harald and Eckbert, Berthold was
commissioned in the artillery—in the year that Claus died.
He saw action in Holland, Belgium and France, as well as
later on in Russia—firing the very same Krupp guns his
father and his eldest brother were helping to turn out by the
score back in Essen. The war's end saw him at his parents'
side at Blühnbach, and although after Alfried's release he in

fact shared a flat with him for a time (Berthold had of course gone to meet Alfried coming out of Landsberg in February 1951) these two particular brothers have never been really close and are not so today. Berthold used the £1 million he received from the Krupp estate as a result of the 1953 Agreement to buy himself a chemical company in Essen and a brake-lining factory in Hamburg. Now he is married and has one daughter.

The one brother Berthold is closest to—they are as a matter of fact business partners—is Harald, the youngest of Gustav's sons still alive and the lawyer of the family. Harald was taken prisoner by the Russians in Rumania in August 1944 at the time of the great Soviet offensive which finally ended the war on that front. The Russians did not release him until the autumn of 1955. At first he had preferred to keep from his captors his connection with the hated Krupp family, calling himself Harald Bohlen, which a Russian jailer later corrupted to Boller. Due to be repatriated to West Germany shortly after VE day he was in fact crossing the Eastern Zone by train when a German Communist from the Ruhr recognised him. The Russians promptly threw him into a jail for political prisoners near Moscow and interrogated him endlessly, even on one occasion requiring him to write them an essay entitled "The Childhood of the Son of a Capitalist". Eventually in 1950 they brought him to trial—and predictably convicted him of war crimes although he had had absolutely nothing to do with administering the Krupp armament factories. Like his other brothers he had, however, been a member of the Nazi party. Sent to Siberia for twenty-five years, he only served five of them before being suddenly selected as one of the 800 chosen to be released as a Soviet gesture of goodwill ten years after the end of the war. The Russians duly handed him over along with his fellow repatriates at a camp near Göttingen. Harald's release had come at a time when Alfried was abroad on business and Berthold was honeymooning in Greece. It fell, therefore, to his younger sister, Waldtraut, to greet him and to take him to meet his mother whom he had not seen for twelve years. Harald has never married.

Waldtraut is in fact the sole member of the family with

whom Alfried maintains any really cordial relations, although today she lives mostly in South America. Besides being now the youngest of Bertha's children still alive, as it happens she is also the most extrovert of the lot. Marrying at an early age a wealthy Bremen wool merchant she eventually divorced him after the war (and also after trying to get him appointed by the Allies in late 1945 as the trustee for the Krupp estates) to wed a few years later an Argentinian shipping millionaire. Her visits to Essen are not all that frequent now, but when they do occur they provide just about the only warm family occasions for Alfried and the other Krupps.

Shyer than her younger sister, Irmgard, the oldest member of the family now next to Alfried, has also married twice. Her first husband, a Prussian baron, was killed in the opening months of the Russian campaign in 1941. Today, living with her second husband and their six children in Bavaria, she seldom sees her brothers, practically never her younger sister.

Like many other large families in this day and age, Bertha's offspring have become scattered and separated. For the most part they prefer to go their own ways. Nor will they ever starve, and so the necessity for a family to stick together for fear of possible hard times is not applicable in their case, for the one clause in the 1953 Agreement which Alfried has done nothing to circumvent is that whereby he gave each of his brothers and sisters roughly £1 million apiece. They could all become even richer, for yet another possibility on the succession issue is that Alfried might choose to divide up his fortune among them all.

Arndt may not be exactly a heavyweight as Krupps go, but it could be that he is also not really interested in expanding the millions and changing the reputations of his family. Presumably too, no matter what the final settlement is, he will never go short of money, but will receive the odd few million by way of recompense in the event of his disinheritance.

If with Alfried's death, or perhaps before, Krupp's were to cease to be either singly owned or family owned, then undoubtedly much of the heat would be taken out of the age-old Krupp controversy—for one thing it is much less easy or satisfying to loathe an institution than an individual. Many ignominious deeds were perpetrated on the premises of IG Farben, for instance, the pre-1945 chemical colossus and manufacturer of most of the poison gases used in the Nazi extermination camps such as Auschwitz, but because these terrible acts are not linked with a single family or a single individual, IG Farben is not nearly so well known or so notorious as Krupp's.

Such a radical change in the constitution of the House of Krupp would also probably mean the end of the now farcical "enforced sale" of the firm's coal and steel assets. Pride on the part of the former Allies presumably precludes any complete repudiation of the 1953 Agreement before such a radical change, and it is clear, as it has been ever since that day in March thirteen years ago, that Alfried never intends to sell of his own accord. In this case, until the radical change in the constitution of the House of Krupp occurs, one can expect the trips to continue by certain American and European worthies every summer to Zürich for the ritual of the annual extensions—to date Alfried has had six such extensions since the original five-year period ran out on 31 January 1959.

It is the single ownership of the House of Krupp that is its uniqueness and that makes it a seemingly glaring anachronism today. For the armament factories to have been in the possession and control of just one man suited Bismarck's or the Kaiser's or Hitler's book admirably. They had only one individual to persuade—only one person to bargain with and to cajole. If they had had to deal with a lot of directors worrying about dividends, having hundreds of shareholders breathing down their necks and asking awkward questions at annual meetings, their task would have been all the more difficult and hence Europe's recent history might have been that bit different.

No business enterprise has ever come in for so much censure as Krupp's. Unlike other giant firms in America, Britain or elsewhere, anonymity was impossible at Krupp's. One man, and one man only, stood for the firm—and it was he who in the eyes of the rest of the world "carried the can" for all its activities. Questions of any great moment were never decided by underlings but purely by the proprietors— so it was always easy to pinpoint responsibility.

Alfried Krupp, sole proprietor could well be his firm's epitaph as well as his own, for it is highly unlikely that the House of Krupp will continue in its present form past Alfried's death.

Léon Blum used to say that the great industrialists of Europe were the Continent's only true internationalists: that as a result they survived the cataclysms that periodically shake Europe.

No doubt the two most incredible facts of the whole Krupp saga are how the firm and family recovered after the two major débâcles their country suffered this century. Because of this, the name *Krupp* has come to take on an almost mythical and immortal quality in German thinking— the symbol of German industrialism that has outlived empires, defied defeats, and adapted itself to every kind of economic situation. If Germans were perhaps to throw off for a while their "sacred cow" attitude towards the Krupps and to think a little more deeply about what the family and the firm have done to Europe and not just to Germany these past 150 years then they might well learn a little more about themselves in the process. They might discover too why others regard them with so much suspicion. Such a realisation could also lead to the evaporation of that "British Krupp trauma" that worries official West German spokesmen so much.

This trauma was born out of disgust for Krupp's treatment of the slave-workers in his care during the Second World War—was born out of distaste for the devilish cunning and lack of honesty shown by Gustav towards the Treaty of Versailles and by Alfried towards the Agreement of 1953. There would be much for the average Englishman or Frenchman or American to admire in the Krupp saga if there were not at the back of many people's minds the disturbing suspicion that perhaps just as the House of Krupp has fallen and risen again so, like the Bourbons of old, the family has seen nothing and learnt nothing, and that just as the name of Krupp has run like a scarlet thread through the unhappy history of our times it could, if we do not watch out, be responsible for a lot more wretchedness in the decades to come. One would like to think that the seamy side of the House of Krupp has gone for ever—but how can one be so sure, for there is nothing in the recent Krupp story to make one convinced that the attitudes of mind of the man at the top have changed. The products are different, but are the principles?

The answer lies with the Krupps themselves. Let them by their actions and their deeds prove our fears and our suspicions to be baseless. If there is silence from them or a shrugging of shoulders or a bland laugh of ridicule then the fears and the suspicions will continue, indeed must continue. The House of Krupp has risen, fallen, and risen again. Let us hope that there will be no further fall and hence no further rise to have to record.

Afterword to the Cooper Square Press Edition

MUCH HAS happened to the House of Krupp since this book was first written in 1966. For one, the year turned out disastrously for the firm. Not only did sales dip for the first time since its postwar reconstruction, but losses for the year amounted to $12.5 million and debts rose to more than $1.3 billion—enormous figures for those days. The latter was due mostly to over-ambitious expansion outside Germany, especially in Spain and Russia, where business had been obtained by offering easy credit terms. In some cases borrowers were offered fifteen years at which to pay and at interest rates lower than the rates that Krupp borrowed at in Germany.

"Krupp Comes a Cropper" was the indelicately eager headline in London's *Daily Telegraph*, a right-wing newspaper. "Krupp Kaput?" asked the *New Statesman*, a left-inclined weekly that went on to claim, somewhat prematurely, that "the end is in sight for the greatest industrial anachronism of the 20th century." It turned out that Krupp had become far too dependent on exports. Many of its managers had worried about Berthold Beitz's overzealousness in seeking out eastern European customers at whatever the cost, but had been afraid to speak out. "Why go to Indonesia or Bolivia when eastern Europe is on our doorstep?" Beitz had maintained on many occasions. But whereas the West German government in Bonn handed the financing for ten years of exports to relatively undeveloped countries like Indonesia and Bolivia, and even guaranteed eighty percent of such payments, it did nothing for exports to Eastern Europe. Quite the reverse, it discouraged business behind the Iron Curtain. Now that particularly foolish chicken was coming home to roost for Krupp. In addition, within Germany nearly $100 million had just been spent on a new wide-strip hot rolling mill in Bochum at a time when the steel market was already oversaturated with such capacity.

Like many an old-style entrepreneur, Alfried had hitherto been inclined to base his business decisions on intuition rather than on painstaking, detailed assessment. But whereas intuition had once been a source of strength for such entrepreneurs, in an increasingly complicated world it was more often than not proving to be their weakness and sometimes their undoing. That was certainly the case for Alfried, who in addition let Beitz handle most of his day-to-day affairs. However, the factor that perhaps contributed most to his downfall was his having clung stubbornly to private proprietorship instead of widening the share-ownership. Four-fifths of Krupp's working capital was borrowed money, and such a high ratio was bound to spell trouble when the boom turned to slump business (as happened in Germany in the mid-1960s).

Alfried now found himself in the classic bankruptcy situation of having lent long while having borrowed short. In other words, he had a cash flow problem. At least half of his debts were short-term loans that the banks had allowed him to roll over continually. But now those banks were reluctant to bail him out further—indeed he was said to be already in hock to 263 financial institutions, some of whom were threatening to foreclose. It was these insupportable debts that caused the firm's collapse.

While any other business would not have been spared, the House of Krupp was still a special case in German eyes. The federal government in Bonn persuaded the banks to extend their existing loans until at least the end of 1968 and chipped in itself with $75 million worth of temporary credits that were matched with half as much from the local North Rhine-Westphalian state government that runs the Ruhr. These credits were eventually extended both in time and amount, the latter by $100 million. However, rival German industrialists were incensed that the government was bailing out a competitor through their taxes.

But aid from the public coffers came at a price. Alfried Krupp and Berthold Beitz turned over the day-to-day running of their tottering empire to a committee of bankers and official appointees, thus allowing, as an insider put it, "strangers to meddle in affairs that had hitherto been thought strictly domestic." Alfried also had to agree to surrender his single ownership of the House of Krupp by making it a public corporation before the end of 1968, and issuing shares in it for sale. The *Financial Times* of London said, "The Krupp concern, last great German stronghold of the individual industrialist who runs his business like a piece of personal property, surrendered today to the temper of the times." Another commentator said, "Where the Allies failed to control Krupp, the bankers have succeeded."

The German press criticized the flamboyant, gregarious Beitz far more than the reticent and reclusive Alfried. He blamed the debacle on Beitz having relished too much his self-appointed role as West Germany's "unofficial ambassador to the Soviets," which distracted him from the realities of the Ruhr. In the midst of the crisis Alfried had become increasingly remote, shunning people and living an almost solitary life. Among his chief pleasures were hunting, shooting, and cruising in his ocean-going yacht, *Germania.* In a surprising outburst the highly conservative *Frankfurter Allgemeine* derided Krupp's business policies as appropriate to a small corner-shop or general store.

In preparation for the changeover, Alfried's heir, Arndt, who had hitherto shown little interest in the family business (preferring the life of a jet-setting playboy), duly renounced his heritage in early 1967 and settled for an annual $250,000 allowance to be doubled on his father's death. This paved the way for the whole of Alfried's holdings to pass into the hands of a foundation, the profits from which would be devoted to furthering scientific research (as under German law Arndt would have been entitled to fifty percent of his father's fortune). But in a Wagnerian twist, Alfried was spared the humiliation of witnessing the end of his family's personal rule over the 156-year old concern. He died of lung cancer in July 1967, just two weeks before his sixtieth birthday. Said the *Financial Times,* "West Germany has lost the last of its great paternalists." Eleven weeks later, Alfried's second wife Vera died of diabetes in Los Angeles, California.

With their deaths the Krupp family name died out, for Alfried's two surviving brothers, as well as his son, bore the name of von Bohlen and Halbach. Hitler's *Lex Krupp* (which circumvented the laws of inheritance that then prevailed, in keeping the firm as a family property) had not encompassed them. Indeed, Arndt's renunciation of his inheritance before Alfried's death had spared the West German government the embarrassment of having to decide whether or not to invoke the *Lex Krupp*. Arndt had declared then, "All my forefathers have experienced much unhappiness from personally owning this enterprise, and I want to break away from it. I am not like my father, who sacrifices his whole life for something without even knowing whether or not it is worth it."

West German President Heinrich Lubke wrote to him when Alfried died, "Your father's life and work were most intimately bound up with the fate of the Fatherland." Six years earlier, on the occasion of Krupp's 150th anniversary, Lubke had written to Alfried, "The history of your firm mirrors the triumphs and disasters of our people." He could have said, without any exaggeration, that the Krupp saga was so saturated in melodrama that the latest act was merely in keeping with what had gone before.

The irony was that if Alfried had sold his coal and steel interests, as the Allies ordained after the war, and moved into more profitable industries as his competitors did, he would almost certainly have avoided the liquidity problems, as it was the slump in coal and steel during the mid-1960s that fatally weakened the House of Krupp. Indeed, coal and steel accounted for more than half of Krupp's $12.5 million losses in the fateful year of 1966. Cheaper American imports steadily undercut demand for European coal, while oil was rapidly replacing coal in power production. German steel also faced strong competition from abroad.

But it was a source of irrational pride of possession on Alfried's part not to sell his coal and steel interests and that stubbornness proved his undoing. His father's contemporary, Friedrich Flick, another convicted war criminal, had faced a similar demand and had chosen to obey. He invested the proceeds profitably in products such as paper, chemicals, and, in particular, automobiles, eventually owning Mercedes maker Daimler-Benz. A year after Alfried's death, the three Allied governments formally annulled the 1953 obligation on Krupp to dispose of its coal and steel interests.

The new managers of Krupp successfully slimmed it down by closing or by selling many of its loss-making subsidiaries, such as truck making, as well as by paring its payroll ruthlessly. They also spun off its coal mines together with those of other companies, into a separate concern that the state was persuaded to finance. Krupp was back in profit by 1970 and the bankers relaxed their grip.

Inevitably, Beitz had been the executor of Alfried's will and had headed the charitable foundation that effectively owned the company. As the bankers took less interest in day-to-day affairs, his influence once again increased and the business pages of the world's press filled with stories of disputes between him and the new managers (few of whom stayed long).

Elsewhere in those same newspapers, the gossip columnists occasionally wrote of how Arndt, having devoted himself to a life of pleasure and having married Princess Henriette von Auersperg (four years his elder and daughter of one of Austria's oldest aristocratic families) was allegedly finding it difficult to make ends meet. His 37,000-acre estate at Bluehnbach, near Salzburg, with its seventy-two-room castle and seventy servants, was said to cost almost $70,000 a year to run. His palatial villa in Marrakesh required $20,000 a year to run. His bachelor flat in Munich, once the residence of the late Pope Pius XII in his Papal Nuncio days, cost $8,000 a year, and his yacht, with its four-man crew, nearly $100,000 a year. Arndt was also paying annual allowances of $50,000 to his mother, and $40,000 to his wife. In 1973 the Austrian government eased his financial worries by buying the Bluehnbach estate for $8 million, allowing him to continue living there. He, and his uncles and aunts had been irritated by their family's unfavorable portrayal, albeit lightly disguised, in Luchino Visconti's recently released film *The Damned*, a dark view of the rise of Nazism. But Arndt outlived his father by less than twenty years, dying on May 12, 1986.

Krupp's profitable spell did not last long and by the mid-1970s it was again in the red. The fault this time, it was claimed, was that, like other West German steel-makers, they could not compete readily against producers elsewhere in Europe whose governments were blatantly subsidizing them, something that the West German government had refused to do. On this occasion the Shah of Iran bailed out Krupp. He bought twenty-five percent of the steel-making subsidiary for $100 million in 1974 and then, two years later, twenty-five percent of the whole concern for $200 million. It was the first time in its 165-year history that an outsider had acquired an interest in Krupp. It was also the Middle East's first major long-term investment in Western Europe, mounting so-called "petro dollars." At that time, apart from Iran's share, only five percent of Krupp was in private hands—so much for the hullabaloo in 1967 over having to go public.

In 1981 the West German government belatedly came to the conclusion that some steel subsidies *were* virtuous. The managers at Krupp, now merely Germany's third largest steel maker, were not slow in elbowing their way to the public trough. The authorities wanted the steel makers to modernize, as well as to rationalize, and were prepared to pay ten percent of the costs of doing so. Krupp Stahl was at that time losing $20 million every month. A merger with Hoesch, then the second largest steelmaker (Thyssen was the biggest), was mooted. The government in Bonn was courted to subsidize the costs of the takeover, but nothing came of it.

Krupp now shifted much of its manufacture abroad to cut costs and to improve access to its markets, fulfilling only about half of its export orders at home. Its sales to East Germany averaged nearly $40 million a year, paid mainly by East German deliveries of steel casings, rolled steel, solid and liquid fuels, and machine tools. However, its liquidity troubles returned when the Russians, among others, postponed their debt payments.

A commission appointed by the West German steel industry to look into the industry's future recommended that the country's five biggest steel makers be merged into two groups protected by tariffs from what was claimed to be "the massive falsification of competition" by other European nations. Imports now accounted for half of German steel consumption, compared previously to a third at most. The steel makers were again arguing that they had to compete unfairly with cheap subsidized steel. Krupp and Thyssen were to form one group, and Hoesch, Kloeckner-Werke and Peine-Salzgitter the other. But after lengthy negotiations Thyssen decided against the merger, because it considered Krupp to be in such a mess that a minimum subsidy of almost $500 million would be needed, which the West German government was not prepared to pay.

Thwarted by Hoesch and Thyssen, Krupp then looked to a

merger with Kloeckner-Werk that would hopefully reduce costs by $100 million a year. Australian mining giant CRA was prepared to back the merger to the tune of $175 million, for which it expected a thirty-five percent stake in the new company. But determined hostility from union bosses and local politicians, as well as opposition from the European Economic Commission in Brussels, stymied that merger, too.

By the mid-1980s, Krupp was profitable, having further diversified so that steel, which had accounted for only a third of its sales, dropped merely a fifth by the end of the decade. But as the Deutschmark grew ever stronger, West German steel was again squeezed out of world markets and Krupp's profits dipped again. An event occurred in January 1988 that would have sent Alfred Krupp spinning in his grave; Krupp steelworkers burst in on a supervisory board meeting at the Villa Hugel to complain of job losses at the Rheinhausen plant. The Krupp payroll had decreased by forty percent since the early 1970s, and for some this was the last straw.

Once West Germany's biggest company (in terms of sales), Krupp now languished in nineteenth place. Daimler-Benz was now number one. Previously associated around the world with German industrial might, Krupp tended these days to be identified with boardroom squabbles, worker protest, and sagging profits. Even Iran, now under the Ayatollahs, wanted out, having pumped more than $500 million into Krupp since 1974 and having received only puny dividends in return—less than $20 million since 1980. Neutral observers argued that Krupp's problems included unclear lines of command and too little cooperation between divisional fiefs. In addition, Berthold Beitz, although he had stepped down as head of the supervisory board, remained head of the Krupp Foundation, the largest shareholder, and continued to interfere in the day-to-day decision making.

In 1991 Krupp bought nearly twenty-five percent of Hoesch for almost $300 million with a view to a complete takeover, which Hoesch's management and its union bosses opposed bitterly. It was almost a year before the merger was pushed through. In March 1997 Krupp took the much more controversial step of launching a hostile $8 billion bid to take over Thyssen, its bigger rival. Hostile takeovers were unprecedented in staid German industrial circles. Indeed, Krupp was accused of adopting "Wild West tactics." Although Thyssen management initially resented the move, within the month an amicable— though much less ambitious merger—had been brokered by what *The Economist* dubbed "elderly notables." It was a merger of the two companies' carbon-steel interests, with Krupp bearing most of the costs as it stood to gain more. Because two-thirds of their businesses overlapped, substantial savings were expected. Indeed, without compulsory redundancies, a figure of $260 million was mentioned. *The Economist* described the outcome as "a failed courtship, followed by an attempted rape— and now an engagement."

Thyssen was by far the larger of the two, with a market capitalization of $6.25 billion compared with Krupp's $3.4 billion, and with sales in 1996 of $22.4 billion against Krupp's $16.2 billion. The joint venture was to be owned sixty percent by Thyssen and forty percent by Krupp. Thyssen would essentially run the company. Both companies' profits had dropped dramatically that year and most financial analysts at the time thought that the deal marked a victory for Krupp. However, because the new name was ThyssenKrupp rather than the other way around, the popular press suggested that this was the House of Krupp's ultimate humiliation. The rump of Krupp, the firm of Alfried Krupp, AG Hoesch-Krupp, does remain an important manufacturer of factories and industrial machinery. Bizarrely, Alfried's remaining relatives, about fifty in all, chose this moment, thirty years after his death, to contest his will. They wanted representation on the Krupp Foundation board, but Beitz refused, maintaining that Alfried did not want his family to be connected in any way. (They had, of course, received generous payments in Alfried's will as recompense for his having locked them out of the family business.)

This time, the European Commission in Brussels readily approved the merger. It had been restricted mainly to steel-making because the bankers had gotten cold feet when faced with determined political and, in particular, trade-union opposition. (Union bosses had claimed 30,000 jobs were at risk and had threatened to encourage their members to boycott the banks involved if a full merger went through.) Even so, the new company is Germany's biggest engineering group by far and at the moment Europe's largest steel maker, numbering sixth in the world (although pending mergers may render this pre-eminence short-lived). Currently employing 193,000 people on five continents, it has a turnover of nearly $42 billion, rivaling ABB, the Swiss-Swedish venture, and even America's General Electric.

The merger has also meant that Krupp will never again be "a special case" within Germany, which can only be welcome. With the family no longer at its helm, the firm has become, in the words of one commentator, "as impersonal and as bland as a General Motors or a Ford," which its executives clearly seem to prefer to the patriarchal leadership of yore. One of the world's greatest politico-business dynasties is no more.

Thus, nemesis would seem to have caught up at long last with the House of Krupp. Indeed what the passing of the last thirty-five years has proved is the certainty that it will never again arouse terror beyond Germany's borders, never again be the personification of German military might. Soon the younger generations might wonder how the Krupp name could have become such a bogy word. No longer synonymous with war and with the ruthlessly cold pursuit of cash and power, some might say that the House of Krupp has ended with a whimper rather than with a bang. While to many an ugly, sordid, and in many respects immoral story, the House of Krupp is still one with an epic quality, worth telling and reading, encompassing the highs and lows of our history during the past four centuries.

PETER BATTY
February 2001
Kingston, England

Bibliography

THE FOLLOWING is meant only to be an approximate guide of the sort of reading I have found necessary in compiling this book.

Balfour, Michael, *The Kaiser and His Times*, 1964.
Barnet, Correlli, *The Swordbearers*, 1963.
Berdrow, Wilhelm, *Alfred Krupp's Letters*, 1930.
Bruford, W. H., *Germany in the Eighteenth Century*, 1959.
Bullock, Alan, *Hitler—A Study in Tyranny*, 1964.
Carsten, F. L., *The Origins of Prussia*, 1954.
Chamberlin, William Henry, *The German Phoenix*, 1964.
Clapham, J. H., *Economic Development of France and Germany, 1815–1914*, 1928.
Clay, Lucius D., *Decision in Germany*, 1950.
Davidson, Eugene, *The Death and Life of Germany*, 1959.
Diebold, William, *The Schuman Plan*, 1959.
Eich, Hermann, *The Unloved Germans*, 1965.
Eyck, Erich, *A History of the Weimar Republic*, 1964.
Frankland, Noble, *The Bombing Offensive Against Germany*, 1965.
Gooch, G. P., *Germany*, 1925.
— *Studies in German History*, 1948.
Gordon, Harold J., *The Reichswehr and the German Republic, 1919–1926*, 1957.
Holborn, Hajo, *A History of Modern Germany*, 1965.
Kirkpatrick, Ivone, *The Inner Circle*, 1959.
Klass, Gert von, *Krupps: the Story of an Industrial Empire*, 1954.
Lister, Louis, *Europe's Coal and Steel Community*, 1960.
Lochner, Louis, *Tycoons and Tyrant*, 1954.
McInnis, E., et al., *The Shaping of Post-War Germany*, 1960.
Menne, Bernhard, *Krupp, or the Lords of Essen*, 1937.
Miller, Henry W., *The Paris Gun*, 1930.

Muhlen, Norbert, *The Incredible Krupps*, 1959.
Neave, Airey, *They Have Their Exits*, 1953.
Pounds, Norman J. G., *The Ruhr*, 1952.
Prittie, Terence, *Germans Against Hitler*, 1964.
Rees, David, *Korea: The Limited War*, 1964.
Rees, Goronwy, *The Multi-Millionaires*, 1961.
Richter, Werner, *Bismarck*, 1964.
Schweitzer, Arthur, *Big Business in the Third Reich*, 1964.
Shirer, William, *The Rise and Fall of the Third Reich*, 1960.
Taylor, A. J. P., *The Course of German History*, 1945.
— *The First World War*, 1963.
Thyssen, Fritz, *I Paid Hitler*, 1941.
Wallich, Henry C., *Mainsprings of German Revival*, 1955.
Wells, H. G., *The War That Will End War*, 1914.
Young, Gordon, *The Fall and Rise of Alfried Krupp*, 1960.

Index

OTHER COOPER SQUARE PRESS TITLES OF INTEREST

HANGED AT AUSCHWITZ
An Extraordinary Memoir of Survival
Sim Kessel
New introduction by
Walter Laqueur
200 pp.
0-8154-1162-6
$16.95

HEROES NEVER DIE
Warriors and Warfare in World War II
Martin Blumenson
432 pp.
0-8154-1152-9
$32.00 cloth

MENGELE
The Complete Story
Gerald L. Posner & John Ware
New introduction by
Michael Berenbaum
400 pp., 41 b/w photos
0-8154-1006-9
$18.95

THE JEHOVAH'S WITNESSES
AND THE NAZIS
Persecution, Deportation, and
Murder, 1933–1945
Michel Reynaud &
Sylvie Graffard
Introduction by
Michael Berenbaum
304 pp., 22 b/w photos
0-8154-1076-X
$27.95 cloth

JULIUS STREICHER
Nazi Editor of the Notorious
Anti-Semitic Newspaper *Der Stürmer*
Randall L. Bytwerk
With a new afterword.
264 pp., 31 b/w photos
0-8154-1156-1
$17.95

CANARIS
Hitler's Master Spy
Heinz Höhne
736 pp., 29 b/w photos, 3 maps
0-8154-1007-7
$19.95

THE MEMOIRS OF FIELD–MARSHAL
WILHELM KEITEL
Chief of the German High Command,
1938–1945
Edited by Walter Gorlitz
New introduction by
Earl Ziemke
296 pp., 4 b/w maps
0-8154-1072-7
$18.95

THE MEDICAL CASEBOOK OF
ADOLF HITLER
Leonard L. Heston, M.D. &
Renate Heston, R.N.
Introduction by Albert Speer
192 pp., 3 b/w photos, 4 graphs
0-8154-1066-2
$17.95

KASSERINE PASS
Rommel's Bloody, Climactic Battle for Tunisia
Martin Blumenson
358 pp., 18 b/w photos, 5 maps
0-8154-1099-9
$19.95

THE DESERT FOX IN NORMANDY
Rommel's Defense of Fortress Europe
Samuel W. Mitcham, Jr.
248 pp., 8 maps, 9 tables
0-8154-1159-6
$17.95

TRIUMPHANT FOX
Erwin Rommel and the Rise of the *Afrika Korps*
Samuel W. Mitcham, Jr.
224 pp., 26 b/w photos, 8 maps
0-8154-1055-7
$17.95

OCCUPATION
The Ordeal of France, 1940–1944
Ian Ousby
384 pp., 16 b/w photos
0-8154-1043-3
$18.95

THE WEEK FRANCE FELL
June 10–June 16, 1940
Noel Barber
336 pp., 18 b/w photos
0-8154-1091-3
$18.95

SIEGFRIED
The Nazis' Last Stand
Charles Whiting
312 pp., 24 b/w photos, 6 maps
0-8154-1166-9
$17.95

SWING UNDER THE NAZIS
Jazz as a Metaphor for Freedom
Mike Zwerin
With a new preface
232 pp., 45 b/w photos
0-8154-1075-1
$17.95

THE HITLER YOUTH
Origins and Development, 1922–1945
H. W. Koch
382 pp., 40 b/w photos, 2 maps
0-8154-1084-0
$18.95

ANZIO
The Gamble That Failed
Martin Blumenson
224 pp., 4 maps
0-8154-1129-4
$17.95

WARLORD
Tojo Against the World
Edwin P. Hoyt
With a new preface
280 pp., 10 b/w photos
0-8154-1171-5
$17.95

DEFEAT INTO VICTORY
Battling Japan in Burma and India, 1942–1945
Field-Marshal Viscount William Slim
New introduction by David W. Hogan, Jr.
576 pp., 21 b/w maps
0-8154-1022-0
$22.95